Praise for *Same Difference*

"My congratulations to Barnett and Rivers for another first-class job of exploring the gender myths affecting our society. They take no prisoners, nor should they, in their cutting analysis, based on solid research and totally accessible writing."

—Marvin Kalb, senior fellow of Shorenstein Center on Press, Politics and Public Policy at Harvard University

"Instead of pitting nature against nurture, Barnett and Rivers present an optimistic and accurate picture of humanity that shows how men and women develop a fuller range of 'natural' life options, including nurturing fathers and women as political leaders."

—Diane F. Halpern, former President of the American Psychological Association, Professor of Psychology, Claremont McKenna College, and Director of the Berger Institute for Work, Family, and Children

"The message of *Same Difference* is compelling: For too long, society has stuffed men and women into ill-fitting stereotypes, and now the tight garments are pinching. This engaging and illuminating book is liberating in the best and healthiest sense—that is, freeing individuals to be themselves."

—Rosabeth Moss Kanter, Harvard Business School, author of *Confidence: How Winning Streaks and Losing Streaks Begin and End*

"A wonderfully provocative book that challenges, one by one, the most popular myths of gender difference, using a combination of compelling science and wise insight. Because it is easier to 'sell' the notion that a wide gulf exists between men and women, books and articles proclaiming gender differences receive cover story attention. I strongly hope that this book receives comparable attention and is widely read—because it will clearly help improve relationships between men and women, boys and girls."

—Ellen Galinsky, President, Families and Work Institute; author, *Ask the Children*

"*Same Difference*, then, serves a practical purpose of helping families reconcile their non-traditional balance between work and home against long-held beliefs, including that men are prehistorically predisposed to be providers and that women lack the hard wiring to do math . . . it is a provocative examination of embedded stereotypes that the authors contend limit the potential of both men and women."

— *Milwaukee Journal Sentinel*

"So, in the name of freedom, I encourage you to sit that insensitive, workaholic boyfriend of yours down in front of a football game and take your maternal, co-dependent self to the bookstore to pick up this fabulous gem."

—*Bust*

Also by Rosalind Barnett and Caryl Rivers

She Works/He Works (1996)
Lifeprints (1983)
Beyond Sugar and Spice (1979)

Same Difference

How Gender Myths Are Hurting Our Relationships, Our Children, and Our Jobs

Rosalind Barnett and Caryl Rivers

BASIC
BOOKS

Basic Books
A Member of the Perseus Books Group
New York

*To Nat and Alan, whose continuous support on
many fronts and unflagging interest and enthusiasm
made all this possible. If we ever needed proof
that caring was as much a male as a female virtue,
our husbands have given us that proof.*

Copyright © 2004 by Rosalind Barnett and Caryl Rivers

Hardcover first published in 2004 by Basic Books,
A Member of the Perseus Books Group
Paperback first published in 2005 by Basic Books.

Books published by Basic Books are available at special discounts for bulk purchases in
the United States by corporations, institutions, and other organizations. For more information, please contact the Special Markets Department at the Perseus Books Group,
11 Cambridge Center, Cambridge, MA 02142, or call (617) 252-5298, (800) 255-1514
or e-mail special.markets@perseusbooks.com.

Library of Congress Cataloging-in-Publication Data

Barnett, Rosalind C.
    Same difference : how gender myths are hurting our relationships, our children, and our
jobs / Rosalind Barnett and Caryl Rivers.— 1st ed.
        p.   cm.
    H.C.: ISBN-13: 978-0-465-00610-6; ISBN 0-465-00610-8
    1. Sex differences (Psychology)   2. Sex role.   I. Rivers, Caryl.   II. Title.

BF692.2.B37 2004
305.3—dc22

                                                                                        2004002183

Designed by Jeff Williams
Set in 11.5-pt New Caledonia

PBK: ISBN-13: 978-0-465-00613-7; ISBN 0-465-00613-2

05 06 07 / 10 9 8 7 6 5 4 3 2 1

Contents

Acknowledgments

It is our great fortune to have Susan Rabiner and Susan Arellano as our agents. Without their insight and grasp of the issues, this book would never have come together. Susan Arellano went well beyond her role as agent to ask probing questions and to put in many hours on the final editing of the manuscript.

Jo Ann Miller at Basic Books believed in the manuscript from the start and helped us shape complex ideas into a coherent whole. Thanks as well to her assistant, Ellen Garrison. We would also like to thank Linda Carbone for her editing work.

Special thanks to Donna Ellis, whose generosity of spirit and careful work added greatly to the success of this project.

I (RB) began work on this project while I was a visiting scholar at the Henry A. Murray Research Center at the Radcliffe Institute for Advanced Study at Harvard University. I owe a great debt of gratitude to Ann Colby, then director, who provided me with the support I needed to undertake this work. In addition, I want to thank Jackie James for her encouragement and wisdom, and Marty Mauzy for her unstinting interest and reassurance. In the course of writing the book, I relocated to Brandeis University, where I was fortunate to find a home at the Women's Studies Research Center. I am deeply indebted to Shula Reinharz, director of the center, for her unwavering support and enthusiasm. She has been a steady source of good cheer and optimism especially at those times when I most needed support. I also want to thank the community of scholars at the center, who showed great interest in the book and offered many helpful suggestions and comments throughout the writing process.

Thanks to the generosity of these two institutions, I had the good fortune to work with a number of outstanding undergraduate students, including Elizabeth Beasely, Madeline Lohman, Rachel Nash, Mical Natoniewski, Rebecca Nesson, Anna Perrici, Erica Pond, Nicole Selinger, Patricia Wencelblatt, and Annie Wong.

CR wishes to thank Bill Ketter and Bob Zelnick, chairs of the Boston University Journalism Department, for their help and encouragement, as well as Dean J. J. Schulz of the College of Communication. Jim Gallagher in the Bebe Research Center at the College of Communication at Boston University was of great help in researching this book. Thanks also to Lisa Becker for her interviewing skills.

Our thanks to Marvin Kalb and the Joan Shorenstein Center for Press and Politics at Harvard University for a Goldsmith Research Award that helped make this book possible.

Preface

In the time since the hardcover edition of this book was published, a series of high-profile events made clear that the issue of gender differences is far from a dry academic subject.

Harvard President Lawrence Summers made comments at an academic conference in 2005 that caused an international uproar. He said that perhaps it was women's innate deficiencies in math and science—not discrimination or the long hours of academic life—that accounted for the dearth of women in top positions in these fields. One world-renowned female scientist who was present, Nancy Hopkins of M.I.T., got up and walked out. The presidents of three elite universities wrote an op-ed in the *Boston Globe*, chastising the Harvard president. "Speculation that 'innate differences' may be a significant cause of under-representation by women in science and engineering may rejuvenate old myths and reinforce negative stereotypes and biases," wrote the authors, Susan Hockfield of M.I.T., a neuroscientist; Shirley M. Tilghman of Princeton, a molecular geneticist; and John L. Hennessy of Stanford, a computer scientist. (On the other side, his defenders accused his critics of political correctness and of being enemies of academic freedom.)

At the conference, Summers called for new research on gender differences in math and science, seeming to believe that little had been done in this area. Some ill-informed members of the media fell prey to the same mistake. The *Washington Post*'s Sally Quinn wrote, "Why don't female mathematicians and scientists, particularly at Harvard, get together and research the issue until they have definitive answers instead of reaching for the smelling salts."

Despite Quinn's Victorian rhetoric, a phone call from president Summers to one of his faculty members could have saved him much grief.

Over the past two decades many large and well-designed studies had found again and again that the differences in math ability between men and women were trivial. (See our chapter "Do The Math" for a full discussion of these studies.)

Summers apologized for his error and proposed new initiatives for women in science. But what will people remember—the fact that good research debunked his statement (as he admitted) or the fact that the president of Harvard said women might not be naturally good at math?

It wasn't only in mathematics that debates over gender differences surfaced. In a fractious squabble over why there weren't more women writers on the op-ed pages of America's newspapers, some people suggested that women's brain structures were the problem. This issue erupted in controversy when law professor and Fox News commentator Susan Estrich offered her syndicated column to Michael Kinsley, editorial page editor of the *Los Angeles Times*. Things got nasty after the column was rejected and Estrich pointed out the paucity of op-eds written by women during Kinsley's tenure. (She suggested his judgment might have been affected by his Parkinson's disease and later apologized for that remark.) Critics used the incident to point out the glaring lack of women among media opinion makers: during a two-month period, they noted 19.9 percent of op-eds at the *Los Angeles Times* were by women; the *Washington Post* clocked in at 10.4 percent; and the *New York Times* at 16.9 percent.

Too often, with brain research, sweeping assertions are made on what one researcher calls "a thimbleful of evidence." Research "findings" about the human brain appear and are debunked faster than hemlines go up and down.

A *Washington Post* article ventured the idea that women's brains made them too cautious to express strong opinions. "Women, being tuned in to the more cautious (and more creative) right brain," said the *Post* story, "are more reluctant to do something unless they're sure they're going to get it right."

Here's an alternate theory about why women don't write as many opinion pieces as men. New research finds that in social arenas that are generally thought to be male-dominated, women are seen as either competent and unlikable, or not competent and likeable. In other words, a woman with strong opinions is far more likely to be disliked than a man. Other research shows that women suffer more negative consequences when they appear to fail than men do. No wonder women are more careful than men—the stakes are higher. The fracas over op-eds illustrates the ways in which generalizations about women's brains are being used to avoid the whole subject of discrimination. Switching the topic to brain structures or hormones usually means taking the focus away from the real reasons that women are often absent from the top levels in many fields. It is being said today that women can't achieve because they aren't risk takers, and their brains are wired for empathy, not achievement. Research demonstrates this is not so, but it's fast becoming the new backlash. (See our chapter "Leading Questions" about this issue.)

However, the media announced in 2005 that even if all these ideas about faulty brain structures and hormones are wrong, and women *do* have the ability and drive for leadership, there's a catch. If they do achieve, they will be miserable. No man will want them. Citing two studies that drew headlines like *Glass Ceilings at Altar as Well as Boardroom* and *Men Just Want Mommy*, New York Times columnist Maureen Dowd asked in 2005 whether the feminist movement was "some sort of cruel hoax." She wrote "The more women achieve, the less desirable they are."

True? No. One study, by psychologists Stephanie Brown of the University of Michigan and Brian Lewis of UCLA, was seriously flawed. It was done on a small sample (120 male and 208 female undergraduates, mainly freshman). The males rated the desirability of a fictitious female, who was described as either their immediate supervisor, a peer, or an assistant, as a dating or marriage partner. Surprise, surprise! The freshman males preferred the subordinate over the peer and the supervisor when it came to dating and mating. But was the study a barometer of adult male preferences—or of teenage boys' ambivalence about strong women? Clearly the latter, given the facts about what adult men actually desire. Men do not reject achieving women—quite the opposite. Sociologist Valerie Oppenheimer of UC Berkeley reports that today men are choosing as mates women who have completed their education. The more education a woman has, the more marriageable she is. And Heather Boushey of the Center for Economic Policy Research found that women between the ages of 28 and 35 who work full time and earn more than $55,000 per year, or have a graduate or professional degree, are just as likely to be successfully married as other working women.

The second study, cited by Dowd and picked up by the *Atlantic Monthly* under the headline "Too Smart to Marry?" found that for every 15-point increase in IQ score above the average, women's likelihood of marriage fell by almost 60 percent. Alarming news for bright women, right? Well, not exactly. The news stories about this study failed to mention that the women in the study are now in their eighties, having been born in 1921. In that era, smart women may have found the constraints of traditional marriage impossible, and since the "ideal" woman of the time was passive, timid, and not given to strong opinions, men may not have found smart women proper marriage candidates. But, despite the media hype, the study tells us nothing about the behavior of today's young men and women.

Still, the "women haven't got the right stuff" narrative is rapidly becoming the conventional wisdom. Unfortunately, women rarely hear the facts about their abilities and their natural inclinations—the drumbeat of bad news and scare stories creates too much of a din. If women believe that they can't really achieve—or that they will suffer if they do—the bright potential of many lives will be forever dimmed.

However, there has been some good news lately. More stereotypes about sex differences are giving way to the insights of technologically sophisticated scientific study. In March 2005 a large international group of 282 scientists (molecular biologists, geneticists, and other specialists) at twenty-one institutions in six countries reported in *Nature* the results of extensive study of the genetic structure of the X chromosome. If a fetus has two X chromosomes it develops into a female; if it has one X and one Y, it develops into a male. At a genetic level, the difference between the sexes boils down to the presence or absence of a second X or a Y chromosome!

The new findings that grabbed headlines across the globe showed that old thinking about the X chromosome had to be shelved. It had been thought that only the genes on *one* of the two X chromosomes every female carries were in fact active; the other was thought to be "turned off." Now, it appears that about 15 percent of the genes on the second copy, the supposedly inactive chromosome, are still busily at work. And, about 10 percent of the genes on the "active" chromosome are in fact inactive. What does this mean? Simply, the combination of genes that are active or inactive on both copies of the X chromosome is very large, leading to far more differences among females than was thought before. In contrast, differences among men are far less dramatic, at least at the genetic level.

These findings contradict the idea that women are stamped out as if by cookie cutters, so that they talk, think, relate, communicate and lead in exactly the same way—as the media would have us believe.

What will tomorrow's scientific breakthroughs reveal? Of course, no one knows. However, it does seem true that previously accepted generalizations about men and women are being dismantled at an astonishing rate. Overall, the most recent developments point to just the trends we describe in this book, namely, that the differences among women and among men dwarf the differences between the sexes.

The Seduction of Difference

NEARLY TEN YEARS AGO we wrote a book called *She Works/He Works*.[1] Drawing on a four-year, million-dollar study of 300 working couples, we examined how the new "working" family—in which both parents were employed—was faring. Currently between 60 and 70 percent of families consist of two working parents and their children, and so it's hard to remember that until recently, this was not the norm. Only thirty-odd years ago, most families consisted of one full-time working parent, the male, and one stay-at-home parent, the female. It was not until 1980, when the U.S. Census Bureau no longer automatically assumed the male to be the head of the household, that the nation put the old *Leave It to Beaver* family to rest.[2] Nowadays most women, including mothers of young children, are part of the paid labor force from their twenties until retirement. This revolution in women's lives, and in the life of the family, is taken for granted today.

Our study, as well as studies done by others, showed that many fears arising from the entry of mothers into the workforce—regarding children's psychological well-being, women's ability to juggle multiple roles, and men's willingness to accept those new roles—were groundless: people are doing well in the new family structure.[3] Most children of working mothers don't exhibit attachment problems or cognitive deficits. Many studies show no meaningful differences between the children of mothers at work and mothers at home.[4] Most working mothers do not turn into emotional wrecks as they perform the family juggling act (in fact, working mothers consistently exhibit fewer emotional problems than stay-at-home mothers), and most men seem to accept the changing power structure at work and on the home front. Clearly something about this new, busy lifestyle confers a major health benefit.

The good news we imparted in *She Works/He Works* was warmly welcomed; the book was widely read and reviewed, and in 1997 it was awarded the prestigious Books for a Better Life Award.

End of story? Not quite. One group of people in our study troubled us. They were having major problems in their marriages, experiencing severe stress at work and at home. What characterized this "out-of-synch" group was that their beliefs and attitudes deeply contradicted the lives they were living. Even though all the couples were actually performing dual roles, the people in this group didn't believe men and women could—or should—be equally competent at both. In their minds, women were more effective in the home sphere because they were naturally more domestic and more nurturing and simply enjoyed that arena more. Men, they believed, were by nature more aggressive and less nurturing, and thus better suited to the competitive world of work than the "touchy-feely" domestic sphere. Because both the men and the women in this group believed they weren't suited to both roles, they couldn't enjoy their dual roles or feel competent performing them. The women were angry that they had to work when they felt their true job was making a home for their families. The men weren't able to take pleasure in caring for their kids because they feared they lacked the natural instinct for it. As a result, the couples—especially the men—felt tremendous stress and often took it out on each other.

We were surprised to discover this group of unhappy couples within our larger study. As veterans of the 1970s women's movement, we had helped broaden opportunities for women, and in the years since then we had witnessed a remarkable transformation in men's and women's attitudes and roles. When RB was getting her advanced degree in psychology in 1964, few women were principal investigators on major grants, held academic chairs, or were sought out as national experts on the science of human behavior. And when CR was studying journalism, there were no female editors or managing editors of major newspapers, no female reporters on network television, few women on the "hard news" beats that led to top jobs. But by 1996, when we published our study of dual earners, all this had changed, as demonstrated by the overwhelmingly positive results of our research. Like us, most people had come to believe that men and women, if not interchangeable, were more alike than different in what they could and in fact did do. The prevailing wisdom was that both sexes would benefit and be happier when there was greater equality at work and at home.

So how to explain our out-of-synch couples? We sympathized with them but assumed that they were simply a holdover from an earlier era and that the traditional ideas they held—beliefs that caused them discord and distress—would soon be a thing of the past.

If we had been right, you would not be reading this book. Out-of-synch couples—faced with overwhelming evidence that women and men could take on the same tasks in the same way and do them equally well—would have faded into history. But, as it turns out, we were dead wrong.

Fast-forward eight years. A best-selling book is published in 2002 by a leading Harvard academic. In *The Blank Slate* psychologist Steven Pinker declares that men and women are *by nature* suited to different roles. Men are inherently "risk-taking achievers who can willingly endure discomfort in pursuit of success," while "women are more likely to choose administrative support jobs that offer low pay in air conditioned offices."

The Blank Slate was the latest in a barrage of backlash books that included Michael Gurian's *The Wonder of Girls* (2002),[5] which urged mothers to disregard feminist messages and focus on their daughters' caring abilities rather than their talents, and Sylvia Ann Hewlett's *Creating a Life: Professional Women and the Quest for Children* (2002), which warns women to abandon serious career plans and have children in their twenties.[6] The acknowledged kingpin of the gender-difference screeds was John Gray's huge best-seller *Men Are from Mars and Women Are from Venus,* which told us that men and women virtually evolved on different planets. Another genre of "difference" books came from a surprising source—women who declared themselves feminists but delivered a message that women are very different from men, which could easily be twisted to diminish women's opportunities. These include Deborah Tannen's best-selling *You Just Don't Understand,* a testament to men's and women's inherently distinct styles of communicating, and Carol Gilligan's *In a Different Voice,* which has profoundly influenced several generations of women's studies students with its message about women's unique caring ability.

The list goes on and on and on. Incredibly, traditional ideas that we thought would soon vanish were back in full force. In the past few years, ideas of innate and rigid gender differences that were hurting some of the families we studied have reemerged, this time from new and unexpected places, dominating best-seller lists and becoming part of the academic canon. Most significantly, they were affecting hiring and promotions in corporations, influencing major legal decisions, and changing educational curricula. In a subtler and perhaps more insidious fashion, these ideas were also influencing the thoughts and feelings of men and women as they made individual decisions about work, child care, and the division of labor in the home.

When we saw how these gender-difference ideas were infiltrating institutions and families, we were puzzled. Why would people, including some of our brightest intellectuals, promote ideas that we thought had been nullified by mothers' advancement into the workforce and fathers' growing involvement in family life. (Women today provide the economic support for most American children.) Our initial confusion soon turned to alarm on two counts: First, all our research and the research of our colleagues contradicted the notion of essential difference. And second, these ideas were not helping the millions of men and women managing multiple roles at home and in the workforce. As with the out-of-sync group in our 1996 study, we were seeing more and more people becoming anxious because their lives were in conflict with traditional sex-role beliefs—newly cloaked in the mantle of "gender-difference" speak. We were seeing these couples in RB's psychotherapy practice, among our friends and their children, in parenting and women's magazines, on television shows, and in an endless stream of new books.

A Closer Look

So, like all good researchers, we went back to the data. We looked closely at the "gender-difference" theories to assess their assumptions and the source of their information. We reexamined our own studies and those of our colleagues to learn why our findings stood in such opposition to the conclusions of the gender-difference theorists. This book is the fruit of that analysis. In each chapter, we examine some of the leading theories in a thorough, systematic way. Eight years of research and writing went into this book, which surveys the latest findings (roughly 1,500 studies) of eminent scientists in biology, primatology, psychology, anthropology, sociology, genetics, and managerial behavior. We rarely rely on a single study. We depend mostly on meta-analyses (which combine the results of many studies), individual studies with well-designed procedures and random samples, and studies with representative samples of the population. These allow us to have confidence in our conclusions. A poorly designed single study may stimulate sensational headlines, but the findings may not hold up when other scientists reexamine the issue. We're confident that the science on which our conclusions are based is sound.

In this book we go beyond data analysis, however, to propose a new way to put together the jigsaw puzzle of research. We hope that our findings, based on a wide array of studies from many varied disciplines, will be of practical use to our readers as they structure their lives.

First, it's important to understand a fundamental difference between our assumptions and those of the gender-difference theorists. We begin with the premise—which we support throughout the book—that people's behavior today is determined more by situation than by gender. In the past, gender was all-important. Whether you were male or female determined your role in society: the way you behaved and the work you did. Under these circumstances, it's easy to assume that the reason men and women were doing different kinds of work was biological. If you look around a community and see only women weaving and only men tilling the soil, you are apt to conclude that the "cause" of this difference is that women are suited for weaving and men for tilling. But that conclusion would be wrong. Being female doesn't automatically give you a talent for weaving. Rigid cultural norms, not biology, are operating here. As gender roles loosen—as they have done in the developed world—women's and men's behavior reflects many forces: their gender, their individual talents and preferences, their personalities, and the situations in which they find themselves.

In our modern technological society, both sexes are doing many of the same things and—lo and behold!—are performing equally well. It's most likely the job that dictates the behavior, not the gender. Consequently we argue that one sex is not inherently better suited to certain roles than the other sex. Certain men and women may have personalities and talents that make them more suitable for a specific role, but personality and talent are individual, not gender based. Some critics point out that there are clear biological differences between the sexes, and obviously that's true, but we don't believe those differences determine most of our behavior or limit the roles we can assume. Because the woman gives birth does not mean that she will necessarily nurture the child better than the father does. Nor does it mean that she will nurture the child differently. (Some might find this difficult to believe, but we will demonstrate its truth in Chapters 6 and 9.) By the same token, men on average may have more testosterone than women, but that does not mean, as some experts have argued, that men are more competitive than women, more suited to be police officers, airline pilots, and CEOs. *Same Difference* acknowledges the existence of gender differences but argues that the part they play in our lives is far less important than most people have assumed.

In contrast to our position, most gender-difference theorists assume that there are fundamental differences between the sexes and that gender absolutely determines behavior; as Freud famously said, anatomy is destiny.[7] According to these theorists, differences between the sexes will determine, for example, which jobs men and women prefer, how they perform on the job, and how they feel about the job. As we've noted, some theorists also maintain that the sexes are inherently better suited to some jobs than others. Women are better nurturers of children, for example, according to Carol Gilligan and Michael Gurian. Steven Pinker and the columnist and erstwhile presidential candidate Pat Buchanan argue that men are better suited to highly competitive arenas, such as certain sales jobs, because they are inherently more aggressive.[8] Some gender-difference researchers believe that men's and women's brains operate differently. For instance, as we'll see in Chapter 7, some theorists maintain that men's (but not women's) brains are hardwired for math, making men better suited to any job requiring math skills. Others argue that men and women look at each other in very different ways, speak to each other differently, reason differently, have different moral precepts, and generally inhabit different worlds (or different planets, in John Gray's parlance). Most of these writers maintain that such differences are innate or are evolutionarily determined and thus not subject to change.

You may wonder why we pay so much attention to what are, basically, philosophical differences among those who theorize about gender difference. We do so because, as we'll show throughout the book, theoretical assumptions have real, practical consequences for the lives and health of men, women, and children. If you believe, for example, that women are better nurturers than men, can you really ask a man to take over child-rearing tasks, knowing he'll do them in an "inferior" way? If you're sure that men are uniquely hardwired for math, won't you discourage women from going into fields that require math—fields that promise to be some of the highest paying in the future? If you're a teacher and you think boys are better at math than girls, does that lower your expectations of the girls? Do you go easier on them? And if you believe that boys don't have the innate verbal skills to write well, do you set the bar lower for them? If you are convinced that men are more competitive and aggressive than women, why would you place women in sales and marketing jobs where a strong competitive streak is an advantage? Perhaps positions in human resources, which generally pay less and require "relational" skills, are the better choice for women. If you're having a problem in your marriage, do you assume that men and women are perfectly capable of understanding each other and, with a little work, can resolve communication snafus? Or do you assume that the sexes are simply fated to speak very differently, making communication problems nearly impossible to solve? These are just a few of the ways in which theoretical assumptions can color our thinking and decisionmaking. Throughout the book, we will bring in many more examples to illustrate this point.

Drawing on a range of sources, we will show how these theories hurt male–female relationships, undermine equality in schools and the workplace, adversely affect the division of labor in the home, and deprive our children of the opportunity to develop their full human potential. Throughout the book we will also step back, at times, and consider why some of these theories emerged when they did and why they remain so seductive. Surely it was no coincidence that just as women successfully moved into the workforce in enormous numbers and challenged traditional male–female stereotypes, theories emerged that defined men and women on the basis of those very stereotypes. It is not lost on us that these rigid gender stereotypes have emerged with particular force as women have been gaining real power. (Similarly, *The Bell Curve*—which argued that maybe blacks *weren't* really as intelligent as whites—didn't appear until African Americans began to make inroads into the monolith of white society.)

This timing would be easier to understand if the theories came out of a conservative base whose goal was to turn the clock back. But at least some of these ideas were advanced by women who defined themselves as feminists and worked to advance the cause of women, not undermine it. Although there is no simple reason why these ideas emerged when they did, part of the explanation may lie in "second wave feminism." (The first wave was the suffrage movement of the early 1900s.) It's important to remember that before women began their large-scale migration into the workforce in the 1970s, certain deeply held beliefs about women's nature and capabilities stood in their way. *Anatomy is destiny* was at its height. It was thought, for example, that women had no need to succeed in the workplace because they bore children, that only "mannish" women had ambition, that any man whose wife worked was "henpecked," that suburban mothers who always put the needs of their husbands and children first were sublimely happy, that women shouldn't "bother their pretty little heads" with issues of the world beyond the home. Even women's menstrual cycles rendered them unfit for leadership. In the 1970s, a prominent physician, Dr. Edgar Berman, told a Democratic Party task force that women's leadership capabilities were limited by their hormones. When Hawaii Congresswoman Patsy Mink protested, Berman labeled her a woman acting under "the raging hormonal imbalance of the periodic lunar cycle."[9]

Attempting to overcome those stereotypes, some women of the second wave asserted that they were not only the equal of men, but carbon copies of them. Women were told to learn the "games your mothers never taught you," to march to work in big-shouldered suits and tailored bow ties, to stop referring to each other as "girls," and, for heaven's sake, never let "them" see you cry. Any hint of femininity in dress, language, or behavior risked censure. When you appear as the first (and sometimes the only) woman in an all-male world, your goal is to blend in and resemble the men as much as possible. A frilly blouse screamed that you were not to be taken seriously. At the Harvard Business school, RB wore her long hair in a bun and dressed exclusively in tailored suits or dresses. CR wore jeans and boots to political meetings—and cheated with discreet eyeliner. In this period, the traditional female virtues were put under wraps, or under power suits in this case.

Although mimicking men helped women move into the workplace and find acceptance there, it also sent an unintended message to women: The traditional male role was what they should strive for, and the traditional female role should be left at home. Can anyone forget Hillary Clinton's stray remark that set off a firestorm? In her husband's first presidential campaign, when the soon-to-be first lady commented that she could have stayed at home baking cookies instead of being out in the workforce, many American women rose up to admonish her. Was she dismissing those mothers who stayed home to bake cookies? Was she suggesting that she was a better, more important person because she was a power broker in the outside world? The response to her remark revealed the enormous tensions and conflicts that women felt as they wrestled with two seemingly conflicting identities.

The bottom line is that women like baking cookies—a metaphor for women's traditional skills. Women value the role of nurturer, and during those early days worried that they either would be forced to jettison that role when they moved into the workforce or, if they stayed at home, would be dismissed as submissive Stepford wives. As we'll see in the next chapter, Carol Gilligan's theories allowed women to legitimately reclaim the nurturer role by arguing that this identity did not make women inferior to men, but simply different—and maybe even better—than the opposite sex.

Although Carol Gilligan intended to raise the status of women, she unintentionally set a trap for both sexes—by giving birth to a school of thought claiming that a woman's nurturing or "relational" self is an essential part of her nature. It is not a role that she can put on or take off at will, but rather one that she—and not the male—is destined to fulfill. This school of thought, which came to be known as "essential feminism," regarded all differences between the sexes as the reflection of "innate" characteristics. It ignored not only the crucial issue of situation as a shaper of behavior but also the huge differences among women. Missing too was the importance of another key factor—power or the lack of it.

Power Trips

Once upon a time, researchers looked at the workplace, lumped all female employees into one group and all male employees into another, and compared them. Because few women held prestigious jobs, the studies wound up comparing apples and oranges: bosses and secretaries.

Not surprisingly, researchers found one group assertive, ambitious, and focused on moving up; the other passive, less interested in promotion, and more interested in making friends and gossiping than climbing the ladder. They said one group revealed typical "male" traits, while the other showed typical "female" traits. But guess what? The real issue was power and powerlessness, not sex—and that reality got ignored. It wasn't that male employees were assertive and focused because they were male. Rather, it was because they were in powerful positions. Put each sex in the other's role, and you see a dramatic shift in behavior. And give each the same work, with the same power and prestige and the same expectations for success, and you find that men and women start to behave in ways that are increasingly similar. Situation outweighs sex. Too often, we've mistaken power behavior for gender behavior.

When it comes to power, situation, and behavior, *Same Difference* offers not only reliable science but also commonsense wisdom that most of us already possess. When we look around, we see clearly that all men are not alike and all women are not alike. One woman is a fearless leader, another is a laid-back, caring friend. One man is a tough boss with a tin ear for employees' needs. Another is a quiet listener with great reserves of patience. And women and men shift their behavior all the time. The CEO who was barking orders at the office might well be a nurturing, "relational" father and husband the minute he gets home. Or he may be pushed around big time by his wife, his daughter, his mother, and even his sister (think Tony Soprano). The deferential secretary may manage the girls basketball team after work—as aggressively and ambitiously as any NBA coach.

Time for a Truce

In explaining behavior, gender-difference experts usually dredge up the "nature versus nurture" argument. For a time, those who espoused the nurture argument—that most gender differences are socially constructed—held sway. Environment trumps nature. Now the nature camp, with its many high-profile adherents, is monopolizing the airwaves. These experts claim massive differences between the sexes that are deeply rooted in our evolutionary history and are relatively immune from the forces of nurture. Nature trumps nurture.

It's time to call a truce in this war. It's not nature versus nurture. It's both. We are not "blank slates" on which experience writes the text. Nor are we so hardwired that we act out inevitable lifelong scripts. We are all a product of many interacting forces, including our genes, our personalities, our environment, and chance. At conception, we are each endowed with our genetic heritage. What happens thereafter—in the uterus, in the early years, and in the rest of our lives—depends heavily on factors other than our genetic heritage. As children begin to explore the world, everything they see and touch stimulates neural activity, which in turn transforms the brain, which in turn changes the way they see and interact with the world.

In short, we are an ever-changing product of continuous learning and interaction that builds on our genetic heritage. But those who endorse the nature-is-all position tend to ignore the immense variety among men and women, boys and girls. Sociologist Michael Kimmel writes of his four-year-old son Zachary, who loves to wrestle and play with his superhero toys Buzz Lightyear and Batman.[10] Zack recently added Barbie to his collection and "she became another superhero, happily flying around with Spider-man and the gang." But, Zachary's father writes, "he also seems remarkably attuned to others' feelings, compassionate and caring. When a child in his preschool is crying, Zachary will offer a hug, comfort, or ask what's wrong." Kimmel worries, with good reason, that the demands of boyhood "which have nothing whatever to do with evolutionary imperatives or brain chemistry, cripple boys, forcing them to renounce those feelings and suppress and deny the instinct to care. And those who deviate will be savagely punished." He also worries about Zachary's little girl playmates who "love to run with him in their playgrounds, who can out-swing him on the monkey bars, who are fearless adventurers in their play."

We worry about what will happen to Zachary and his female classmates when the difference juggernaut comes their way. Such views polarize the sexes: Men are aggressive; women caring. Men are rational; women emotional. But in truth we exhibit all of these behaviors at one time or another. Men and women both experience aggression, but given social sanctions, they differ in how often and how directly they permit themselves to express it. Aggression is not the property of one sex or the other.

Of course there are differences between the sexes—how could it be otherwise? But more important is the size of the differences *between* men and women compared to those *among* women and *among* men. In most areas of life, the latter are much larger. If you are a woman named Sarah, you may be very different from Jessica, Elizabeth, or Susan in the way you tackle a math problem, deal with subordinates, relate to your spouse, soothe your child, feel about yourself. In fact, you are just as apt to be like Richard, Tom, and Seth in these areas as you are to be like other women.

Looking Ahead

Arguments over gender difference aren't merely academic exercises; they have real consequences. If we believe that men and women are inevitably and innately different, we won't regard policies that limit women at work as discrimination, but rather as the logical outcome of women's "choice" not to seek good jobs. We won't expand parental leave for fathers (as much as they may want it) because men are not "natural" caregivers. We'll try to resegregate the military and the workplace, and we'll abandon efforts to spend more money on women's sports because women are "naturally" less interested in sports than men are. We'll set up separate educational facilities for boys and girls, and teach all girls one way and all boys another, so lots of kids won't get the kind of teaching that's right for them. We'll create suspicion rather than trust between men and women by teaching men to view women as being interested only in men's paychecks and women to believe that men are biologically programmed to have sex and run off.

Our goal in this book is to look beyond junk science, pop psychology, and media spin to see what is real and what is not. We want to tell a new story for a new century, one that will empower both men and women to make good choices and take advantage of the opportunities that await them. For a long and complicated life, women will need skills beyond those of bearing and caring for children. In a life that will increasingly depend on relating to others at home and at work, men will need much more than aggression and fertility. As people live longer and want to thrive, not merely survive, both sexes must be allowed to draw on, as Michael Kimmel puts it, "a full—and fully human—emotional palette."

To this end, we will paint a richer portrait of the sexes, one based on research, that will enable women and men to take maximum advantage of the opportunities and challenges that lie ahead and to confront the future unencumbered by the myths and stereotypes of the past.

part one

Relationships

The Caring Trap

MIRIAM, A SUCCESSFUL executive at a major retail firm, married Don, the wealthy owner of a car dealership, and followed him from Boston to Washington, D.C. A cheerful, outgoing woman with a wide network of friends, Miriam was one of five children and grew up in a happy family. She had always wanted a large brood of children and imagined herself as an energetic, creative mother, the kind who would invent games and sew costumes for her kids and take them on adventures to parks and museums.

But when Miriam had two boys in less than two years, she found herself overwhelmed. "I'm always tired, I'm edgy—I'm not the person I want to be with the boys," she laments. After much soul searching, she decided to put the children in day care two days a week. It seemed like a reasonable, affordable plan for an overburdened mother, but Miriam was wracked by guilt: "I don't believe I can't manage this. My mother had five kids and never had outside help. What's wrong with me? I'm supposed to be able to do this."

Miriam sees herself as an imperfect woman, deficient in the special caring abilities that women are supposed to come by naturally. Even though she feels less exhausted with the children in day care, she feels ambivalent about needing it. She believes that every moment she spends with her sons has to be memorable and special. Instead, she finds herself sprawled across the bed watching Sponge Bob Squarepants with the boys and drowning in self-loathing.

Janelle is a magazine writer in her early forties. Frank, her husband, is the major breadwinner, but he's a demanding, self-centered man with a sense of entitlement. Over the years of their marriage, Janelle has assumed the role of understanding Frank, and she tries to accommodate even his most outrageous demands. Since they have no children, Frank expects to be the center of her attention. "He's more work than a whole bunch of kids," she complains. Frank's position as a university professor gives him a flexibility that Janelle's monthly deadlines don't permit. But Frank, who loves to travel, is always booking trips for them without consulting her. Once he presented her with airline tickets to London two days before she had a major project due.

Janelle feels she can't say no or even tell him that he has to cut down on his ambitious plans if he wants her to join him. "Look, I know these trips are really important to him—but they make it very hard for me to plan my work," she explains. Unable to assert herself, she is often depressed and angry. "He never hears me when I say I have to meet my deadlines. It's like I'm talking to the wall. One time I said to him, 'Frank, October is going to be a killer for me!' but he went ahead and made hotel reservations in Montreal over Columbus Day. I convinced him to cancel, but we had a huge fight over it." Now that Janelle is in therapy, she's beginning to understand that this pattern will go on forever if she doesn't break it. But it's hard for her to let go of the notion that she has to meet his needs—because "taking care of people" is what women do.

Miriam and Janelle are caught in a "caring trap." It's their job, they believe, to take superb care of the other people in their lives. Consequently Janelle can't tell Frank he needs to plan his life around her schedule once in a while, and Miriam can't wean herself away from the ideal of the perfect, omnipresent mother. They are both in a trap from which, it seems, they can't escape.

It's not a trap of their own making, though. Miriam and Janelle, like millions of other women, have been powerfully influenced by a tradition with deep roots in history. The idea of women as sole and "natural" caregivers goes all the way back to Genesis, in which Eve was created to take care of Adam. ("It is not good for man to be alone.")[1]

Throughout history, the "good woman" was the one who sacrificed for others. In the *Odyssey,* while Ulysses wandered around having adventures, faithful wife Penelope stayed home, raised his children, and kept his kingdom in good order.[2] Almost never, in the Bible, other sacred texts, or world literature, is the woman ambitious for herself without suffering some terrible fate. In fairy tales, notes the late feminist scholar Carolyn Heilbrun, aggressive, self-motivated women are usually cast as wicked stepmothers or witches.[3]

When the founding fathers proclaimed the Declaration of Independence, it was understood that only men had an inalienable right to the pursuit of happiness. A century later, Theodore Roosevelt compared women who were not loving wives and mothers to cowardly draft dodgers, declaring, "The woman who, whether from cowardice, from selfishness, from having a false and vacuous ideal, shirks her duty as wife and mother, earns the right to our contempt, just as the man who, from any motive, fears to do his duty when the country calls him."[4]

Women who tried to change society for their own benefit often had to do so in the name of others. Advocates of women's suffrage argued that women ought to have the vote precisely because they care for others. Suffragist Julia Ward Howe insisted, "Woman is the mother of the race, the guardian of its helpless infancy . . . upon her devolve the details which bless and beautify family life."[5] In the Victorian era, the "Cult of True Womanhood" portrayed women as fragile angels of the hearth, too delicate for the perils of the world beyond the home.[6] Ironically, motherhood was decreed to be woman's sublime gift—at a time when wealthy women were hiring more and more servants to deal with the daily care of children. The 1950s sanctified suburban mom—an outgrowth of the effort to get women out of the jobs they held during World War II and didn't want to leave.[7] Starting in the 1970s, the women's movement began to transform the American landscape.[8] In one of the greatest mass movements of American history, women flooded into the workplace, and attention focused less on woman's ability to care, and more on her ability to achieve.

And then along came Harvard's Carol Gilligan.

Gilligan (now at New York University) presented a new narrative for women's lives, which says that women have a unique, caring nature that men do not share. Her ideas have revolutionized the psychology of women and influenced their life choices to an unprecedented degree. Beginning in 1982 with *In a Different Voice*, her books have sold over half a million copies in the United States.[9] Why do women respond so strongly to the idea that they alone can hear the imperative to care for others? Carol Gilligan's books didn't become best-sellers because they were saying something new or different to women. To understand Gilligan's appeal, you have to look not only at history but at the complex details of her argument.

The Gilligan Juggernaut

Before Gilligan, every major theory of how human beings grow and thrive took males as the norm; these theories influenced parenting, education, and careers. Sigmund Freud, for example, focused heavily on the father's role in children's early development.[10] Central to his ideas was the Oedipal crisis in the lives of young boys, who have to surrender their primary attachment to their mother and develop a "superego" that will propel them through life. A male child who makes a successful passage through this crisis has a healthy sense of himself as a whole, competent person able to assume his role in the world of work and form a loving relationship with a woman. In contrast to the clarity with which Freud described boys' progress, his treatment of girls was less precise. The girl's major milestone is her discovery that she doesn't have a penis, and the only way she can make up for this deficiency is to marry and have a child. Girls can never develop a sense of autonomy before that; alone they are incomplete.

Freud's follower Erik Erikson laid out a sequence through which children move on their way to maturity. He too believed that until a young woman marries, her sense of identity is incomplete.[11] According to Freud, women can never be as self-directed, rational, or driven to succeed as men in the world outside the home. For Erikson, since adolescent girls can't achieve a full sense of identity until they marry, girls must be indecisive and their plans open-ended, pending the arrival of the man of their dreams. All future plans are tinged with a sense of uncertainty for women. Not so for men. For them, sense of identity formed in adolescence *precedes* the formation of intimate relationships, allowing them to plan their careers without this sense of tentativeness.

But for a woman, if you accept the idea that only a man completes you, you feel impermanent. You can't plan your future because you have none without "him." A divorced middle-aged woman (quoted by Carol Gilligan) says:

> As a woman, I feel I never understood that I was a person, that I can make decisions and I have a right to make decisions. I always felt that I belonged to my father or my husband in some way. I still let things happen to me rather than make them happen. I think that if you don't grow up feeling that you ever had any choices, you don't either have the sense that you have emotional responsibility.[12]

Carol Gilligan broke ranks with her male predecessors on the idea of female inferiority. In male theories, she said, "the qualities necessary for adulthood—the capacity for autonomous thinking, clear decision making and responsible action are those associated with masculinity, but considered undesirable as attributes of the feminine self."[13] She proposed a new theory of human development based on the experiences of women and articulated the idea that women have a "relational self," which sees reality in terms of connections with other people. Moreover, this relational self is innate only to women. Because boys are typically reared by the opposite-sex parent, whom they must repudiate in order to grow up as men, they do not sustain the awareness of—or connection with—other people that women develop naturally.

In this view, the sexes look at the world through different lenses. If you could put on the "male" lens like a pair of sunglasses, you'd see a landscape on which individual objects stand in isolation, distinct and unconnected. But when you put on the "female" glasses, new items appear. No longer are the objects in your field of vision isolated; now they are tethered together by brightly colored lines and moorings that previously lay hidden.

Imagine a meeting between a senior male executive and a group of midlevel managers of both sexes. In Gilligan's scenario, the male executive would see a room full of individuals, whom he would judge on their distinct performances. He'd decide to give Allen, the marketing manager, a prime assignment because he knows him to be an efficient worker. The female senior executive, in contrast, would be acutely aware of how each manager relates to the others and how they work together—just as she is aware of how her coworkers, her friends, and her teenage children relate to one another. She might decide that although Allen was indeed competent, his hair-trigger temper too often ruffled team dynamics, so she'd give the assignment to a manager who could be counted on to keep people working together well.

Such connections, Gilligan argues, shape the development of women's entire web of thought—and the way they make decisions. Women build their lives around their connections to other people and judge themselves on the quality of those relationships. If women are completely enmeshed in their connections to others, it follows that their moral decisions, their ideas about right and wrong, and the ways in which they confront life's moral choices will be colored by these experiences. Men, unable to see such connections, operate as if the individual is paramount. They make their decisions based on rules and abstract principles.

Seeing women as "different" was hardly a new idea, but this time it was coming not from men who believed that women's brains were tiny and their bodies frail, but from a woman who saw value—and even moral superiority—where men had seen weakness and inferiority. According to Carol Gilligan, women's moral judgment proceeds from "an initial concern with survival, to a focus on goodness" and finally to a principled understanding of connection as the moral basis on which to act. The implications of this claim are enormous. Indeed, if women are the better sex, then the entire weight of the goodness of society rests firmly on their shoulders. This not only takes men off the hook but puts an impossible burden on women.

Gilligan's ideas penetrated public practice and private belief with unprecedented swiftness. Her ascension was akin to Dr. Benjamin Spock's, whose ideas of more liberal, "permissive" parenting swept away a previous generation's belief in strict disciple and rigid child-rearing practices.[14] Let's examine how one psychologist's leanings brought about such widespread change, and how her theory was turned on its head to once again relegate women to domestic, caring roles.

Gilligan's Message

Early in her career as a psychologist, Carol Gilligan became deeply unsatisfied with the scholarly work on how people develop a moral sense. She was particularly skeptical of the research of one of her mentors at Harvard, Lawrence Kohlberg, who had developed scales to measure the ways in which people make moral decisions.[15] At the low end of his scale were people who simply followed such moral authorities as religious leaders, politicians, or social arbiters. At the high end were people who had internalized a set of moral principles and acted on those principles in situations where moral decisions were required.

Kohlberg used the now classic "Heinz dilemma" to measure moral decisionmaking. In this scenario, Heinz's wife is severely ill and may die without her expensive medicine, which he can't afford. Should he break into the store to steal the medicine to keep his wife alive? Kohlberg believed that Heinz may indeed break into the store because justice places the right to life above the right to property. He was less concerned with what people decided than with how they reached their decision. He used their decisionmaking process to rank people on his scale.

Gilligan claimed that women scored lower than men—meaning that their moral development was less mature. But was it really? Gilligan asked. Were women at fault, or were Kohlberg's methods in some way lacking? "This repeated finding of developmental inferiority in women may . . . have more to do with that standard by which development has been measured than with the quality of women's thinking per se," Gilligan said.[16] She claimed that when women are judged by masculine standards, they are seen as undeveloped, more like children than adults. She proposed an alternate theory. Women, she said, based their decisions not on the abstract ideas of justice that Kohlberg relied on for his ranking but on beliefs about human connection and caring.

To support her argument, Gilligan cited two of her own studies. In one, she asked twenty-five of her Harvard students to respond to the Heinz dilemma. In the other, she and a team of researchers questioned twenty-five women grappling with moral issues as they contemplated whether to end their unwanted pregnancies. Gilligan analyzed the women's language and claimed to find clear evidence that the women in the studies used what she calls "care reasoning" instead of the "justice reasoning" Kohlberg admired. In the Heinz study, she says that women voiced "an injunction to care" while the men reported "an injunction to respect the rights of others . . . and to uphold the right to life and self-fulfillment." Gilligan claims that for women "the moral person is one who helps others; goodness is service, meeting one's obligations to others, if possible, without sacrificing oneself." Gilligan believes that women's moral decisionmaking proceeds in three stages. First is a focus on the self, second is the concept of responsibility as the basis of a new "equilibrium" between the self and others, and third is a stage in which condemnation of hurt or violence to others becomes the guiding principle of action.[17]

In Gilligan's abortion study, a married twenty-four-year-old Catholic woman found herself pregnant two months after the birth of her first child. She decided to terminate the pregnancy, because, she said, she was thinking of her husband and his financial and emotional needs, and of her aging parents, with whom they were living, as well as her own reluctance to handle another pregnancy so soon. She thought the fetus was indeed a life, though an unformed one. "Am I doing the right thing? Is it moral?" she asked. In the end, she decided to have the abortion, not because she wanted it but because she thought that having the child would be too great a burden on others. She came to this decision via her own sense of what she owed to others, not because she was being pressured by her husband or family. "I can't be so morally strict as to hurt three other people because of my moral beliefs," she said. Gilligan sees her as striving to "encompass the needs of both self and others, to be responsible to others and thus to be 'good' but also to be responsible to herself and thus to be 'honest' and 'real.'"[18]

Based on these two studies, Gilligan, as already noted, makes a sweeping claim: male and female moral development takes different paths, due primarily to what happens to them in early childhood. Boys are urged to separate from their mothers. Girls, in contrast, are held close by their mothers, making the connection between self and other the hallmark of female socialization. For boys, concern with individual rights and justice dominates their moral development: "justice reasoning." For girls, relationships and issues of care and responsibility for others are at the core of morality: "care reasoning." "Thus," Gilligan says, "males tend to have difficulty with relationships, while females tend to have problems with individuation."

Gilligan's Critics

Despite the runaway success of Gilligan's ideas (*In a Different Voice* has been translated into fourteen languages), there was rampant skepticism from the beginning among her fellow psychologists. A number of other researchers read her students' responses and found them complex and hard to fit into neat categories; no clear gender voice emerged to them. Furthermore, a review of Kohlberg's data found that women did not fare as poorly as Gilligan suggests. Psychologist Lawrence J. Walker concluded that if "educational and occupational backgrounds of subjects are controlled, there are no sex differences in moral judgment."[19] In other words, when you look at the education people have and the jobs they do, you discover that those two factors—not their sex— account for the differences that had been erroneously attributed to sex.

Critics also questioned Gilligan's research methods. Her abortion study consisted of only twenty-five women (an additional two miscarried and another two had unknown outcomes), and Gilligan herself notes that the women varied widely in age (from fifteen to thirty-three years) and race, as well as socioeconomic and marital status. From such a small sample, it would be impossible to draw any conclusions; at best, hypotheses could be generated to test in a better sample. (Gilligan admits that her theory of men and women "awaits for its confirmation on a more systematic comparison of the responses of both sexes.")[20]

Gilligan simply observed her subjects' decisionmaking processes. When they seemed to use "care" reasoning, she assumed it was because they were women. But might it have been due to their race, socioeconomic class, level of education—or some other factor? She had no way of knowing.

Most glaringly, Gilligan's sample included no men. Would the husband of the twenty-four-year-old Catholic woman have made an argument similar to his wife's? Would he have said that the needs of his newborn son and his wife (advised by doctors that the new pregnancy could endanger her health) were paramount in his decision about an abortion? We have no way of knowing.

Moreover, Gilligan reported only some of her data and conducted the interviews herself or with her associates. (Usually scientists hire interviewers who are "blind" to the ideas being tested.) She provided no statistics or coding scheme to allow independent researchers to assess the criteria she used or replicate her work. Consequently one of the critical tests of good research—the ability of its findings to be replicated by other scientists—was not passed. Only now, more than two decades after her work was first published, is she giving researchers access to some of her data.

Psychologist Faye Crosby gave the same tests to her undergraduates and found no consistent pattern among their answers.[21] She also designed a series of questions in 1991 to investigate women's "relational" qualities. She asked both male and female undergraduates the following questions: Is your self-concept wrapped up in social interactions? Do you need and enjoy the company of others? Do you learn in social situations better than in impersonal or mechanical situations? Are you swayed in your opinions and attitudes by others?

Crosby found that females' self-concept depends on social approval—but so does males'. Males enjoy being in the company of others—just as much as females do. Social factors such as approval by teachers or supervisors are important for women—and just as important for men. And women are not easier to persuade than men. "Under some circumstances, everyone acts like a spineless jellyfish; and under other circumstances, everyone shows strength and independence."[22]

Crosby methodically examined all the scientifically well-designed studies comparing males and females with regard to empathy, altruism, cooperativeness, nurturance, and intimacy and found "no conclusive evidence to show that men and women differ from one another in the extent to which they attend to and are good at interpersonal relationships."[23] It's clear, says Crosby, that many factors affect how you relate to other people—your social class, age, religion, nationality, education, personality, and especially the situation you're in at the moment. Your sex is only one variable, and not necessarily the most important one. Situation, not sex, is often more important. This is a key concept to which we will return.

Ann Colby and William Damon[24] at Stanford and Debra Nails[25] at Michigan State also took issue with Gilligan. If women and men are as different as she purported, they argued, then we'd have to rethink everything we know about human behavior. Gilligan, said Colby and Damon, represented "no less than a sweeping critique of all major developmental theories on the grounds that they are biased against women . . . if Gilligan's charges are justified, developmental psychology must return to the drawing board, since it has misrepresented a majority of the human race."

Other voices began to weigh in as well, including Supreme Court Justice Sandra Day O'Connor. In 1986 Suzanna Sherry, a professor at the University of Minnesota law school, analyzed the language of O'Connor's decisions and identified her as a voice of this new feminism.[26] Sherry concluded that women's jurisprudence would be "merciful, just and compassionate." Justice O'Connor was not pleased. She debunked Sherry's idea that men and women adjudicate cases differently. (She proved to be right. A major study published in the *Indiana Law Review* found that "most female judges do not decide cases in a distinctly feminine or feminist manner.")[27]

In a speech at NYU in 1991, O'Connor said, "This 'New Feminism' is interesting but troubling, precisely because it so nearly echoes the Victorian myth of the 'True Woman' that kept women out of law for so long . . . asking whether women attorneys speak with a 'different voice' than men do is a question that is both dangerous and unanswerable."[28]

Dangerous indeed. And prophetic. O'Connor correctly intuited that such a notion would ultimately hurt women. Not, as in the past, because their "difference" would be used as an excuse to close doors of opportunity, but because women would be held to an impossible new standard. The following examples reflect today's and maybe tomorrow's headlines:

1. If you're an executive, your company may send you to a mandatory retraining program because you're seen as too assertive, not "relational" enough. This happened to a group of female managers in California who, to their chagrin, were marched off to a Bully Broads seminar in 2001. "I was sent here," one of the women said, "because of my intolerance for incompetence and for having a passion for my job that scared people to death."[29]

2. New research finds that a kinder, gentler image of managers brings with it hidden costs to women. Suzanne Edmonds, a sales representative for a large pharmaceutical company, was promoted to regional manager—but her promotion hinged on a performance review. Even though her technical competence was rated very high, she got a lower grade on "interpersonal skills" and lost the promotion. She was a victim, say Laurie Rudman of Rutgers and Peter Glick of Lawrence University, of a "trend toward the 'feminization' of middle management," as corporations recognize the value of more collegial leadership styles.[30] The researchers found that the new trend actually winds up discriminating against talented women. To get hired, both men and women have to ap-

pear competent, decisive, and in command. Men don't get punished for such traits after they get the job, but women do. Simply by being in charge, say the researchers, "women may be seen as violating the feminine-niceness prescription of society."[31] Like the "bully broads," they are punished. Of course, if women are seen as too nice and too feminine, they don't get hired for top jobs in the first place.

3. If your daughter is a math whiz in middle school and wants do an independent project on the new Mars expedition, her teacher may insist that she work on the project with a team because "that's the way girls learn." When your daughter objects, you get a note from the teacher saying that she is being "uncooperative" and hurting the feelings of the other girls. The teacher reads to you from a story in the *Boston Globe*, in which a psychologist says that for women, "the apex of development is to weave themselves zestfully into a web of strong relationships that they experience as empowering, activating, honest and close."[32] Your daughter, but not your son, may lose the opportunity to develop the skills that independent research hones.

4. A book about female friendship called *Girlfriends: Invisible Bonds, Enduring Ties*, by Carmen Renee Berry and Tamara Trader, cites Carol Gilligan as its inspiration.[33] The authors celebrate the fact that when thirty-four-year-old Eileen was feeling blue about returning to work after the birth of her baby, her friend Jenny jettisoned her own plans and offered to care for Eileen's baby. In addition to making the mother feel guilty, this proposal sets the bar for female friendship too high for almost anyone to meet.

5. If you are a woman who is depressed or anxious or suicidal, your therapist may judge you entirely on your relationships—not on your work or other areas of your life. Women who check into the women's psychiatric unit of the Weill Cornell Westchester Hospital in White Plains, New York, take part in daily teatime and are observed to see how well they relate to other patients.[34] A senior social worker confidently justifies this practice: "Carol Gilligan's

work suggests that women's sense of well-being comes from their relationships."

Gilligan's Impact

If Gilligan's view is accurate, the basic and indisputable fact of our gender determines, to a large degree, who we are and how we behave. Our maleness or femaleness dictates our moral development, as well as our preferences, values, priorities, and communication styles—which, once established, don't change. Women's "different voice" is not just different, it's nearly incomprehensible to the opposite sex. As with any influential notion that seeps into the cultural consciousness, this new theory morphed into a simplified, bastardized version of its original. In his phenomenally best-selling Mars and Venus books, John Gray tells dozens of stories of men and women whose lives seem to be on separate tracks.[35] Patrick, a restaurant designer, comes home from work and wanders into the kitchen, where his live-in girlfriend, Jennifer, is making dinner. He watches her, then asks, "Why are you using those spices?" Jennifer, feeling angry and criticized, blurts out, "I feel like it— that's why." Echoing Gilligan, Gray attributes the tension to deep male and female emotional styles (Martian rationality and Venusian emotionality) when it might just be that Patrick is tired and Jennifer is stressed. If it was Jennifer coming home and Patrick cooking, isn't it possible that the same exchange might have taken place?

It's hard to overestimate Carol Gilligan's impact on nearly every facet of modern life. If you're female—even if you've never heard of Gilligan—your life has been affected by her theories. Do you find yourself excusing men's insensitivity because "that sort of thing is easier for women"? At work, do you turn only to women to help mend rifts and soothe tempers? If you're a manager, when it comes to raises, do you disregard the "people" work one of your female subordinates does every day, since caring comes naturally to her? Do you hesitate to criticize a colleague, even on an important issue, because you don't want to be seen as uncaring?

Gilligan's ideas have also deeply affected the way many men think about women. A woman may find her partner taking it for granted that she'll listen to his problems but not offer to do the same for her. Many women write off that kind of behavior as caused by men's "natural" relationship deficiencies. When a woman expresses her opinion forcefully at work, her male boss may see her as lacking in appropriate feminine skills.

Even at the movies, you see reflections of a Gilliganesque world. In *You've Got Mail*, Tom Hanks is the workaholic owner of a huge bookstore chain when he meets Meg Ryan, the sensitive owner of a venerable children's bookstore. His new store, located in the same neighborhood, drives her out of business, but she puts him in touch with his feelings and teaches him how to be a more humane entrepreneur. He opens a children's department in his new store and hires a PhD in children's literature to run it. Countless other films and television broadcasts pair a thoughtful, caring woman with an aggressively hard-edged man, reinforcing these essentialist notions in the culture.

Gilligan herself has become a media icon. In 1996 *Time* named her one of America's twenty-five most influential people.[36] In 2001 Jane Fonda gave Harvard $12.5 million in Gilligan's name to fund a center on gender issues. (The gift was later rescinded because of the stock market downturn.)[37] Recently the *New York Times* cited Gilligan in stories as varied as the review of a TV movie on the life of civil rights pioneer Rosa Parks, an article on a 9/11 fireman, and a story on whether playing with toy soldiers hurts boys.[38]

More than Gilligan's fame, it's her influence that makes her so important. Her work has spawned a whole body of belief in women's "otherness" from men that has come to be called "female essentialism." You encounter it everywhere—in management texts, newspaper and magazine articles, best-selling books—maybe even in chats with your best friend over coffee.

It's easy to understand why women find Gilligan's theories both familiar and reassuring. Her message resonates with women. *Yes, I really do care about my children, my husband, my friends, and my community. And my caring is a big part of who I am.*

When Gilligan published *In a Different Voice*, women were relieved to see themselves defined not as the second sex or as imitation men or second-class citizens. As the women's movement burgeoned and more and more women found themselves operating in previously all-male domains, some women began to get the message—from society, the media, and their friends—that the only path to personal and professional success was to be as hard-nosed as men. Many were uncomfortable with that model. They did not want to dress like men, talk tough like men, or compete like men. One of Gilligan's research subjects said of her experiences on the job, "I have a great mother complex. I want to help people and be kind to them. I was told to work on that stuff—be more aggressive."[39] The time was right for a new message, and Gilligan was there to provide it.

At the time, pundits—male and female—suggested that men would do well to emulate women, and this argument continues to be heard today. *Business Week* decreed "As Leaders, Women Rule," saying that men could take lessons from women about participatory management.[40] The *Virginia Law Review* suggested that female judges were more compassionate and tuned in to people than male judges were.[41] Gilligan herself suggested that women in the military would humanize the institution.[42]

If Gilligan had only said that the experience of being an outsider assigned the job of caregiver, peacemaker, and relationship doctor gave many women a valuable angle of vision, her work might have encountered little scientific objection. But she seemed to be arguing that a certain way of thinking and feeling was natural *only* to women but not to men. Others took this idea and built on it—from *Women's Ways of Knowing*[43] by Mary Belenky and her colleagues to John Gray and his Mars and Venus books[44] to Michael Gurian's *The Wonder of Girls*[45] to a spate of books on management, parenting, friendship, education, marriage, careers. The idea blossomed that women have ways of knowing, ways of thinking, and ways of feeling that are inaccessible to the male mind.

No wonder droves of women embraced her message. Gilligan appeared to be elevating women from the "second sex" to the "better sex":

women as better than men. Better as friends, better as parents, better at everything having to do with relationships, even at the workplace.

There is hardly a sphere of thought and practice that has not been in-filtrated by the idea that "care" is central to women's psyches. The prestigious Stone Center at Wellesley College was founded to develop Gilligan's theories (and those of psychiatrist Jean Baker Miller) and apply them to psychotherapy. McLean Hospital, the renowned Harvard teaching hospital, set up a women's center based on these notions. A book on brain function argues that women's brains are actually constructed for caring. "The female brain is predominantly hard-wired for . . . a natural desire to 'care' about others. The male brain is predominantly hardwired for understanding and building systems," says Simon Baron-Cohen, professor of psychology and psychiatry at Cambridge University.[46]

By the early 1990s, Gilligan's ideas had reconfigured much of the theory underlying training and practice in psychology, psychiatry, and social work; they had been used to argue precedent-setting legal cases on gender discrimination and had made deep inroads into the ranks of educators, reshaping ideas about education and adolescent development around the world. The Linden School in Toronto completely revamped its academic program to conform with Gilligan's theories, aiming to "help young women develop their sense of self by encouraging non-competitive learning."[47] At this school and many others, math classes were reorganized so that girls would work exclusively in cooperative teams to overcome math anxiety. Female teachers, doctors, judges, managers, journalists, and scholars, essentialists said, would be the ones to restore "care" to the world. How could one slim book (184 pages) exert such far-reaching influence?

Harvard professor Anne Alonso, director of the Center for Psycho-analytic Studies at Massachusetts General Hospital, is dismayed by the lightning speed at which Gilligan's ideas, based on slender evidence, have been absorbed into psychotherapy.[48] Usually new theories go through a long, rigorous process of publication in peer-reviewed journals before they are accepted by the field. "None of this work has been published in [such] journals. It's hard to take seriously a whole corpus of work that hasn't been [peer-reviewed]." Charging that no clinical research supports these theories, Alonso calls the "relational self" an idea du jour (she calls it "penis scorn").

Ironically, it wasn't long before the new theory was called on to bolster claims of women's incompetence. Gilligan could never have imagined the ways her work would be used to hurt women. When forty-two women sued Sears, Roebuck and Company in 1984 for sex discrimination, the company cited Gilligan's theories to argue successfully that women do not want better-paying jobs and cannot handle stress, competition, or risk.[49] The fact that so many women are in low-level jobs is the result of "women's choices," not discrimination, the company argued in this highly publicized case. The state of Virginia cited Gilligan's work in arguing that the Virginia Military Academy should not admit females, even though Gilligan herself wrote a brief saying that her work was being misrepresented.[50] Despite its author's intentions, Gilligan's theory has become the favorite foundation for arguments that innate differences—not gender discrimination—are responsible for women's slow pace of advancement in the workplace. The essentialist emphasis on gender difference, says Judith Shapiro, president of Barnard College, too often is "feminism doing the work of sexism."[51] (But men, as we will see, can also be damaged if they believe they are deficient in the caring arena.)

Relational theories (and the "caring trap" they engender) have been forcefully challenged over the past two decades, but they remain stubbornly entrenched, still affecting women's and men's jobs, relationships, and personal decisions. In a 2002 Oxygen Media survey, 62 percent of women said that "women in power need to act more like 'real women' and less like men."[52] Women clearly held other women to a higher standard. Did the belief that women must be kinder, gentler, and more tuned in to others influence their thinking? How could it not have, with Gilligan's ideas so firmly embedded in our culture? (In fact, research shows that people expect women to be nicer than men, and so to get any credit, women have to be "supernice." Men get credit when they're just civil.)[53]

The recurrent media narrative proclaims that women, since they are so relational, are willing to quit good jobs more often than men are to stay home and care for their children. In March 2002, the *New York Times* ran such a story, referring to Massachusetts Governor Jane Swift and TV host Rosie O'Donnell.[54] One boldface tag line read: "Some say women have less psychic investment in careers." This idea lingers in spite of solid evidence that it's false. Studies show that male and female managers leave good jobs for exactly the same reasons—for better career opportunities. Staying home with children is not a major reason for men or women to leave their managerial jobs.[55] But if you are female and your employer believes that you will probably drop out of the workforce, why should he move you up the ladder?

Situation, Not Sex

Can you surmise a person's gender from a description of his or her relationships? You can, if Gilligan is correct. Consider the following comments: "I get almost smotheringly close to people and show my real self. People tell me they're smothered and feel like they lose their identity . . . I guess I am looking for some love affair which takes the mystical 'two are now one' kind of thing. But that frightens a lot of people I have run into." Typical female, right? Actually, the speaker is a man, interviewed by Gilligan herself for a 1980 paper.[56]

The essentialists view the world through the lens of gender, but they ignore a much more important perspective: power. When women use care reasoning, it is because they tend to occupy less powerful positions in society and not because of an innate quality they possess. People in power expect others to listen to them. Aides scurry when Condoleezza Rice or Hillary Clinton wants something done. The aides, however, have to find a way to appeal to their bosses to get what they need and may use care reasoning as a strategy. Those without power develop a sharp attentiveness to the needs of those with power, often resorting to manipulation and duplicity. A political aide, for example, may "suck up" to the candidate's husband and make himself available for any favor needed. A wife in an abusive relationship may lie and keep secrets in an attempt to avoid her husband's wrath. But people who have power don't have to resort to manipulative techniques; they promote the rules because they benefit from them.

It's crucial to recognize too that people behave differently in different situations—and their behavior is often determined by how much power they have in a given situation, not their sex.

When men control most of the resources in marriage, wives emphasize caring while husbands emphasize rules. (Husband: "The last time your mother was here, we almost got divorced. You agreed that she couldn't stay more than a week." Wife: "But I can't say no to her this time. She can't do anything for herself with a sprained ankle and I'm all she's got." Husband: "We made a deal. I'm not going to change it!") The scenario shifts, however, when these same women deal with their children, now from a position of relative power. (Child: "I really want to stay over at Vanessa's tonight. All the kids will be there." Mother: "You didn't finish your term paper, so no sleepover this time.")

When power shifts, behavior shifts with it. From Carol Gilligan's scholarly publications to John Gray's down-market prose, essentialist feminist writings all miss the mark when it comes to this issue. We'll discuss power in more detail in the next chapter. Gray tells the story of Tom, on his way out the door when he asks his wife, Jane, to pick up his dry cleaning.[57] Jane responds, "I'm already in a hurry. I have to pick up Mary at school, make two bank deposits, return Timmy's library books, buy groceries for tonight's dinner . . . I just don't know how I can do it all . . . there are so many things I have to do. I still need to give you your phone messages." Gray sees this as a case of the sexes misunderstanding each other because of their innate differences. How about an alternate explanation? Jane has to deal with the kids, the shopping, the banking—she even has to act as Tom's secretary and handle his phone messages. And he has the nerve to ask her to pick up his dry cleaning too? This little drama is really all about who has the power to make demands, and who does not.

If we operate within Gilligan's system, however, anybody who doesn't fit the template—such as the ambitious female or the nurturing male—is an anomaly. She says: "Women not only define themselves in the context of human relationships—but also judge themselves in terms of their ability to care."[58] Is this true? In our thirty-five years of interviewing hundreds of women and studying women's lives, we have found few women who judge themselves *primarily* on the basis of caring, although they do see caring as important to their lives. Miriam and Janelle, whom we cited at the beginning of this chapter, fell into what we call the "caring trap," putting too much emphasis on doing for others at their own expense. Most women, however, have far more balance in their lives. They value caring, but they do not see it as a central defining quality. A writer who concentrates on politics says being a caring person should be a given, for a man or a woman. "But I judge myself on how much of an impact I can make on the world beyond my own little circle."

Hillary Clinton is a highly visible example of power—and caring. In her valedictory speech at Wellesley College, she didn't hesitate to chastise Senator Edward Brooke for supporting the Vietnam War. The justice of her cause was more important to her than his public humiliation. In the White House, she rarely backed off from championing causes that did not win her popular approval. And instead of running for cover after the trauma of her husband's impeachment, she risked more public scrutiny of herself—and her daughter—by entering the Senate race. Despite her not inconsiderable ego, she consistently puts forth a vision of politics based on caring and community. In this, she's a lot like Jimmy Carter, who travels the world promoting peace and picks up a hammer and nails to build inner-city housing.

Circles of Care

Though there is much to take issue with in Carol Gilligan's findings and methodology, she must be applauded for rescuing "care" from the dustbin of second-rate virtues. (For Freud, Erikson, and others, female caring was attached to an incomplete sense of identity, while male achieving grew from strength.) Women, though they may not define themselves by it, are often in charge of caring for others, and the perspective and compassion that go along with such a role must be appreciated, not demeaned. When Joyce Fletcher at the Simmons School of Management "shadowed" women engineers at work, she discovered that the women got no credit for mentoring others, giving advice, and engaging in other caring activities—and this is true in many workplaces.[59] Neither men nor women get organizational credit for caring. Professors who spend too much time with students are unlikely to get tenure because they aren't spending the bulk of their time churning out scholarly papers.

Care reasoning and justice reasoning may be distinct ways of making decisions—and this idea may turn out to be Gilligan's major contribution to understanding moral development. Gilligan might say that the sexes are stuck with one mode of operating, but we'd like to build on her model of two types of reasoning, and add flexibility. Then both sexes can move from one to the other as the situation demands. A district court judge—male or female—may mete out sentences to criminals based on the magnitude of their crimes, an example of justice reasoning. But when the judge comes home to discover that a daughter broke the neighbor's window playing baseball, he or she will probably use "care reasoning" in deciding what the child's punishment should be.

Gilligan believes that all women have a "circle of care," and that the people within it have first dibs on their attention. One frazzled young working mother recalled asking her own mother, "When is it going to be my turn?" Her mother's answer was blunt. "It's never going to be your turn." To get their own needs met more directly, Gilligan believes, women first have to learn to put themselves inside their own circle of care. But how can this be done? Caring is what you do for others. In this respect today's young women are no different from their mothers and grandmothers, especially when they become mothers themselves.

Some women discover—to their shock—that once they quit their jobs to stay home with a baby, they fall into "subservient" behavior. They begin to defer to their husbands and put their own desires well behind those of their husbands and children. Psychologists Philip and Carolyn Cowan of the University of California–Berkeley studied the impact on couples of having a first child; they found that the women's major complaint was dissatisfaction at slipping into traditional roles, doing more housework and child care than they expected.[60] One woman says of her journalist husband, "Jim has never changed a diaper in his life . . . sometimes I feel like a single parent with a visiting boyfriend who pays the bills."[61] RB found much the same situation with female doctors who cut back their work hours.[62] They picked up many more of the routine household tasks that have been shown to be associated with high psychological distress.

These women are among many people struggling to resolve problems that are stubbornly entrenched, partly because of belief in the notion of gender differences. Jill, twenty-five, a realtor, is dating Steve, a twenty-six-year-old building contractor. She admires his easygoing temperament but finds he makes commitments and doesn't follow through. He said he would pick up theater tickets for them and her visiting parents, a special surprise. But when her parents arrived, she found out that he had never gotten the tickets. He repeats this pattern over and over. Steve rarely follows through, but he's always apologetic afterward. Jill struggles because a part of her thinks she shouldn't make a fuss: "Look, this is a relatively minor flaw, and there are so many other qualities about him that I like."

Her need to forgive him every time is blocking her access to an important emotion she needs to express: anger. She's furious with Steve's behavior, and she's also angry at herself for feeling annoyed at him. "I hate the way I feel when I'm angry," she says. "When I'm like this, I don't feel like myself." Jill thinks that she's the one who is supposed to be accommodating and understanding—the one with the "relational self." She's afraid that if she makes any real demands on Steve, she will chase him away. If she has to see herself as always kind, always caring, always the "relational" partner, then her anger has to be deflected someplace else—all too often, back at herself. Jill has created this problem by not allowing herself to make any demands in the relationship. In fact, by silencing herself, she's being unfair to Steve because she's not giving him the chance to be understanding or to respond positively to her needs. If she had expressed her annoyance in past instances and discussed his pattern of unreliability, Steve may well have remembered to pick up the theater tickets.

Phyllis, thirty-five, a highly paid executive, has just given birth to her first child. Her husband, Chet, a thirty-eight-year-old unemployed dot-comer, has been unable to get so much as a job interview for six months. Economically it makes perfect sense for Phyllis to continue to work and for Chet to care for the baby full-time. Phyllis is up for a promotion that will give her even more income and security. But when Chet suggests the obvious—"Let me stay home and take care of the baby"—she feels uneasy and unreasonably upset. She knows he's a caring person and she trusts him more than she would trust a baby-sitter. What holds her back is the fear that even his best care won't be good enough. No one else can be *mommy*. "All my friends think I'm the luckiest person around, that I'm nuts to be worried about this. He's too good to be true. Why is it so hard for me to just let him do this?"

Another couple, interviewed by *Newsweek* for a story titled "She Works, He Doesn't," is also shackled by gender expectations.[63] Laurie and Jonathan Earp of Oakland, California, thought they had the perfect life. He was earning a six-figure salary at Napster, while she was consulting part-time as a fund-raiser. Then Jonathan got laid off and couldn't find another job. Laurie stepped into the breech and became the breadwinner; Jonathan cared full-time for their five-year-old son, Dylan.

The only one happy, apparently, was Dylan, who called his dad a great "mom." "This is not the life I wanted," said Laurie as she headed off to an after-dinner meeting. As for Jonathan, he declared of his new life, "I hate it all." If Laurie could admire Jonathan for his ability to care for their son and if Jonathan could be proud of Laurie for keeping the wolf away from the door, they could both get through this rough patch in their lives a lot more easily. This flexibility would allow them to grow as individuals and tap into strengths they never realized they had.

Rigidity is one downside of the caring trap; another is the turf battle that can undermine relationships. Some women have used their care imperative to shut their husbands out of close relationships with their children. Roger and Marilyn, now in their fifties, are divorced and estranged. They married in their early twenties and had a child two years later. Marilyn devoted herself exclusively to caring for their daughter, Gwen. Roger worked long hours at a public relations firm, and he very much wanted his wife and baby daughter to be happy. But whenever he was at home and tried to engage with Gwen, Marilyn stepped in. "Don't give her soda; it'll rot her teeth," she'd tell him. "Don't try to dress her, you don't know where anything is." When he'd offer to take Gwen skating, she'd claim that Gwen wasn't steady on her skates and needed her mother to keep her from falling. Roger's own father had been very distant, so he had no model for being the kind of father he wanted to be. Understandably, he thought it was "right" for Marilyn to be the special parent, so he pulled away. As a result, Marilyn formed a close bond with Gwen and he remained the outsider.

They lived in Cleveland, but Marilyn loved the Berkshires and insisted on taking their child there every summer. Roger resisted. He could only get away for an occasional long weekend and didn't want to spend so much time away from his daughter. In the end, Marilyn prevailed because Roger believed in the natural rightness of Marilyn's decisions about their child: "Hey, she was the mother. Was I supposed to second-guess her?"

Denied any real emotional connection to his daughter, he was relegated to being a checkbook. When the marriage broke up, Roger tried in vain to keep in contact with his daughter. Marilyn had already planted a "family narrative" in Gwen's mind, in which Roger was responsible for all their problems. Gwen, now an adult, accepts her mother's story. When Roger remarried, Gwen refused to go to the wedding and rebuffed every overture Roger made for Gwen to join him and his wife on any number of occasions. Today Roger has no relationship with his daughter, which he bitterly regrets. And Gwen blames her many problems on her father. If he had been able, early on, to challenge Marilyn instead of withdrawing, Roger might have formed a real connection with his daughter. Instead, both father and daughter miss out.

For Cynthia Danaher, buying into a Gilliganesque idea of what a woman manager should be nearly sabotaged her career.[64] A newly promoted Hewlett-Packard executive, she confided to her employees that she was scared and needed their help. "I was brought up to believe that if I did what was best for everyone, and made others comfortable, I was a good person." She soon learned that what people—and the company—really wanted was a skilled manager who could make tough decisions. She exchanged her tentative management style for a more decisive one and now cringes at her old words. "People say they want a leader just like them but deep down, they want to believe you have the skill to move and fix things they can't."

Danaher was able to change, but others who buy into essentialist stereotypes never figure out how to ask for what they really need in their relationships or how to step out of rigid roles without feeling like failures. The "relational self" is simply old wine in new bottles. Whether women's "otherness" comes from perceived frailty and weakness or from perceived moral superiority and strength, it remains a harmful stereotype.

What About Men?

At first glance, relational theories may seem to be win-win for men. They get to be taken care of, and they can opt out when an aging parent needs care, a friend is in trouble, a coworker needs help, or a child wants to be comforted. But probe a bit more deeply, and you see that men too are harmed by essentialism. They may well shrink from situations that call for caring abilities. They may pull back from involved parenting, as Roger did, in the belief that it belongs in the natural sphere of their wives. But in doing so, they are damaging their marriages and cutting themselves off from a prime source of emotional enrichment.

One study showed that when men do almost as much child care as their wives their psychological well-being soars and they get an added bonus—their wives evaluate the marriage more positively.[65] This was true for men whether they held conventional ideas about child care or more liberal views. Conversely, men who see caring as woman's work pay a high price in diminished physical and emotional health.

In another major study, men who had good relationships with their kids and were deeply involved with them had fewer illnesses than more distant fathers. What's more, job problems create high distress for men unless they have good relationships with their children, which buffer them from career stress.[66] You see young fathers carrying their babies in Snuglis in the supermarket, coaching their daughters' soccer teams, picking their toddlers up from day care. Many young men want this closeness and focus more on fatherhood than did men in earlier generations. A national survey by the Radcliffe Public Policy Center, released in 2000, found men between the ages of twenty and thirty-nine more likely than older men to give family matters top billing over career success.[67] Eighty-two percent put family first and 71 percent would sacrifice part of their pay to have more time with their families.

In contrast, men who don't have close relationships with family or friends are at higher risk for heart attacks and other health problems— they die at four times the rate of men who have such ties. Gilligan's claim that men are poorly equipped to succeed at relationships is literally a death sentence.

Life After Gilligan

Women are moving with astonishing speed and in large numbers into what used to be exclusively male turf. They are being told that there's nothing they can't achieve; they should "Just Do it!" as the Nike ad says; they can be "An Army of One." In films, swooning females have been replaced by tough, killer dames like Lara Croft, tomb raider, the kickbutt new Charlie's Angels, and Xena, warrior princess. These days, the female of the species is more deadly than the male—at least in Hollywood's eyes.

But many women don't want to be professional athletes, killer executives, or karate queens. Carol Gilligan gives them a gentler, kinder narrative, and that's a big part of her enduring popularity. At the same time, global terrorism and economic uncertainty have made Americans feel they are in dire peril. At times like this, people cling to the familiar, and the idea of the caring female and traditional "family values" have a comforting resonance.

Today's young women find themselves in a particularly tough bind. They are the best-educated group of females in history, they have unprecedented access to good colleges, medical schools, law schools, business schools. They can aspire to be judges, cops, DAs, astronauts, pro basketball players, tenured professors, members of Congress, heads of companies. Yet, even as women take these advances for granted, they realize they are dealing with an incomplete revolution. They are shocked by how little help they get when they try to combine their work and family lives. They lag far behind their European sisters in the support systems that make juggling work and family possible. They have little paid maternity or paternity leave, little paid family leave in the event of sickness or emergencies. While more professional women get paid leave than lower-level workers, it's still spotty. Nevertheless, contrary to media stories about high-powered women dropping out, the data don't show any such trend.

At the same time, a woman's circle of care seems to put more demands on her than ever before. Once upon a time, a young mother was content if her child was basically happy and healthy. Today she has to make sure that her daughter can read by three, isn't picking up eating habits that lead to obesity, isn't watching violent television, is relating well to her peers, and is primed to enter a good preschool that will start her on the road to a top-notch college. This vigilance starts even before her child is born. A popular pregnancy manual instructs mothers to avoid sugar: "If you feel a need for sweets, don't eat the cake or the cookie—take a bite, savor it in your mouth for a minute, then spit it out." A bit extreme? We think so.

Asked to do an impossible job—care for everybody—women find themselves overwhelmed. The need for care flows like a stream of water that never dries up. And as we live longer, the stream gets wider, carrying our children, our parents, maybe our husband's parents, our siblings, our friends, our children's schools, our community, a whole range of volunteer organizations.

A recent National Academy of Science study found that people caring for relatives with Alzheimer's suffered damage to their immune systems and were vulnerable to sickness, including heart disease and cancer.[68] Women who spend much more time caring for others than they spend doing what they want to do risk feelings of helplessness and chronic depression.

We can wear the straitjacket of the relational self, which hinders us from ever putting ourselves first and diminishes men's opportunities for fully realized lives. Or we can break free of the caring trap and see both sexes as resilient people who behave differently in different situations. The choice is ours.

That Old Black Magic

FRANK SINATRA SINGS for lovers everywhere in his velvet baritone about "those icy fingers up and down my spine," trying to explain the magic of love. Most of us like to think the sensation he croons about, along with glances across a crowded room, moonlit nights, the sigh of violins—the whole romantic thunderbolt—describes what happens when lovers find each other. But some say that "old black magic" is no more than a collection of drives and impulses for which the score was written eons ago, and that women and men hear completely different tunes, to which they have been hardwired for centuries to respond.

Their ideas comprise the sexiest fodder in the media's insatiable maw, as well as a lively topic in academia. "Evolutionary psychology" has spawned a slew of professional articles and books, academic journals, undergraduate and graduate courses, magazine covers, TV specials, and newspaper columns. Its disciples decree that back in prehistory, perhaps millions of years ago, in what they call an evolutionary environmental adaptation (EEA), our forefathers (nomadic hunters and gatherers) emerged through natural selection and mutation. So far so good. But some go on to claim that, although the environment (as well as many other aspects of our lives) has changed dramatically over many thousands of years, "our species has not changed genetically since that time."[1]

Drawing on Darwinian theory, these researchers—whom we have dubbed the Ultra Darwinists—argue that humans' basic drive is to pass their genes on to the next generation. Because males and females confronted different reproductive problems, their bodies and brains were shaped by the characteristic ways they developed for coping with those problems: their reproductive strategies. Women had to deal with the long time required to nourish and protect a growing fetus and then a dependent baby. As a result of this great investment, women had few children compared to females of most other species and made a relatively large investment in them. Given their need for assistance in nurturing and caring for their offspring, successful women (those who reared more children who lived to reproductive age) chose mates who were "good providers"—strong, aggressive men who were successful hunters.

In contrast, men's investment in their offspring could be comparatively small, so their reproductive success would be increased by inseminating as many females as possible. The challenge for them was to select fertile females and then keep them from consorting with other males. Because these differing strategies became encoded in our genes and shaped female and male brains and behavior early on, the argument goes, we are "hardwired" to behave in the same ways today.

There is an almost religious fervor about this doctrine. Harvard's E. O. Wilson, considered the founding father of the new Darwinism, writes that the "evolutionary epic" will supplant existing religions and become the "sacred narrative" of society.[2] Robert Wright, author of the best-selling *The Moral Animal*, decrees that evolutionary theory can proclaim what is worthy in life and what is not.[3] One critic calls it "a theory of simply everything."[4] And what does our genetic programming propel us to do, according to the sacred narrative of Ultra Darwinism? Here is a sampling of the most frequently described behaviors.

1. Women are by nature coy, teasing, modest, and monogamous. Think Carol Brady of *The Brady Bunch,* think Doris Day in the old 1950s comedies with Rock Hudson. Women with many partners, such as Madonna, Elizabeth Taylor, and Jennifer Lopez, are aberrations. Rutgers anthropologist Lionel Tiger says, "Women want good genes and resources . . . so a woman agrees to be faithful."[5]

2. Men are by nature aggressive skirt chasers. Natural selection instructs them to spread their seed; therefore, Senator Robert Packwood soul-kisses a startled employee, and Bill Clinton handles the help. (Harvard psychologist Steven Pinker cited "genes" in the *New Yorker* as the reason for Clinton's dalliance with Monica Lewinsky.)[6] Your boyfriend or husband will do the same thing, given the chance.

3. Women are less ambitious than men. They either can't or won't compete with males for high-level jobs, partnerships in law firms, chairs in academic departments, and so on. So they should not expect equal representation with men in upper levels of the job world or even equal pay for equal work. As we noted earlier, Harvard's Steven Pinker claims that men are risk takers but women "are more likely to choose administrative support jobs that offer lower pay in air-conditioned offices."[7]

4. Women want successful men (an updated version of the mighty Neolithic hunter), and older men generally have more resources than young men. Women would run right past Brad Pitt if he was a struggling actor instead of a rich and famous one, and fall into the arms of, say, Dennis Franz (Andy Sipowicz of *NYPD Blue*). The press agent for the portly, aging actor claimed she got letters from women who found Franz sexier than the show's younger, more handsome leads, David Caruso and Jimmy Smits.[8] The Ultra Darwinists would not blink an eye at this news. Former Guess jeans model Anna Nicole Smith wed a wealthy (now dead) nonagenarian and went to court to wrest his fortune away from his children. A gold digger, or just a woman acting on her genetic programming? Robert Wright says that evolutionary forces make wealthy older men "an attractive package in the eyes of the average woman."[9]

5. Men lust after very young, presumably fertile women. University of Texas psychologist Davis Buss proclaims this in his book *The Evolution of Desire,* and pop culture revels in this notion.[10] It was the mainstream press, not just the tabloids, that salivated when GE CEO Jack Welch cheated on his second wife with a younger woman, an editor at the *Harvard Business Review.* Donald Trump

dumped his beautiful first wife for a beautiful, younger second wife and then divorced her to pursue even younger women. This is the natural behavior of a successful male; it's what all men would do if they owned Trump Tower.

6. Men are uninterested in investing in their kids. Long-term monogamy and fatherhood are not natural to men. When they sometimes hang around, it's to have sex with the mother, and that connection is tenuous. Their true inclination is to father kids and move on, in search of another female to impregnate and abandon, says biologist Robert Trivers.[11] Even when they don't follow this scenario, their genes make them want to.

How do these conclusions stack up as legitimate science? One valid measure of a theory's worth is whether or not it can be either verified or discredited. However, in a 24/7 media culture that doesn't always bother to wait for that next step, speculative theory can too often be fobbed off as scientific fact on the evening news or in magazine features like one in *U.S. News & World Report:* "It May Be a Many-Splendored Thing, But Romance Relies on Stone Age Rules to Get Started."[12] Researchers sometimes make provocative statements to the media that would never be spoken before an audience of their peers or in a journal article (like Pinker's comment about Monica Lewinsky).

Many scientists in the evolutionary camp offer measured speculations that aren't sound bites; some are even avowed feminists. But they rarely make headlines. The scientists who get most of the ink put forth an untestable evolutionary narrative. "How can we possibly know in detail what small bands of hunter-gatherers did in Africa two million years ago?" asked the late Harvard scientist-essayist Stephen Jay Gould:

These ancestors left some tools and bones, and paleontologists can make some ingenious inferences from such evidence. But how can we possibly obtain the key evidence that would be required to show the validity of adaptive tales about an EEA: relations of kinship, social structures and sizes of groups, different activities of groups, different activities of males and females, the roles of religion, symbolizing, story-telling and a hundred other aspects of human life that cannot be traced in fossils. We do not even know the original environment of our ancestors—did ancestral humans stay in one region or move about? How did environments vary through years and centuries?[13]

In the absence of any verifiable facts about the inclinations, behaviors, or strategies of our remote ancestors, many evolutionary psychologists have decided to portray them as the idealized 1950s American family: breadwinning, dominant males and domestically oriented, passive females. A "Flintstones version of history," as one critic puts it.[14] In doing so, they have garnered widespread attention while ignoring new research which assures us that Fred and Wilma are as fictional as the cartoon world they inhabit. (It's easy to understand, however, why outdated ideas are readily embraced; this version of the "natural" family plays every night on Nickelodeon.)

In a major review of the origin of sex roles, psychologists Alice Eagly of Northwestern University and Wendy Wood of Texas A&M debunk the idea of a universal EEA. The evidence suggests, they say, that the earliest human societies were based on foraging and scavenging, not hunting.[15] Women during the Pleistocene era (the time of the EEA) were as active as men in providing food for the group: "Indeed, anthropological and historical evidence indicates that simple foraging societies tended to be strongly egalitarian and that strongly patriarchal social structures developed later as byproducts of social and technological innovations."[16] Imagine a group of relatively weak but agile prehumans, all of whom—men, women, and children—spent time scavenging and gathering, only occasionally bagging large game. No one had the luxury of waiting around for someone else to find food, and males didn't have the luxury of spending most of their time trying to keep females in line. Sheer survival was their primary concern.

Evidence for this scenario can be found in contemporary hunter-gatherer societies, in which male dominance is hardly universal. An extensive cross-cultural study of preindustrial societies shows a wide range of behavior: male dominance, egalitarianism, and some types of female dominance. Eagly says unequivocally that the primate record and research in anthropology and ethnology do not support the picture that is essential to the Ultra Darwinist thesis: "male–female relations based on male effort to control female sexuality, male dominance and a distinct division of labor."[17]

The early feminist search for a past when women ruled a domain of harmony and peace has proven just as illusory as a simple picture of dominant males and passive females. The evidence does suggest that women in prehistory had higher status and more equality with men than did women in later eons, when a settled, agricultural way of life led to property rights and increased male control. Many historians believe the discovery that every child born has only one father led to the understanding of paternity and to the related idea of private property that could be inherited at the same time. And the rise of agriculture meant that women no longer roamed far in search of food and became easier to control.[18]

Women's "Nature"

The idea that we humans were hardwired back in the Stone Age has become a favorite theme in the media despite its speculative nature. But a careful review of the Ultra Darwinists' major claims, in the light of relevant studies by biologists and primatologists, shows them to be unsubstantiated conjectures. Let's begin with the idea of the naturally monogamous, libido-challenged female.

The Myth of Coyness

It is hard, in any age, to lift the veil of culture and gaze at nature in an unbiased way. Even Charles Darwin failed to pierce the fog of Victorian sensibility regarding females:[19] "The female . . . with the rarest exception, is less eager (to copulate) than the male . . . she generally requires to be courted, she is coy, and may often be seen endeavoring for a long time to escape from the male."[20] (What a coincidence that this notion of female behavior fits perfectly with Victorian sexual mores.)

Was the coy female, resurrected by the Ultra Darwinists, a figment of the male imagination? As primatologist Sarah Blaffer Hrdy states, "The appellation 'coy' which was to remain unchallenged dogma for the succeeding hundred years, did not then, and does not now apply to the observed behavior of monkey and ape females at mid-cycle."[21] Darwin, she says, in many ways misunderstood and misinterpreted the female primate. Though he introduced the idea of female sexual choice as one of the driving forces of evolution, he saw the mechanism of that choice imperfectly.

Of course, he didn't have access to the myriad field studies available to scientists today. Those studies largely show, Hrdy believes, that natural selection drives female primates to seek many male partners. In a closely studied group of female chimpanzees in West Africa, half of the offspring turned out not to have been sired by the males in residence. Hrdy notes that although Darwin observed female sexual swellings, "he apparently never had the opportunity to observe the 12-day period around a chimpanzee's maximum tumescence, when she typically mates about one to four times an hour with thirteen or more partners."[22] A far cry from Darwin's coy mistress waiting to be courted. Female bonobos, perhaps our closest primate relatives, copulate with as much energy and variety as their male counterparts. Studies of many primate species show that females often initiate sexual activity and take part vigorously.

Cornell anthropologist Meredith Small reports this provocative vignette in a group of Barbary macaques. "The large, pink rump of a female macaque bobbed through the juniper scrub. The monkey was in estrus, and like a lighthouse beacon, the huge swelling on her backside signaled that she was near ovulation. She paused for a moment among four or five males. Surely, one would corner her, mate, and become the father of her next infant."[23] Instead, the female monkey "approached a low-ranking young male and presented her rear, enticing him to mount. After screeching a passionate mating call, she left him, then sashayed up to an older male, presented, and urged him as well." This field experience trumped old theories. "The story that unfolded that autumn changed my views forever," Small writes.

"Female primates," agrees Hrdy, when they are in heat "act as if they are trying to select multiple partners."[24] Rather than wait for her evolutionary Prince Charming, what if the female best protects her genetic future by seeking out a whole pride of Charmings? That would put a crimp in the Ultra Darwinist worldview. Brown University biologist Anne Fausto-Sterling wonders why promiscuous human males who spread their seed are considered the important players in evolution.[25] Why isn't it just as likely that the females "were the ones who hedged their bets and slept with more than one male?" Fausto-Sterling, along with Patricia Gowaty of the University of Georgia and Marlene Zuk of the University of California–Riverside, says that in the past, "the vast majority of research on sexual selection has recorded and theorized male behaviors while ignoring, undervaluing and presenting cardboard cutouts of female activities."[26] That began to change in the 1970s when a large cadre of female researchers spent a lot of time in the field, watching many species and many interactions over time. The picture they brought into focus was more complete and nuanced than the old story, and females emerged as just as active—and sexual—as males.

A mother could indeed gain an advantage by copulating with many males, who would then be invested in her offspring. This behavior might prevent males from attacking her babies or might elicit other forms of protection from a group of males rather than just one. Observations of a number of species support this view. As Hrdy notes, in species as varied as savanna baboons, Barbary macaques, and humans, possible suitors as well as former consorts of the mother appear to look out for the well-being of infants. Males will not kill infants of their species to which they have any kind of connection. Even male baboons in South Africa, who kill 41 percent of infants born, will not kill the infants of females with whom they have mated.[27]

A substantial number of human societies offer evidence that having many consorts works to the advantage of women and the survival of their children. In the lowlands of South America today, there's a common belief that all men who have intercourse with a woman share the biological fatherhood of her child. Among the Bari people of Venezuela, married women often take lovers after they are pregnant. At the birth, they announce to each lover, "You have a child," and these men become "secondary fathers" who recognize obligations to the child (most often gifts of fish and game).

Researcher Stephen Beckerman and his colleagues found that the survival chances of children who had secondary fathers were better than those without such relationships—80 percent, as compared to 64 percent.[28] (This is not an isolated oddity; such patterns are found in many societies in Africa, Australia, and Melanesia, among others.) Hrdy concludes, "Clearly, female primates are more sexually assertive than Darwin and his successors realized, and by extension, so were our remote ancestors."[29] It is unlikely that the behavior of our hominid ancestors was totally unlike that of their primate kin.

The Myth of Monogamy

The evidence suggests that whether either sex strays or remains faithful has more to do with cultural mores, existing laws, economic realities, and individual preferences than with gender. The notion of ancient hardwiring falls flat in light of the great variety in sexual behavior. Worldwide, over time, mating patterns change in every culture. Evolutionary psychologists claim that men are programmed to protect women with whom they have mated from any incursion by other males. But in these primitive societies, men seem to benefit when other men have sexual relations with their wives because their children then get more food and other resources. Men who encourage secondary fathers are more likely to see their genes passed on than those who jealously guard their wives from other men. Moreover, the faithful wife puts herself and her offspring at risk by not having secondary fathers to care for her and her children.

The notion that, throughout history, women would best protect their interests by having only one partner (who was always off hunting, according to some evolutionary psychologists) seems to make little sense.

How would a lactating mother, perched by the fire at a campsite, protect herself and her children from predators? Life was harsh in the Pleistocene. The chances that a woman's mate might not survive a virus, an injury, or an encounter with a predator must have been high. Clearly, it would have made better sense for her to have had more males invested in her offspring than to have been a coy, monogamous female.

The situation of the Stone Age female in a resource-poor environment seems much more analogous to that of the Bari women than it does to that of, say, 1950s homemakers. Not many of *their* husbands would be eaten by something in the neighborhood, so fidelity was probably a successful strategy for their survival and that of their children. Not so for our ancestors. The female roving eye has deep roots in prehistory and is probably as natural as the male's.

This point was ignored in a large-scale study of mating behavior that garnered a great deal of attention in 2003. "Desire and DNA: Is Promiscuity Innate?" asked the *Washington Post*.[30] The paper reported that for men, the answer was yes. Dozens of other media outlets picked up the story, and it was featured on Web sites around the world. The article discussed a study of 16,000 college students from every continent except Antarctica. It found that males everywhere said they wanted many more sexual partners than did women. Because these differences seem so "universal," the media reported, they must be "hardwired."

But the researcher, David Schmitt of Bradley University in Peoria, Illinois, argued that the press got it "exactly wrong" in reporting the finding that men were promiscuous and women weren't.[31] Both sexes, he claimed, have a promiscuous streak; women, however, tend to be somewhat more selective. Critics also noted that what someone says he wants is one thing; what he actually does can be quite another. Schmitt asked the men and women only about desires or fantasies. "There's a big difference between wanting lots of partners, and actually getting them or seeking them." And it turns out that men and women don't differ much in their actual behavior. A major study of extramarital affairs found that, overall, 23 percent of males strayed, as compared to 12 percent of females. But for those under forty (the prime dating years), there were no differences between the sexes—roughly 3 percent for each. Yet in self-report surveys, men say they would like to have eighteen partners, while women would settle for four or five. In a National Opinion Research Center poll at the University of Chicago of 3,432 adults in 1992, a fourth of the men and a sixth of the women reported at least one extramarital affair—not a major difference.[32]

Can we believe what women say about sex when they know somebody's listening? Psychologist Terri Fisher of Ohio State asked men and women whether they ever masturbated or watched pornography.[33] On a scale of 0 to 3, the men scored 2.32 and the women 0.89. However, the women's scores jumped dramatically—to 2.04—when they were assured of privacy and anonymity. (The men's scores did not change with the promise of privacy.) In Schmitt's study, men and women answered the survey while sitting together in classrooms, hardly a private setting.

We must back up from these miniportraits to see the big picture: both sexes overwhelmingly opt for fidelity. In a major representative sample (1997) of more than 2,000 adults, 4 percent of married men and 1.7 percent of married women had had affairs during the preceding year.[34] Thus 96 percent of men and 98.3 percent of women stayed true to their mates. Even over a lifetime, 67 percent of men and 88 percent of women stay faithful to their mates.

Researcher Michael Wiederman of Ball State University, in an extensive review of the research, concludes that because gender differences in fidelity are so small and influenced by so many social factors, trying to explain these differences with any single cause is "merely speculation."[35] The major pattern for both men and women seems to be that miserable couples do not stay married—but those with good marriages do. This is so despite the new firepower directed against the old institution. The media story is that marriage is in tatters. "Clearly, the lifetime, monogamous marriage is being abandoned and falling apart," says the *Toronto Star.*[36] In her much hyped book *Against Love*, author Laura Kipnis calls marriage an affront to human rights.[37] "The domestic captivity that is marriage is complete and relentless, with surveillance, repression and prohibition built into its very structure." Then why do so many of us stay married?

In today's modern urban society, couples depend on each other for financial and emotional support and make long-term investments in their children. Monogamy is the strategy that best guarantees the survival of their genes. For our ancestors, having many children helped ensure that at least some would live to maturity and reproduce. Today, with infant mortality in the developed world at an all-time low, parents have fewer children and invest significant resources in each of them. These days, when it's estimated that it costs well over $100,000 to raise and educate a child, monogamous partners can muster those resources better than single parents.

In the evolutionary script, a major reason for female fidelity was that males would provide food and protection for the woman and her children. But in the Pleistocene, was the male the most reliable provider for women and children? There's evidence that in contemporary hunter-gatherer tribes, males don't give first dibs on the food they have killed to their offspring, but use it to advance their status and curry favor. Since women provide an estimated 80 percent of the food in hunter-gatherer groups, they might have been better served by relying on aunts, sisters, and grandmothers to provide for their children. Anthropologist Kristen Hawkes studied the Hazda people of Tanzania and found that children did better when grandmothers or other older women were on hand.[38] It was women's gathering, not men's hunting, that determined whether a family received adequate nutrition. Her intriguing suggestion is that perhaps women live on well after their fertile years because they are so important to the survival of children.

The Myth of Low Libido

The idea that female monogamy evolved through natural selection as a means of ensuring the survival of the species is suspect. Obviously, it was in women's own genetic self-interest to seek out many partners.

This view, better than the monogamy story proffered by some researchers, appears to match both the scientific record, as it is now understood, and experience with primates.

To take this notion further, the story of mankind can be seen, through one lens, as an ongoing, desperate struggle by males to repress female sexuality. Wright asks, "Can anyone find a single culture in which women with unrestrained appetites aren't viewed as more aberrant than comparable libidinous men?"[39] A number of anthropologists would say they can. Bari men, for example, seem not to view women's sexual activities with alarm. But even if Wright's scenario were true, women's restrained sexual activity would be due less to nature's dictates than to male anxiety.

The historical record shows that as human societies evolved into large, settled social groups, the control of female sexuality was solidified into custom and written into laws across many cultures. The need to control female sexuality is powerful, explains *New York Times* science writer Natalie Angier: "Women are said to have lower sex drives than men, yet they are universally punished if they display evidence to the contrary—if they disobey their 'natural' inclination towards a stifled libido."[40]

The list of attempts to control female sexuality goes on and on: genital mutilation, purdah, suttee, veils, the scarlet letter, chastity belts, stoning adulterous women. As Angier notes, "Men have the natural higher sex drive, yet all the laws, customs, punishments, strictures, mystiques and anti-mystiques are aimed with full hominid fury at that tepid, sleepy, hypoactive creature, the female libido."

What Is Natural About Natural Selection?

Given the new studies of primates and the span of human history, it might make sense to suggest, as does primatologist Barbara Smuts, that natural selection is a three-legged process, with all three supports bearing equal weight: male–male competition, female choice, and coercion of females by males.[41] Females may be coy in some situations, insatiable in others, faithful at times, unfaithful at other times.

Still, there is a yearning in some quarters to resurrect the passive, eternally faithful female. After September 11, for example, some conservative pundits rejoiced that at last women were going to need brave, noble, manly men. Social critic Camille Paglia couldn't help noticing, she said, "how robustly, dreamily masculine the faces of the firefighters are. They're not on Prozac or questioning their gender."[42] Former Reagan speechwriter Peggy Noonan famously declared, "I missed John Wayne. But now I think . . . he's back."[43] And the *Economist* managed to link Bridget Jones with September 11.[44] The magazine bemoaned the fact that the fictional Bridget, and by extension all her real-life single gal pals in the United States and Britain, are finding work and single life too much fun to think about babies and marriage. But in the wake of the terrorist attacks, "Bridget Jones may be willing to settle sooner for marriage and less eager to find fulfillment at work." Could love, the *Economist* seems audibly to sigh, "really be what matters most to single women in their 30s?"

Will young women abandon their jobs and march cheerfully back to 1950s domesticity—and lifelong monogamy—starting at an early age? Don't count on it. There seems to be no letup in the rate at which women enter college and secure good jobs. Little more than a year after the *Economist* predicted women would choose early marriage over work, American women in unprecedented numbers joined men in going to war in Iraq and performing more types of jobs than ever before, under trying circumstances.(One airport runway construction project was directed by three female engineers.)

Yet the sentimental attachment to the notion of an "old-fashioned" female dies hard. Wendy Shalit, just out of college in 1999, wrote a best-seller titled *A Return to Modesty*, calling for a march back to retro values: conservative dress, celibacy before marriage, and fathers who rule their daughters with an iron hand.[45] Sexual harassment and date rape, she says, are basically women's fault: "I believe a lot of these problems are due to the breakdown of modesty and a lack of respect."

Maybe her new brand of modesty is an updated version of the romance novel—this one designed for men. Women aren't really coy and monogamous, but wouldn't it be nice if they were? Today, however, as women work side by side with men, they have the same temptations that men have always had—and they give in to them at about the same rate. And, like men, women choose monogamy—when they do—because it suits their emotional as well as sexual needs. Women today feel much freer to fantasize about sex and talk about it as one of life's delights—whether they act on their fantasies or not. Though the data tell us that few married women (or married men) actually cheat, they can enjoy entertaining the possibility.

Men's "Nature"

If women are governed by iron laws ensuring that anatomy is destiny, men are no less constricted by the story the Ultra Darwinists tell. They are as anchored to their unchanging biology and Stone Age–honed genetic drives as women are. Although on the surface, this narrative gives men a natural claim to such gifts as ambition, power, and achievement, it also paints a picture of males that leaves them bereft of many of the joys of being human. In particular, they are seen as deficient in the ability to love, nurture, and connect deeply with their children.

The Myth of Don Juan

If women are passive and coy in the Ultra Darwinist view of the world, men are naturally programmed to spread their seed far and wide with little concern for the children they beget. This picture derives from biologist Robert Trivers's notion of differential investment in parenting, in which females are the "parenting gender," with males only tangentially involved.[46] Another author speaks of men as having "love-'em-and-leave-'em genes."[47]

Can this be the best strategy for a man to pass on his genes? Angier, among others, does not think so.[48] Since the human female does not go into estrus, the male doesn't know when she's fertile—two or three days a month. Even if she's ovulating, there's only a 20 percent chance that he will impregnate her. She may already be pregnant; he can't tell. And even if he does impregnate her, she has a high chance of miscarrying. Since he's soon off to find greener pastures, he won't be around to know whether another male will step up and win the genetic lottery. The Pleistocene was a tough world for infants. If a father invested no energy in feeding and guarding his young, there was a good chance that none of them would survive.

Another strategy may make more sense. As Angier puts it, "if a man were to spend more time with one woman rather than dashing breathlessly from sheet to sheet, if he were to feel compelled to engage in what animal behaviorists call mate-guarding, he might be better off, reproductively speaking, than the wild Lothario." Mating with one female more often, he would have a better chance of getting her pregnant, and if he stayed around, his infant would have an enhanced chance of survival. (And the father would be less likely to be killed or injured by males whose favored females he would be attempting to seduce.) Perhaps, as Nicholas Blurton Jones of the University of California–Los Angeles, has argued, marriage was invented by males as a form of mate guarding.[49] Having regular sex with one woman was a lot easier than roaming from female to female, and possibly more effective in terms of reproductive success. So maybe marriage works better for men than women. According to the Ultra Darwinists men are by nature unsuited for marriage. This belief isn't supported by the data. Married men are healthier, both emotionally and physically, than single men. Men thrive in marriage more than women do, in fact. The cliché is that a man chases a woman until she catches him. The truth may be quite the opposite.

The Ultra Darwinists have some explaining to do, say psychologists Kay Bussey of Macquarie University and Albert Bandura of Stanford, who did a major review of the mating strategy research and found that most males mate monogamously.[50] Relatively few roam around impregnating young, fertile females to populate the gene pool for future generations. "If prolific, uncommitted sexuality is a male biological imperative," they write, "it must be a fairly infirm one that can be easily overridden by psychosocial forces."

When men stay with one mate, they can be reasonably sure that the children produced by the union will be their own. And if they stay around, those children will grow and thrive. At the same time, they get a human connection, which they desire as much as women do. One man, for example, discovered that an enduring relationship could be more exciting than a string of one-night stands. "There was no more challenge at the bars. Everybody knows your name, but when you leave, you feel empty." Then he met the woman who became his wife. "And here she was—we were doing other things, exciting things. I learned a lot from her, we enjoyed each other, so why not get married?"[51]

But a man who has tired of the dating rat race and is ready to commit might find that the woman he believes to be his soul mate is skittish because she has deep reservations about his basic male nature. Yes, things seem wonderful now—but wouldn't he inevitably head off for greener pastures? Can you ever trust a man to be faithful if his unchanging nature is to stray? The popularity of the Don Juan image of men sends the message to women that they must always watch for signs of their husbands' cheating. If he's a half hour late from work, was he with a lover? If he comes home looking rumpled, has he stolen an hour in a motel room with his secretary? If he has to go out of town on short notice on a business meeting, is he really spending his night with a new love?

One woman's marriage nearly crumbled under the weight of her anxiety. Thirty-five-year-old Rebecca constantly rummaged through her husband Sam's phone bills and credit card statements, checking for numbers or places she didn't recognize. She was always calling him at work to find out when he'd be home and demanding to know where he'd been if he was the slightest bit late. The only concrete evidence she'd found to support her suspicions was a receipt from a fancy restaurant they had never patronized. Her "proof" elevated her suspicion to a near frenzy. When she calmed down enough to talk reasonably to Sam—instead of blindly accusing him—she learned that he had been entertaining a prospective business client. It took a lot of work for Rebecca to trust Sam and for Sam to get over his anger at her unfounded jealousy.

Statistically, Sam is not much more likely to stray than Rebecca is. If she's always distrustful, always doubting whether he can be faithful, her suspicions can undermine their marriage. Ironically, they might even lead him to search for someone more trusting. Buying into old gender-difference beliefs can create a woman's worst-case scenario.

What about men's scenarios? If a man believes he is unable to make a long-term commitment to a woman because "men just don't do that," he may wind up spending his life in one unsatisfying relationship after another. He may never connect with a woman in a joyous way. Men who fall into this pattern can develop deep anxiety about their lack of ability to commit and choose intermittent loneliness because this is "natural" for men. For example, Neil, an architect in his forties, had a number of short-term relationships but never married. Finally he fell in love with Joanne, a warm, loving woman with whom he was unusually comfortable. Neil at last seemed to overcome his belief that he wasn't designed for marriage. He proposed, the wedding plans were set, the guests were invited—and then Neil's doubts about his ability to commit kicked in. A month before the wedding, Neil insisted on a punitive prenuptial arrangement that convinced Joanne he had forged a weapon to drive her away. And it worked. The wedding was called off and Joanne moved out of Neil's house—and out of his life. Neil is back into his on-again, off-again relationships. From the outside, many men might envy Neil. He's affluent and attractive, and he's not tied down. But those close to him see a lonely, troubled man who sabotages his chances for happiness. Joanne still carries scars from Neil's behavior. Men who are trapped in this "evolutionary" straitjacket wind up not only hurting themselves but doing great damage to the women who love them.

The Myth of the Uninterested Father

Men's genes, the Ultra Darwinists tell us, render them uninterested in—and unfit for—involvement with their young. Early primate studies appeared to bolster this belief, but they centered on certain species in which males are indeed remote from offspring, such as rhesus monkeys, baboons, and chimpanzees.[52] In the past twenty years, an explosion of field studies has demonstrated a remarkably high level of male caregiving among many species. Their parental behavior, we've learned, is wide and varied. Cotton-top tamarin mothers and fathers each carry their infants 50 percent of the time. Males also share food with infants at the time of weaning, assisting in their transition to solid food. Among tamarins and marmosets,[53] adult males do more carrying of juveniles than do adult females, and in captivity Aotus males carry infants 70–81 percent of the time during their first month. In the wild, Callicebus males carry infants 80–90 percent of the time. And male rhesus monkeys in captivity have been found to groom infants as much as the females do, playing with them and serving as powerful attachment figures.

Researchers have also observed special relationships between baboon mothers and males that may not be the fathers of the infants, in addition to noting males of a number of species who "adopt" orphans and develop close, long-lasting relationships with them. When new infants are given to juvenile male and female rhesus monkeys, there are few differences in their responses to the babies. Psychologist Charles T. Snowdon of the University of Wisconsin notes, "To the extent that a male's assistance during the female's lactation improves infant survival, or that male assistance and protection assures that weaned infants survive until they can reproduce, then males may be making a parental investment that may be comparable to that of the female."[54] In tamarins, for example, researchers found a 40 percent survival rate in groups with three caregivers, compared with the 87–100 percent survival rate in groups with five or six helpers, male and female.

Among humans, male parental care is more likely when mothers make important economic as well as child care contributions to the family. In hunter-gatherer societies such as one tribe of pygmies in East Central Africa and the !Kung of the Kalahari Desert, where women gather two-thirds of the family's food, male parental care is high.[55] In many modern two-income couples, when women work outside the home, both males and females are heavily engaged in both nurturing and breadwinning. When sociologist Barbara Risman from North Carolina State University studied single fathers and involved married fathers, she found that fathers can "mother" just as well as women, and in just the same way.[56]

Among the Aka pygmies of Central Africa, the father holds his infant more than 20 percent of the time and remains within arm's reach of his baby 50 percent of the time.[57] He marries just one wife. And when he goes off to hunt, his wife and kids go with him. Males do not "naturally" avoid infant care but sometimes need the mother's permission to interact. As Snowdon concludes, "Males are not by nature prone to love 'em and leave 'em but can form long-term relationships with mates that are defended against intruders of either sex. Finally, males of many species appear to be highly interested and motivated to take care of infants. Even in highly promiscuous species in which males are rarely observed to display parental care, males have the potential to express highly competent parental care."

Increasingly, researchers argue that ancestral environments would have favored strong male–female bonds and high levels of paternal as well as maternal investment in offspring.[58] The solitary, aggressive male is not a huge success in the modern world, either; often he's cooling his heels in jail, hardly a place conducive to ensuring the survival of his genes.

As Bussey and Bandura point out in their review of sexual differentiation, "Aggressive skill may have had reproductive advantage in ancient times when males could lay claim to females at will, but cultural evolution of social norms and sanctions has essentially stripped it of reproductive benefit. Some males rule females by physical force, but most do not. Would male aggression be the trait most favored by natural selection? The opposite may be true."

Because both men and women in the Pleistocene faced a harsh, difficult environment, humans would instead be selected for capabilities such as social competence and the capacity to invent culture. In this view, our ancestors organized themselves in small, cooperative groups, and the fittest of these would be the most social, promoting such norms as loyalty to the group, cooperation, and adherence to social norms.[59] Seen in this light, "survival of the fittest" takes on a new meaning: less about "tooth and claw" than intelligence, sociability, and cooperation.

For a theory of sex differences based on the absence of male involvement with children, another problem becomes apparent. In the United States, fathers are spending more time with their children than they did twenty years ago, and they express a strong preference for further involvement.[60] In today's world of growth and abundance, mere survival isn't enough. Children's chances for success depend on access to such resources as education and the ability to navigate in the job world, and a father's involvement improves the child's chances of getting that access.

As one father puts it, "I look at my boys and realize that I am helping them turn into men. I see them changing from soft pudgy children with all the emotions of children; I see them becoming the kind of people whose work you can rely on. That's my image of a man. And I want to be a man who is there for them."[61]

Ultra Darwinist theories about men seem far off the mark, when real men talk about their connections to their children. The idea that the promiscuous male is the most "successful" male in the game of propagating their genes is off-kilter too.

Pleasure Poker Versus the Genetic Lottery

The evolutionary narrative suggests that only male genes count, and that male "swingers" win both the pleasure poker and the genetic lottery. In fact, a great deal of attention is being paid to what females contribute to the next generation. Women pass on more of their genetic material to both their female and male babies than men do. Most of the genes a baby possesses come from the X chromosome. "The Y has but seventy or so elements that code for proteins compared to ten times as many on the X," says British writer Steve Jones, author of *Y*.[62] He explains that women have two X chromosomes, while men have one X and one Y. All males must get their X chromosome from their mother. The Y chromosome they inherit from their father carries much less genetic information. It turns out that males, not females, are the also-rans in the story of whose genes have the most influence on who you turn out to be.

Another intriguing idea is that effective contraception may have a huge impact on which men emerge as winners in the genetic lottery. As Rutgers University philosopher Colin McGinn notes, "Contraception breaks the link between sex and babies. . . contraception cuts the Gordian knot."[63] No longer does male copulation regularly lead to offspring. Indeed, a man may want the pleasure of sex without the consequence of babies—especially in a time when he can't procreate and run but will be forced by the legal system to provide for the child he has fathered. Legal and economic concerns may outweigh genetic imperatives. At present and in the future, McGinn suggests, the man with the most number of copulations will be the man with the *fewest* children, since in the developed world, a very active sex life may go along with the wish (and the means) to avoid pregnancy.

When New York University sociologist Kathleen Gerson studied contemporary men (average age 36), she found them clustered in three distinct groups: involved fathers, career-oriented breadwinners, and autonomous men. The last category, about a third of the group, ducked family responsibilities entirely. Zachary, a divorced business manager, explains, "I won't have had that love relationship of a father and child. I know that's what I'm giving up. But how important is that? It's not something I feel bad about; it's just something I know I won't experience. But I say no matter what you do, if you're married with children or single and not with children, you can screw your life up and really feel depressed. You've got to make your own moves." Jeremy, a forty-year-old single computer consultant, says, "Nobody has a hold on me. I do as I wish. And tomorrow, if I don't want to, I don't have to."

McGinn notes, "Certainly in developed countries an active sex life does not always go with a large family." If this trend persists, he says, the most promiscuous males will clearly be losers in genetic roulette.

What does all this mean? That the old black magic is not merely a distant echo from the Pleistocene past, making us dance a series of preordained steps. There is no evidence of the rigid patterns of sexual behavior that the Ultra Darwinist scenario mandates. Rather, there is an enormous variety of male and female behavior around the globe. Depending on the culture and the social class, men and women can behave very differently or in much the same way. We are not puppets waltzing to a preset tune. If we believe we are, our options will be limited, our lives will be constrained, and our future diminished.

The Mating Game

"WHY DID THE CHICKEN cross the road? If it was male, probably for a tender young pullet; if it was female, probably for a powerful old rooster."[1] This "joke" appeared as a headline in the *Houston Chronicle*, reporting one of the ideas revived by the Ultra Darwinists as newsworthy science. In this skewed version of male–female history, the newspaper was inspired by David Buss, University of Texas psychologist and author of *The Evolution of Desire* (1994).[2] The notion that men everywhere prefer very young women was a central finding of a major study by Buss, who proclaims great differences between men and women in their choice of mates, all harking back to the Pleistocene.[3]

The story, with its irresistible mix of sex, beauty, and Stone Age man and woman, was made for the media. The *Washington Post* wrapped the message in a familiar romantic lyric: "The fundamental things apply, as time goes by."[4] *Newsweek* ran a cover displaying two fetching young people titled "The Biology of Beauty," with the subtitle "What science has learned about sex appeal" as if these speculative theories were established science.[5] *U.S. News & World Report* decreed that "the sophisticated sexual strategies of modern men and women are shaped by a powerful Stone Age psychology."[6] The writer went on to say, "Within the human skull is a Stone Age mind that was shaped by the mating concerns of our ancient ancestors and continues to have a profound influence on behavior today. Indeed, this ancient psychological legacy influences everything from sexual attraction to infidelity and jealousy." Let's examine Buss's study to see how much truth there is to this assertion.

Buss set out to test five hypotheses derived from evolutionary theory about gender differences in mate preference. In choosing a mate, he predicted, females would value earning capacity, ambition, and industriousness more highly than would males, whereas males would value youth, physical attractiveness, and chastity more highly than would females. He collected data from 10,047 people drawn from thirty-seven cultures in thirty-three countries located on six continents and five islands—the largest sample ever obtained to test hypotheses on mate preferences. He developed questionnaires and sent a team of some fifty interviewers (who were natives of each country) to administer them. Sometimes the interviewers had to read the questions aloud to illiterate people, especially in rural Africa. This ambitious study had serious problems, many of which Buss acknowledged. The samples vary widely in size—from 55 people (Iran) to over 500 (China)—and representativeness. Some subjects were recruited through newspaper advertisements, some on university campuses, and some through more scientifically sound sampling techniques. (Although Buss cautions that the data from some of these samples may thus be unreliable, he nevertheless gives equal weight to each one.)[7]

His findings echo the theories of the evolutionary psychologists we have been discussing. His data, he claims, provide strong support for three of the five hypotheses he studied:

1. Women prefer men with high earning potential.
2. Men prefer very young women.
3. Men select physically attractive mates.

The hypothesis that women seek ambition and industriousness in men received only partial support, and the one concerning chastity in mates received even less. Despite the problems with the sample, Buss claims to have found "among the most robust psychological sex differences of any kind ever documented across cultures."[8] As we shall see, scholars who reanalyzed Buss's data came to different conclusions.

Importantly, *both sexes* ranked kindness-understanding and intelligence higher than earning power and attractiveness in *all* samples—a finding of enormous significance that the evolutionary theorists all but ignore. Could it be because there is no way to trace these qualities back to the Pleistocene?

What a Man Wants
(Youth Isn't Everything)

Buss says males select mates on the basis of particular features of physical appearance that are associated with youth—such as smooth skin, good muscle tone, lustrous hair, and full lips—and behavioral indicators of youth, such as high energy level and sprightly gait.[9] In accordance with natural selection theory, he argues that sexual attraction and standards of beauty have evolved to correspond to these features, which in turn should transcend cultural variations and all men everywhere should be attracted to them. "The physical and behavioral cues that signal youth and health and are regarded as attractive should be linked with reproductive capacity among human females in all cultures."[10]

The notion of a universal female type beloved by men—young, unlined, with baby-faced features—goes back to Darwin's day, although Darwin himself did not promote it. He believed that sheer physical appearance would act more forcefully on primitive man than on modern man. "Civilized men," he wrote, "are largely attracted by the mental charms of women, by their wealth, and especially by their social position."[11]

Yet Ohio State University psychologist Terri Fisher says that whenever she teaches her college students about the Ultra Darwinian take on the power of youth and beauty, the young men smile and nod and the young women look appalled.[12] But college students aren't the only ones who simplify the complicated business of mate selection. Some of today's Ultra Darwinists, betraying their namesake, do indeed claim to have discovered a universal beauty that all men desire. Buss, for example, says that because a fourteen-year-old may be able to have more offspring in her lifetime than a twenty-four-year-old, she is more desirable. She may also have the baby-faced features that signal fertility: small nose and ears, large brow relative to the chin, short stature.

Some researchers went to absurd lengths to quantify the ideal female face:

> The chin length is short—exactly one fifth the height of the face. The distance from the bottom of the eyebrow to the center of the face is relatively long—one-tenth the height of the face. The individual eye width is large—consistently it was three-tenths the width of the face at eye level. The visible eyeball is large too—one-fourteenth the height of the face—and so is the width of the pupil—one fourteenth of the distance between wide cheekbones.[13]

Are baby-faced teenagers what men want? And is extreme youth an accurate indicator of fertility?

One answer comes from our primate cousins. Biologist Sarah Blaffer Hrdy says, "To a primatologist, reported preferences for young females' neotenous [baby-faced] traits are puzzling. There is not a *shred of evidence* [italics ours] for any primate that youth or [baby-faced features] affect male willingness to mate. Instead, for every monkey or ape species for which information on male preferences is available, priority is given for fully adult females who have had one or more offspring."[14] Across primates, including humans, younger mothers actually suffer higher rates of infant mortality than older mothers. "Clearly, it makes evolutionary sense for males to select females not only on the basis of fecundity, but on the probability of producing offspring that survive," notes Hrdy.[15]

If a human preference for very young females diverged sharply from the behavior of other primates, we might ask why. Hrdy says, "Why would Homo Sapiens, unique among primates, be so attracted to neotenous females?"[16] Not, she says, because of fecundity; perhaps it is because male humans do not simply mate with females; in some societies they try to control or even own them—as wives with few legal rights, slaves, or concubines. Such coercion may be much easier with a very young female than with an experienced woman. Elvis Presley, for example, a man who wanted to control nearly every waking moment of his wife's life, chose fourteen-year-old Priscilla Beaulieu as his future wife. Priscilla obeyed for a while, but then grew up, divorced Elvis, pursued a thriving career of her own, and competently managed his estate after he died. Unfortunately for some men, little girls get bigger every day.

If there is a universal beauty, there should be agreement on what it is. There isn't. In another study David Buss asked 107 newly married couples to rate each other's attractiveness.[17] He also asked independent observers to rate the attractiveness of each man and woman. Everybody should have agreed on which women were attractive and which weren't, but the findings threw a monkey wrench into this notion. There was no significant correlation between the husbands' and the observers' ratings of the attractiveness of the wives. Beauty really is in the eye of the beholder. People tend to find their own spouses attractive, whether others do or not. Individuals vary widely in what they find attractive in a partner.

In fact, what men and women look for most are people like themselves. Cornell biologist Stephen T. Emlen reported in 2003 that "attractive people tend to value attractiveness, wealthy people value mates with money and ambitious types and family oriented souls tend to gravitate to others like themselves."[18] He found that the desire for similar mates was *five or six times* more powerful than the desire for beautiful or wealthy ones. One lively couple in their thirties we spoke to found that a similar sense of humor first attracted them to each other—and still helps keep the relationship strong. "I don't like fart jokes," says the wife. Then she reconsiders. "Well, sometimes I do—if *he* tells them. He's funny. He makes me laugh all the time." The good news is that a reasonably attractive person, male or female, stands a good chance of finding another reasonably attractive person who likes the same things.

If, as the Ultra Darwinists claim, beauty has played the major role in all societies, then how do they account for societies with arranged marriages, in which mate selection is based not on physical attractiveness but on tribal and family affiliation, family relationships, social status, and wealth?[19] Only in societies in which men and women have freedom to choose could physical attractiveness conceivably play a major part in mate selection. Indeed, that notion is backed up by a 1972 cross-cultural study of the ethnographic records of twenty-nine societies.[20] Spouse selection for qualities such as physical attraction rather than for skills, rank, alliances, and increasing family wealth were positively correlated with the freedom that people had to select spouses according to their own preferences. Buss's data were drawn predominantly from cultures in which individual mate choice was likely to be high; but were our early human ancestors free to mate as they chose? Or did kinship ties, alliances, primitive religious beliefs, or tribal strife place constraints on them? And how did these factors affect the process of evolution? We cannot even hazard a guess. There were no Kinsey studies during the Pleistocene.

Why should we assume that what worked a million years ago would be related to what works for modern humans? Perhaps our male hominid ancestors were much like our primate cousins, looking for a mate who had already produced offspring, rather than a Stone Age Britney Spears. Perhaps qualities that are unknown to us played an important role.[21] Maybe our male ancestors were attracted by the gracefully feminine way a potential mate dug up roots and tubers. Maybe a series of melodious grunts or a particular male gait proved irresistible to a female. With no record to sift through, these theories may be no more far-fetched than the "biology of beauty" argument. The unanswerable question is, How would Stone Age men recognize the women most likely to be fertile?

Baby Bait

If there were a universal male preference for beautiful young women, it would have to be based on a strong correlation between beauty and reproductive success. Richard Gere chose Julia Roberts in *Pretty Woman* because of her beauty and youth, but those qualities hardly ensure enhanced fertility. Having a pretty face as a young adult has no relationship to the number of children a woman produces or to her health throughout a lifetime.[22] And, among married women, physical attractiveness is unrelated to the number of children they produce. The homeliest of women can be star breeders. If beauty has little to do with reproductive success, why would nature insist that men select for it? It seems more likely that having a young beauty on his arm indicates, instead, that a man is living up to certain cultural and social norms.

Despite the popularity of the "universal" beauty notion, studies show, furthermore, that ideas of beauty vary greatly across cultures. Psychologists Bussey and Bandura say, "Many of the human characteristics that are sexually arousing—corpulence or skinniness, shiny white teeth or black pointed ones, distorted ears, noses or lips, light skin color or dark—not only vary markedly across cultures but bear no relevance to 'good genes' or reproductive fertility and value. Human sexual arousal is driven more by the mind through cultural construction of attractiveness than by physical universals."[23] Chinese men in a certain era found tiny, crippled, bound feet erotic. Some African tribes find nose rings sexually charged—as do some contemporary American teenagers. And extreme swings in notions of beauty can occur in a short time span.

In the 1950s, when the American birthrate jumped to an all-time high, curvy women like Marilyn Monroe, Jane Russell, and Jayne Mansfield were the paragons of beauty. In those days, the average model was a size 12. Now she's a size 4. Extremely thin models and actresses like Kate Moss and Calista Flockhart are proclaimed as icons of beauty. Monica Lewinsky, by Ultra Darwinist standards, should be the ideal woman. She was only twenty-one when she became famous, and she had a beautiful face with symmetrical features. She was the perfect picture of female fertility, with her ample bosom and hips. And she seduced the most powerful man in the world. Instead of toasting her as the new Cleopatra, the media derided Monica as fat—and she agreed. Not hard to understand, when magazine covers are routinely emblazoned with supermodels and actresses who resemble famine victims. One result of hyperthinness in women is cessation of menstruation, making the contemporary construction of beauty the exact opposite of fecundity.

This ideal is a throwback to earlier times. Authors Barbara Ehrenreich and Deirdre English note that about 100 years ago, "a morbid aesthetic developed, in which sickness was seen as a source of female beauty."[24] The beautiful woman was pictured as "sensuously drooping on her cushions, eyes fixed tremulously at her husband or physician or already gazing into the Beyond." In 1900 "society ladies cultivated a sickly countenance by drinking vinegar in quantity, or, more effectively, arsenic. The loveliest heroines were those who died young." Yet men were attracted to these women, so ill that they were about to drop dead or so thin that they couldn't even menstruate. How can this behavior be reconciled with a need hardwired in all men to seek out visible manifestations of fertility?

The evidence that men prefer very young females is questionable, at best. And if it ever existed, we argue that it is fading, thanks to new economic realities. If men and women are now having fewer children, with both parents heavily invested in them, reproductive success does not mean that a man will seek out a woman who will have many children. The drive to make sure one's genes survive can be expressed in many ways. Having lots of kids was probably a good gamble in the premodern era, when child mortality rates were sky high. But it may not be such a wise strategy now, when infant mortality is so low. How many men today want lots of children to support through college, when they can pass on their genes by having just a couple of kids.

And what of the forty-five-year-old man who divorces his forty-something wife and marries a twenty-eight-year-old woman? He's probably not driven by reproductive urges either. After all, most men don't divorce their wives at midlife, and those who do change wives don't normally produce large second families. Surprisingly, most divorces in the United States are initiated by women. Among women with children, the woman is the initiator in 65 percent of the cases; among wives with no children, the figure is 56 percent. If an inborn need of men to mate with young women were driving the divorce rate, then that arithmetic would be reversed.

On the contrary, these days many men with resources are marrying women of substantial means. In elite social circles, having a high-powered lawyer or businesswoman on his arm wins a man more points than a showgirl would. *Management Today* points out that marriages with two supersuccessful spouses are on the rise: Cherie and Tony Blair, Bill and Hillary Clinton, marketing guru Matthew Freud and his media mogul wife Elisabeth Murdoch, and Diane Sawyer and Mike Nichols are among them. "Two high-flyers can use each other's talents as effectively as one high-flyer with a steadfast support at home."[25]

Show Me the Money

Perhaps the most dramatic evidence against the Ultra Darwinist scenario for mating is an unexpected recent trend: Men's mate selection is increasingly influenced by women's earning potential. Recent data show that men are becoming *more* likely to select as mates women who have finished their education, forsaking youth for earning capacity.[26] Today the more education a woman has, the more marriageable she is. This trend is in direct contrast to Buss's findings and challenges the idea that a preference for very young women is in men's genes.

Blind to this shift, the media cling to the old beliefs. Magazines aimed at young women are still filled with instructions on how to perfect nearly every body part. *Elle Girl*, for example, offers "Fun Stuff for the Beauty Buff," including eye makeup, skin products, hair bleach, lip lacquer, mascara, and a range of other diet and beauty aids. Its editors might be wise to include articles on higher education.

Far from being hardwired, men's mate preferences change when situations change.[27] Men's wages have been stagnant or declining for fifteen years now, and the "family wage" of the industrial age has been replaced by the job insecurity of the global era. Most couples require two paychecks to stay in the middle class, a math lesson that is not lost on men. Judge Richard Posner, author of *Sex and Reason*, suggests that "economics is not divorced from mate selection. People change their behavior as costs and benefits change."[28] The popular dating service J-Date automatically requests information on women's incomes because their male clients ask for it.[29] Mary Balfour, director of Drawing Down the Moon, an executive dating agency, says that men in their twenties and thirties now want women who match their intellectual and earning abilities. "It is only those in their fifties and sixties who tend to take a deep breath when introduced to powerful women," she says.[30]

Today, more than 40 percent of white, college-educated married women earn more than their husbands.[31] According to evolutionary theory, these couples should be highly divorce prone. But a 1999 nationally representative sample of 4,405 couples found that divorce is *more* likely when a woman has no earnings than when she brings home a paycheck.[32] In particular, the marriage of a woman with no earnings was *more than twice as likely* to dissolve than that of a woman who earned up to $18,000. The traditional homemaker—who stays by the hearth and wastes no energy on earning money—is commonly thought to have the most stable marriage. But having an income of her own in fact protects a woman's marriage. This is especially true when *his* income goes down—the situation facing a lot of couples today. If he's getting $10,000 less in his paycheck every year, the odds of the marriage breaking up are *four times* greater when his wife has no earnings than when she has income. These findings make sense. Unemployment creates chaos—the suicide rate among men shadows the unemployment rate. In traditional couples, not only does the man suffer the blow of losing his breadwinner status, he may also feel diminished in the eyes of his wife and children. A wife may panic, since the family's economic structure has collapsed. A cycle of guilt, blame, and fear can set in, especially if he can't make up the lost earnings or get a job right away commensurate with the one he lost.[33] But when the wife has a paycheck, the husband's reduced earnings have only a minor disruptive effect.[34]

In our own study of 300 dual-earner couples (funded by the National Institute of Mental Health), we found that women who earned more than their husbands were no more or less likely to devalue their marriages than were those who earned less.[35] Women's magazines no longer tell readers they *shouldn't* earn more than their husbands if they want to hang on to them. Assuming that many women will be in this situation, they offer advice for negotiating this new terrain.

In 2003, a *Cosmo* headline read "Reversal of Fortune: When You're More Successful Than He Is." The magazine offered "Secrets of Happy Breadwinners"—tips on "how to deal with a low-income lover from women who have one."[36] (For example, "I remind myself that if I was with someone who worked long hours like I do, I'd go crazy. He's the yin to my yang and provides the balance I need.") Emily, twenty-six, a Denver sales rep, makes close to six figures while her boyfriend Peter, a lab scientist, makes $30,000. Emily says, "If Peter and I get married, I won't have the choice [to stay home.] He's probably going to stay home and raise the kids, but I think we'll be OK with that." Todd, an actor, has no problem with the good income that his wife, a dancer, brings in. "We agreed in the beginning that we'd go fifty-fifty . . . even if I had the money to take care of things myself, my wife has a calling, a vocation that she needs to fulfill and I want her to fulfill."

As more and more women outearn their partners—and as more men value themselves for something other than money—Emily and Peter's situation will not seem odd. One male artist in his thirties says it used to bother him that his doctor wife earned more. "I used to have pangs about the money thing—feeling that I ought to be contributing an equal amount." But as he has come to appreciate the value of his own artistic talent, the income gap "doesn't bother me at all."

In our dual-earner study, only men with traditional attitudes about sex roles were unhappy when their wives earned more. As for sex, women's earning power does not appear to get in the way of pleasure. When psychologist Janet Hyde and a few colleagues conducted a longitudinal study of 500 couples, they found the highest sexual satisfaction, for both men and women, among couples who both worked and experienced high rewards from their jobs.[37]

These days, with so many people clinging to the middle class by their fingernails, a woman's salary may make the difference between a reasonable life for a couple and one of constant struggle. A very young woman with little earning potential may not seem like much of a bargain to a man today. Indeed, the "right" age of marriage for women changes with time and culture.[38] In Edith Wharton's novel *The House of Mirth*, heroine Lily Bart sees herself, at 29, nearly an old maid in the stratified world of nineteenth-century New York society.[39] Certain her beauty is fading, she has, she believes, precious little time to snare a husband. Compare that to the hit television show *The Bachelor*, in which one man looked askance at a twenty-two-year-old vying for his hand and said, on camera, that the thirty-something beauties in the competition were more desirable because they knew more about life and were more sophisticated. On a segment of *Queer Eye for the Straight Guy*, the gay guys "made over" a twenty-four-year-old straight man who wanted to look good when he proposed to his thirty-year-old fiancée. The age difference was commented on only in passing. Further evidence comes from a study reported in *New Scientist*, finding that men prefer "aging" beauties (36, 41, or 45 years old) to younger, plainer women.[40] Asked to pick a "life partner" from photographs, groups of men (200 in total) all picked the beautiful older woman over the younger, plainer one. The beauty of the woman mattered, but fertility—or lack of it—did not. In this case, "beauty" is clearly a cultural prescription, not an evolutionary one.

Men seemingly don't define beauty strictly in terms of youth. One scientist told the BBC, "You'd think men would always go for the 20-year-olds, but they don't." Although in movies older women don't get to play the primary sex object (remember how much was made of fiftyish Diane Keaton playing a nude scene with Jack Nicholson in *Something's Gotta Give?*), in real life they do. Mary Tyler Moore has been married to a man some twenty years her junior for years. The buzz in Hollywood as of this writing is that forty-year-old Demi Moore is dating twenty-something Ashton Kutcher. Forty-year-old Meg Ryan had a fling with thirtyish Russell Crowe. Melanie Griffith is wed to the younger Antonio Banderas, and *Sex and the City* author Candace Bushnell recently wed a man nearly a decade younger.

This isn't just true of female celebrities with lots of money. Partnerships between younger men and older women are becoming more common across the board. U.S. Census figures from 1998 show that 21 percent of American women live with younger men; among women aged 35–44, the figure is 39 percent.[41] By 2010, thirty-something men will outnumber women five to ten years younger by two to one, so even men who are looking for a much younger wife will soon have a harder time.[42] Because the overall birthrate dropped 40 percent between 1955 and 1973, men in their forties looking for a younger mate will have a much smaller pool to draw from. They may have to choose between marrying a woman their own age or older—or not marrying at all.

What a Woman Wants
(Depends on What She's Got)

Today's courtship rituals couldn't possibly follow the narrative set out by the Ultra Darwinists. Barbara DaFoe Whitehead, codirector of the National Marriage Project at Rutgers, observes, "Today, getting married at 19 or 22 is not a steppingstone to independent adulthood; it's an obstacle."[43] Also, she notes of today's young women, "their mothers had to struggle to find a place in the world of work. For the daughters, however, the struggle is to find their way in the world of love. What they need is a contemporary form of courtship that respects the new timetable of women's lives." (Much the same could be said of men, who are not leading their fathers' lives.) To the extent that people believe the old evolutionary ideas, the new rituals that Whitehead says are needed won't emerge. Everybody loses.

Some evolutionary psychologists and writers, however, cling to the idea that men must always be dominant and always control resources, a stance they can take to absurd lengths. Robert Wright suggests that polygamy would be a better alternative for modern women than divorce, since getting at least a share of the wealth and attention of a wealthy male is better than getting stuck with a poor provider or none at all.[44] (However, recent research shows that women in polygamous marriages around the world fare badly.)[45] Completely missing in Wright's prescription is the idea that females can provide for them-selves—as they do throughout the animal kingdom and increasingly in many human societies. In any event, few modern women would rush out for a spot in a harem as an alternative to a good paycheck of their own and the chance of a liaison with one suitable man.

Another problem with the idea that women are programmed to seek out males who control resources is the assumption that males *always* have the power. In the nonhuman primate world, it's not clear who con-trols the resources. Early studies centered on species (rhesus monkeys, chimpanzees) in which males clearly had control. But in some species, fe-males compete or cooperate with other females for resources, while males distribute themselves to have access to the females that defend and control the resources. Among certain Asian monkeys (langurs) "the most persistent defenders of the troop's territories are often female relatives who inherited this feeding area from their mothers and grandmothers."[46]

Not all researchers in the biological camp take a simplistic view of the world, however. Evolutionary biologists such as Sarah Blaffer Hrdy and Patricia Gowaty declare themselves feminists, and careful scientists of all stripes do not subscribe to sound bite notions. Unfortunately, the synergy among science, the media, politics, and social policy favors sim-ple, usually conservative ideas. "What begins as a scientist's cautious speculation moves rapidly into a headline in *USA Today* and from there becomes received wisdom that directs public policy and influences girls' career choices," says biologist Sarah Blaffer Hrdy.[47] Soon everyone "knows" that women prefer wealthy men and that guys want young babes and that women are naturally better parents than men. In a *New York Times* article on polygamy in Utah, the author simply states as fact that men are programmed to be promiscuous, while women are not.[48] Alternative hypotheses get lost along the way.

And, as we have seen, there is the question of whether people tell the truth. Psychologists Kay Bussey and Albert Bandura, in a major review of Buss's study, showed that while more men than women *said* they would select a mate for physical attractiveness, in reality both sexes are equally influenced by attractiveness.[49] Whether women are more reluctant than men to admit this or whether they are unaware that physical attractiveness is driving them as much as it is, they know they are *supposed* to say that they want someone with a sense of humor who enjoys long walks. But advertisers seem tuned in to the importance of the male body. The famous Coke ad in which a group of women in an office crowd around the window to see the hunky, shirtless construction worker chugging down the amber liquid was a favorite of many female viewers. Scantily clad males are a staple of women's magazines. The September 2003 *Cosmo*, for instance, showcased a department called "Man Manual: Guy Without His Shirt." Below the headline appears a full-color, full-page portrait of a pro soccer player whose bikini jeans fall so far beneath his navel as to risk an X rating.

According to the Ultra Darwinists, though, there is no mystery about women's preferences in a mate. The man with resources to feed and protect the woman and her future children is always the winner in this mate-selection saga. Those who believe gender roles are shaped at least as much by culture and environment as by biology point out that women's preference for "older good providers" fits perfectly with the rise of the industrial state. This system, which often called for a male provider and a female domestic worker, arose in the United States in the 1830s, remained dominant until the 1970s, and declined thereafter.

If this idea about the demise of the male breadwinner is correct, then we should see a declining preference for older, "provider" males, particularly among women with resources. Researchers Alice Eagly and Wendy Wood used U.N. data to determine which societies have achieved the most equality for women, enabling them to participate equally with men in economic, political, and decisionmaking roles.[50] As measured by this index, the most egalitarian societies (in order) are Norway, Sweden, Denmark, Finland, New Zealand, Canada, and the United States.

Next they reanalyzed the Buss data and found that as gender equality in society increased, women expressed less preference for older men with greater earning potential, and men expressed less preference for younger women with domestic skills. Their major conclusion is that the primary predictor of mate selection is the degree of gender equality in society. In other words, what you look for in a mate depends on whether your society is very traditional or relatively liberal. As the industrial state—with its male-breadwinner dominance—fades, as women move into the workforce and gain more resources, so-called universal mate choice preferences diminish as well. According to Eagly and Wood, these findings strongly suggest that the evolutionary scenario will fade and perhaps disappear entirely as gender equality grows.

Their theories are bolstered by the work of another scholar who re-analyzed Buss's data, sociologist Norval Glenn.[51] He found that in more developed societies, both males and females prefer smaller age differences between themselves and their spouses than in the less developed ones. In more industrialized cultures, both sexes place less importance on the financial prospects, industriousness and ambition, and chastity of a spouse. These data suggest that living in the developed world tends to diminish some of the male–female differences predicted by evolutionary theories.

Ubiquitous media stories that use modern, urban people to illustrate evolutionary theories—men and women flirting in big-city bars or the dating habits of movie stars—are badly out of date. Of course, this puts journalists in a quandary. Would an article that featured Third World people for whom the theories are more appropriate—shepherds on the African plains, say, or nomads in Mongolia—be as eye-catching as photos of chic young Manhattanites? Buss himself has come to recognize that culture plays a significant part in who mates with whom. In his revised edition of *The Evolution of Desire* (2003), he acknowledges that "prevailing cultural norms" and other nongenetic factors strongly affect the mating dance. With this admission, he's making a bow to Darwin—something the Ultra Darwinists are not wont to do.

Despite research contesting his findings and Buss's own revisions, the media continue to hold sacred his original, more rigid ideas. Prize-winning science writer and zoologist Matt Ridley stresses the interplay of genes and the environment in his best-selling 2000 book *Nature Via Nurture:* "Genes are not puppet masters or blueprints."[52] He veers from this commonsense path in only one area—when he decrees that Buss has "proved" mating strategies to be largely determined by genes. Again, the media picked up this narrative. The *Los Angeles Times* reports that "Ridley insists that what men look for in a mate is beauty, while what a woman wants in a man is money." This steady media refrain drives evolutionary biologist Patricia Gowaty to distraction. She can't believe that the old Buss study is still being cited, despite the "seriously damaging" scientific critique. Why on earth, she asks, "a decade after their original publication," are Buss's thirty-seven cultures data "still a topic of discussion?"[53]

That's easy. It's because the argument is simple and sexy. Such notions tend to get repeated so often that even people who should know better parrot them as established fact. But the scientific enterprise relies on better studies and more sophisticated tools to pose a constant challenge to the prevailing wisdom. The more textured ideas of Eagly, Wood, and Glenn make sense of the data and don't require us to make a great leap backward through history to explain the behavior of modern people. Their work underscores our point: Freed from social and economic constraints, men and women want the same characteristics in a mate. Not many young women today pass up an eligible contemporary mate for a considerably older, wealthier prospect. Demographic data show a long-standing tendency for women to marry men two or three years their senior—hardly the rich old rooster. One thirty-four-year-old woman we know says that among her peers, a woman who marries a rich older man isn't envied. She's seen as having a "pathological father complex." So the story currently favored in the media goes against the economic and psychological reality of today's women. Clearly the media do not dictate people's lives—but could be creating a sense of uneasiness about them. A woman who decides to marry a man who is obviously not on the high-earning track may have doubts along the way about whether she's doing the right thing. Even if she doesn't, her parents or girlfriends may. And the man who chooses to marry a woman who earns more than he does may worry about his manhood and may face doubts about whether she will stay with him for the long haul. After all, if she's programmed to find a "provider male," at some point she may indeed find one.

Once again, a popular myth stands in stark contrast to a new reality— this time the myth that a woman is attracted to a man because of his resources and a man is attracted to a woman because of her youth. Just when women have begun to acquire their own resources, they are ostensibly drawn to the male because of his. And just when men have begun to factor in a woman's earning potential when selecting a mate, we are told by the media it's only nubile looks that count. Why are women buying this idea? First, it's an old message, so it has a familiar ring. Second, it may have more weight today. Since women are getting married later than in the past, they may pay more attention, for a longer time, to keeping themselves looking good. After all, if you don't plan to get married until you're thirty, you don't want to be in the back of the pack. Nobody has ever said that men don't care about women's looks, even if they are taking a woman's paycheck into account these days.

In the recent past, with hardly any high-paying jobs open to females, a woman's future depended almost entirely on the earning power of her husband. Mothers instructed their daughters that it was just as easy to fall in love with a rich man as a poor man. Any preference, to the extent that it existed, for older, wealthier men was the product of women's own lack of resources as well as strong, consistent social messages.

Today, however, women's relative earning capacity is growing and will probably continue to grow, with women now outnumbering men in colleges and universities and with men's wages continuing to stagnate or decline. Not surprisingly, it is becoming more and more common for women to choose younger men as partners. Unfortunately, the U.S. Department of Vital Statistics stopped collecting the ages of brides and bridegrooms in 1989, but anecdotal evidence is all around us. Australian census figures reveal a growing trend for women in their thirties to marry men in their twenties.[54] When women have their own resources, they seek qualities other than earning power in men—and the capacity for caregiving may be chief among them. On a *Today* show segment about new brides, one of the young women said she knew her new boyfriend was Mr. Right when she came down with strep throat and he took care of her and did her laundry for a week.

The National Marriage Project at Rutgers reports that in a 2001 poll of 1,003 young adults aged 20 to 29, both sexes wanted to find a "soul mate" with whom they could share their hopes and dreams for a lifetime.[55] These young people would seem to have little in common with the desperate, scheming females in dating guides such as *The Rules*, which echo the Ultra Darwinists.[56] Contemporary twenty-somethings more resemble our second president and his outspoken wife. John and Abigail Adams shared a love story that lasted a lifetime. She began all her letters to him with "Dearest friend" and he "poured out his heart and soul to her," says Adams biographer David McCullough.[57] "And they weren't just lovers gazing at each other but rather lovers gazing out in the same direction together—in many ways a stronger definition of love."

The Evolutionary Narrative

Why do the popular media latch on to outdated ideas of gender relations like those in the Mars and Venus books and in *The Rules*, when the real behavior of young people bears so little resemblance to them? These books are just two more in a long, dreary line of best-selling advice guides that instruct women to be submissive. Marabel Morgan's *The Total Woman* (1973) taught women to gaze at their husbands adoringly and greet them at the door wearing nothing but Saran Wrap. In 2002 Laura Doyle's *Surrendered Wife* said women must defer to men and let them manage the money.

Why do people turn these books into best-sellers when their own lives veer so far away from these tired formulas? Philosopher Susan Bordo, author of *Unbearable Weight*, says they provide simple answers that satisfy a craving to know things with certainty in a time when gender roles are in tremendous flux. All of us live, Bordo says, "in a culture in which knowledge is really up for grabs." We're mapping the human genome, finding the underlying causes for disease, performing surgery in utero, cloning mammals—we are beginning to think we can know everything. This makes us vulnerable to theories that seem to tell us what men and women are all about. In this climate, we are "all the more fascinated with the possibility of nailing it down."[58]

Given this uncertainty, ideas that resonate with stereotypes—what we think we *do* know—seem intuitively "right." But as Harvard psychologist Jerome Kagan warns, "Just because an idea feels right doesn't make it right. Most of the time, intuition is wrong. I mean, intuitively the sun goes around the earth, right? Intuitively, the earth is flat, right? Why is psychology the least advanced science? Because our intuitions aren't very good."[59] Not so long ago, two other theories about men and women seemed to be intuitively right and were buttressed by impressive scientific pedigrees. Penis envy, the Freudian notion that women who tried to achieve were displaying a maladjusted desire for a part of the male anatomy, was accepted dogma among psychoanalysts in the 1940s, 1950s, and 1960s.[60] In that same era, Erik Erikson's theory of "inner space" was used to turn women's ambitions into a disease.[61] Men, it was said, were motivated to build skyscrapers, compose symphonies, and fly airplanes because they did not give birth to children. In contrast, Erikson said, childbirth satisfied all of women's psychic needs. Such theories seem laughable now, but they were offered with great seriousness in respected academic and social circles in the recent past—just as evolutionary narratives about males and females are today.

The Rambo Effect

One tenet of Ultra Darwinist dogma—that females naturally go for the alpha male who dominates all the resources—doesn't seem to be true even in the animal kingdom. When biologist Barbara Smuts studied baboons in Kenya, she discovered close friendships between opposite sex baboons who had not mated.[62] The males groomed the females, helped care for the offspring, and came running if the female was in distress.

Smuts speculates that by befriending the females, the males were getting into their good graces and increasing their chances of mating with them in the future. The males who waited—some for as long as two years—often succeeded in transforming those friendships into long-standing mate relationships. Like our cousins the baboons, "our prehistoric ancestors probably experienced intimate friendships long before marriage and norms of sexual fidelity were invented."

Indeed, the male at the top of the heap may be there not because of his aggression but because of his social skills. Psychologist Shelley Taylor notes in *The Tending Instinct* that the reason certain male nonhuman primates become dominant has as much to do with social savvy as aggression.[63] They're good at forming alliances, they cajole, they appease other animals when they are agitated, and they ostracize those who are too aggressive and don't play by the rules. Harvard Business School professor Rosabeth Moss Kanter notes that the management skills needed to succeed in the global information age are teamwork and partnering, and this probably held true for our early ancestors. Among our nonhuman primate cousins, Taylor notes, males have to pass muster in the eyes of the troop's females. If an abusive leader rises to dominance, "the females may throw their support to another leader or to a coalition that will oust the leader, sometimes with fatal force, and replace him with a socially skilled leader who enjoys the broader support of the females."[64]

Dominant males don't mate more often than other males, nor do they produce more offspring. A study that used biochemical tests to determine paternity of primates concluded there was no direct correlation between paternity and rank.[65] Some low-status males—and even some juveniles—fathered as many offspring as the highest-ranking males. (Recall the Barbary macaque that Meredith Small observed, who passed up the high-ranking older male for the young stud who caught her eye?)

The Rambo image of Ultra Darwinism tells us that the biggest and strongest and meanest guy gets the women, but that's not always so. Chimpanzee females, for example, often neglect the most dominant males (established in fight or threat hierarchies) in favor of the more sociable and less disruptive males. While male-on-male aggression certainly exists, these and other studies challenge the notion that such competition gives the dominant males the breeding advantage. Anthropologist Adrienne Zihlman suggests that among our hominid ancestors, the "matrifocal" or mother-focused group structure would have put a premium on cooperation and skill learning.[66] Aggressive, disruptive males would not have been the most successful suitors. Instead, males who could cooperate and help with child care and guarding would be the most acceptable mates. Nice guys do finish first.

Among our own species, women more and more are looking for men with the kind of cooperative social skills that served our early ancestors well. Ana Scott, a twenty-six-year-old college administrator we spoke to, was first attracted to her husband, Dave, a systems analyst, because of the way he supported her. As undergraduates together, "He encouraged me to lead a collegewide event," she remembers. Dave told Ana she could do it, and he focused on *her* abilities, not his own—even though he was a campus leader himself. Today, she says, when she falls into stereotyped thinking and says she can't do something, he is her primary cheerleader. "I don't just encourage him because he's the man. We both encourage each other—he as much as me," she says.

Clearly Dave does not much resemble the males in today's "lad magazines," *Maxim* and its ilk, in which men are portrayed as dim louts interested only in sports, cars, and girls with gigantic breasts. These magazines have a strong scent of satire clinging to their pages. The guys may be leering at empty-headed silicone maidens—but they don't seem to be marrying them. Forty years ago, when women had virtually no power outside the home, feminists could get hot under the collar about *Playboy* magazine. But today, when women outnumber men in college classrooms and can command high salaries in law firms and Fortune 500 companies, such images of women seem more an annoyance than an issue of concern. At the same time, the workplace model for women of a generation ago has become anachronistic. Drab power suits and sensible shoes have been replaced by ultra-high heels, tight miniskirts, and Victoria's Secret underwear. Young women today have no notion that they need to dress like men to be successful. But as women indulge a sense of femininity in a previously male domain, men have lost their casual attitude toward the mating game. Not long ago, a presentable fellow with decent financial prospects was attractive enough. Now women are choosier. Men are trying almost as hard as women to make sure their wardrobes, bodies, and hair look good enough to make them viable prospects. There's even a new word, "metrosexual," to describe straight urban men who are fashion conscious and eager consumers of hair sprays, deodorants, nail polish, liposuction, and jewelry. In *Queer Eye for the Straight Guy,* gay men advise straight guys on how to dress and decorate.

As British cultural critic Mark Simpson writes in *Salon,* "The more independent, wealthy, self-centered and powerful women become, the more they are likely to want attractive, well-groomed, well-dressed men around them . . . by the same token, the less men can rely on women, the more likely they are to take care of themselves. For men, narcissism has become a survival strategy." Both men and women will find the Ultra Darwinist notions unreliable guides to today's mating game. The payoff for discarding them is finding "rules" that really work. Looking for a soul mate is not a bad place to start. Being in tune with your partner, sharing common ideals, and having a similar vision of how you want to live your lives are important. You need to be honest with yourself about what you want and be able to communicate that to your partner. Is it important to you that you're not the one always picking up the socks? Say so. If you don't aspire to be the hard-driving, high-earning CEO of your company, make that clear. We know that over the long haul, when marriages last, it's because each partner makes room for the strong preferences of the other, even when they are not shared. Both partners must be able to communicate and compromise, trusting that the other person will reciprocate. Also, each must know that the other will be there when it counts.

How It Harms Us

It's hard for people to erase the tapes that keep playing in their heads when they believe there's "scientific" evidence for these stereotypes. They can lead both men and women to make poor life choices.

One of RB's therapy clients, Elizabeth, is a forty-year-old real estate broker with a large clientele who has been divorced for a number of years. She owns her own house and is comfortable paying her way. She's been dating Matt, a forty-one-year-old documentary filmmaker who is funny, kind, and warm. Because of the type of work he does, he goes from project to project, with an uncertain income. No stable, high-earning guy here. Matt wants to marry Elizabeth, but she's reluctant.

RB asked Elizabeth why this was a problem. At first she was reluctant to talk about the money difference. She said that he traveled too much, that he didn't know where he was going to be based, that it wasn't clear he'd ever have a real job. But when pressed, Elizabeth admitted she was concerned because he didn't fit the picture of the ideal mate painted by the plethora of best-sellers of the Ultra Darwinist genre. She worried that he wouldn't be able to take care of her financially. But she also worried that she'd never find anyone who could make her as happy. RB tried to encourage her to follow her heart instead of the sounds of those old tapes.

Joe, who's 32, makes a good salary as a civil engineer. But he's miserable because he would prefer to be working closely with people. He once thought about becoming a physical therapist but rejected that idea when he realized there was no way to earn big money and high esteem in this "helping" profession. He hates what he does and wakes up every morning not wanting to go to the office, but he knows that other people think he's living up to expectations of male success. When he looks ahead to thirty more years of doing what he's doing, he becomes depressed. His unhappiness is wrecking his relationship with his fiancée, Sara, who is anxious to get married and start a family.

RB asked Joe what he thought it would be like to be a physical therapist. His face lit up and he said, "It would be great to see people getting back on their feet, or recovering from a stroke, or from sports injuries. I'd love to have a real impact on people's lives—doing something that really matters to people." When RB asked him why he didn't pursue this career, he admitted that it would be hard to live on the salary he would earn. But there was more to it: "The guys I hang with tend to spend money pretty freely. I worry that I couldn't keep up with them. They're pretty high-powered, and I think they'd tell me I was taking a dead-end job that wasn't going anywhere. Sometimes I tell myself the same thing. But I really feel that my life would have more meaning if I made the switch."

As these stories show, stereotypes aren't just harmless abstractions. Joe's depression and Elizabeth's ambivalence about Matt are preventing both of them from moving on with their lives. Today's employed woman might well need a partner to share child rearing and domestic tasks more than she needs someone to provide economic security. A man may be better off with a mate who can share the economic responsibilities for the family than with one who is focused solely on child rearing. If they can shake loose from the old gender straitjackets, men and women get a double benefit. They'll be promoting their genetic self-interest as well as securing their own personal happiness.

Flawed science, in addition to harming our private lives, can have wider consequences. Most worrisome, it can be used to taint women's ambitions with a dreaded word: "unnatural." It's odd how this notion persists, from the cruder sexist versions of yesterday to the subtler sexism of today. Robert Wright suggests that both feminism and communism violate human nature. In "Feminists, Meet Mr. Darwin," which appeared in the *New Republic*, Wright says that "history has not been kind to ideologies that rested on patently false beliefs about human nature: Communism, for example, isn't looking very robust these days." He suggests that "feminism is where Communism was at mid-century." Feminism, like communism, "will fall under the weight of its doctrinal absurdities." Wright is so focused on the male's aggressive sexuality that he can't seem to imagine a workplace that is not plagued by sexual harassment. "Human males are by nature oppressive, possessive, flesh-obsessed pigs," he says.[67] He also believes that men are naturally more ambitious than women—and work much harder—which is why there is "a gross underrepresentation of women in high-paying jobs."[68]

Wright outraged several prominent female biologists when he wrote, "Not a single well-known feminist had learned enough about modern

Darwinism to pass judgment on it." Three distinguished scholars (Anne Fausto-Sterling, Patricia Gowaty, and Marlene Zuk) begged to differ.[69] They wrote, "Some of us were studying Darwin and working as professional biologists years before Wright was old enough to attend college." (Wright gave Fausto-Sterling a C– in Evolutionary Biology 101, despite her PhD and many scientific publications. Wright has done no primary research on his own and has no terminal degree in the sciences.) The three professors, who have done groundbreaking research in biology, approached the *New Republic,* where Wright was an editor, to respond to his article. But they were rebuffed. As far as the magazine's readers are concerned, Wright's speculative narrative stands as uncontested truth. They didn't get to hear the scientists argue that, far from being "unnatural," feminism's notion of women as active players in the history of *Homo sapiens* fits the new field research much better than Wright's dubious version of Darwinism.

Too often the rights to our evolutionary past are claimed by people who seem determined to look in only one direction—backward. The advice implicit in their views suggests that men and women can best find a mate and live happily ever after, if they accept—perhaps even revel in—traditional roles, roles dictated by ancient scripts. But new research indicates that this advice is scientifically invalid and potentially harmful. Yesterday's formulas—no matter how invitingly packaged—are unreliable road maps to a future filled with change and uncertainty.

The late Stephen Jay Gould predicted that evolutionary psychologists would suffer the fate of the Freudians, "who also had some good insights but failed spectacularly, and with serious harm imposed upon millions of people (women for example, who were labeled 'frigid' when they couldn't make an impossible transition from clitoral to vaginal orgasm) they elevated a limited guide into a rigid creed that became more of an untestable and unchangeable religion than a science."[70]

If, however, our genetic past has bequeathed to us adaptability rather than fixed behaviors, then evolutionary theory can be seen as an agent of change rather than an obstacle to it. In this scenario, as women's and men's needs for certain attributes in a mate change with the changing circumstances of their lives, so too will their criteria for mate selection—in keeping with the Darwinian principles of variability and adaptability. As Matt Ridley points out, just *having* a gene is meaningless—it has to be expressed to have an impact.[71] Culture, learning, experience, the fetal environment, nutrition, education—all act on our genetic inheritance.

Evidence suggests that the lessons to be learned from our ancestral heritage lie in complexity rather than simplicity; in flexibility rather than rigidity. We are who we are because of our biology *and* our culture. We created a culture that acts on us as we live inside it. Our minds imagine something, and we then create that something, and our creation changes who we are and who we will become. The idea that we passed, rigidly unchanged, through eons of history does a disservice to our magnificently rich and varied existence as human beings.

Talking About Power

"YOU JUST DON'T UNDERSTAND!" is a simple plea to be heard correctly—perhaps from a friend, family member, or coworker. But when these four little words became the title of a book, they turned into a powerful shorthand for the failure of women and men to communicate with each other. In this 1990 best-seller, Deborah Tannen, a Georgetown University linguist, jumped headfirst into what she admits is a controversial area of study—gender differences in communication.[1] The book was wildly successful and Tannen's ideas, like Gilligan's, were swallowed whole by therapists, corporate trainers, journalists, and the general public. A female manager at Fairchild, thought to be lacking in "people skills," was sent to a corporate trainer who told her to read Tannen's book.[2] At a seminar sponsored by the Ministry of Community Development and Sports of Singapore in 2001, the organizer said the book he recommended most was *You Just Don't Understand*.[3] Reporters seek Tannen out to assess the speech of presidential candidates, teenagers, CEOs, married couples, working women, and network anchors. Tannen's subsequent books, including *Talking from Nine to Five* (2001) and *I Only Say This Because I Love You* (2002), were also very popular.

What groundbreaking message elevated Tannen to this rarefied status? Women, she says, use their unique conversational style to show involvement, connection, and participation, while men use speech to indicate independence and position in a hierarchy. (This also echoes Carol Gilligan, who set up the equation Connection + Care = Female.)

Women seek connection and want to be liked, Tannen says, so when they talk, they tend to qualify their statements and turn declarative sentences into questions. Instead of saying, "Let's go full steam ahead on this merger," a woman might say, "Let's go ahead with this merger, if we're sure the timing is right." Or she might say, "It's a good plan—isn't it?" Tannen also charges that women apologize far more than men. "In one meeting I sat in on at an insurance company," she recalls, "the sole woman in the group, whom I will call Helen, said, 'I'm sorry' or 'I apologize' repeatedly."[4] Tannen cites Charlotte, one high-ranking officer at the company. She began her evaluation of a subordinate with the words, "I'm really apologetic, Bruce, that I laid this on you so soon."[5]

In addition, according to Tannen, women don't interrupt and tend to agree with what others are saying. She gives the example of "Meredith," the only female in a college writing class.[6] Meredith, when she does speak, spends her time affirming the men in the class. When one of the males tells another student, "You just got to . . . elaborate more on it," Meredith chimes in, "Yeah, I mean, you need to elaborate." Six times, when she tries to make a contribution to the class, she is interrupted and backs off. Even women who are assertive when talking to women colleagues become mute and reticent in mixed-sex situations, Tannen observes.

Men, she says, are concerned mainly with status and independence, using speech to jockey for position. Women ask questions to establish connection and soften the sting of any possible disagreement. Men, in contrast, ask questions to engage in public sparring. A man is likely to express his opinion forthrightly—"You're wrong!"—and to interrupt others when he has something to say. And men tend to move on after altercations. Tannen gives the example of two men in a large company who argued heatedly and then were friendly afterward. Asked by a woman colleague, "How can you pretend that fight never happened?" one of the men said, "It happened. And it's over."[7] In contrast, "Kristen," critiquing a subordinate's draft of a report about the company's foreign sales, says, "You know, you might put in parentheses, you know . . . dollars per unit, and then in parentheses, put, you know, dollars per

FFC."[8] Because of their different ways of communicating, women feel men just lecture and criticize. Men, for their part, wonder why women never get to the point.

Tannen's books may have resonated with millions of readers in part because her prototypes are familiar—the guy who interrupts women all the time, the woman who doesn't speak up in mixed company, the man who doesn't apologize, the woman who expects her husband to read her mind, the guy who never asks for directions. Tannen says her book "makes it possible to explain these dissatisfactions [between men and women] without accusing anyone of being crazy or wrong, and without blaming—or discarding—the relationship."[9] She links patterns she finds in women's speech—indirection, a tendency to apologize too much, hesitation—with caring and connection. It is no coincidence that researchers find these same qualities in the speech patterns of subordinates—the folks who aren't in charge. Research tells us that power is central to how men and women communicate, but once again its importance seems to have been lost along the way.

Downplaying power while overemphasizing gender, as Tannen does, translates into practical problems for real women. Not surprisingly, Tannen gives women few useful strategies for addressing communication issues with their partners or at work. Jane, a thirty-three-year-old woman we spoke to, is a highly regarded fifth-year associate at a major East Coast law firm specializing in entertainment law. But she comes away frustrated from weekly staff meetings. In the latest one, a male colleague suggested that the firm get more actively involved in financing motion pictures, and he won plaudits from his colleagues for his entrepreneurial initiative. Jane was surprised and angry because a similar suggestion she made just two weeks earlier had been ignored. She feels that nobody hears what she says, and she can't come up with a way to break into conversations when she needs to be heard. "How come this keeps happening to me over and over again?" she laments. Jane worries that she'll never make partner because she's seen as ineffectual in meetings. "I really know my stuff. How do I get that across?" she asks. She fears she simply can't because this is how women and men *naturally* behave.

Charles and Bette, both in their forties, struggle relentlessly over their inability to talk to each other. Every time Bette brings up a relationship issue, Charles immediately takes over the conversation, tries to diminish the problem, and focuses solely on "fixing" it. Bette resents Charles's behavior. She never gets to tell her side of the story and feels he's only interested in hearing what *he* needs to make the problem go away. Sometimes when Bette gets angry, Charles throws up his hands and says, "You're too emotional for me. But what can I expect? This is how women are!" Other times, Charles keeps up a monologue and Bette, in frustration, says, "Do anything you want!" and walks away in disgust. From her point of view, he's so linear and rational that he ignores the emotional undercurrent of the exchange.

Jane and Bette and Charles are locked into thinking the sexes inevitably communicate in particular ways. If Jane keeps butting up against male behavior that she can't change, then all she can do is "understand" the guys. She can't confront them about their behavior or insist that they treat her with more respect. She either stays where she is and runs into a dead end or leaves the firm to find a more congenial work environment—a tall order in an aggressive field like law. The idea of "natural" male and female speech does broader damage as well because it may give managers reason to stereotype their employees. If you have an all-male team, why bring in a woman—who will not be able to communicate and will likely disrupt the team's functioning?

Is this really happening? Male managers certainly wouldn't say so, but research shows women managers leaving companies at a higher rate than men, due to lack of opportunities. They want to go to jobs where their work is recognized and their views listened to. If male managers believe they can't communicate with women on their team, they are losing out. Meta-analyses show that while all-male groups may be better at some things, and all-female groups better at others, mixed-sex groups are slightly superior to both all-male and all-female groups.[10]

Meanwhile, Charles and Bette are playing the same tape over and over. She says that Charles is "hardwired" to behave the way he does; he's incapable of understanding emotions. He says that she is overly emotional, which keeps her from being able to hear him. Either they have to look elsewhere to get what they need or they must try to step over the land mines—a hopeless task. Seeing each other the way they do, there's no way they can resolve their issues.

But the best and newest research says men and women are not doomed to act out inevitable gender scripts. Let's look closely at Tannen's arguments to see why.

Yes, We Do Understand

Tannen relies heavily on the work of other scholars, but even when she accurately presents their data, she often changes or ignores their conclusions. While these scholars stress the *similarities* between men and women in their own data, Tannen sees only *differences*.[11] She gives the example of a manager, Sid, talking to his secretary, Rita, about the plans for a special event: "Oh, and I was meaning to ask you about that. When I meet them Sunday, I'll have the invitations for Sunday night's activities and also I have an agenda for the following day. In fact, an agenda for the following week for them—to give them. Is that right?" Rita says it is, and Sid continues, "and, uh, if it could just be in an envelope or something for each one of them."[12] Tannen says that though Sid is indirect, because he doesn't say "thank you" his speech does not display a "feminine" lack of confidence. But does his speech differ much from Kristen's, quoted earlier, who is supposed to exemplify uncertain female speech?

Remarkably, Tannen's own data consist largely of personal anecdotes. She analyzes two and a half hours of dinner table conversation among herself and five friends to draw endless conclusions to support her views.[13] And she makes sweeping generalizations on the basis of meager evidence. She states as fact that men interrupt women: "I've never seen a popular article on this subject that does not cite this finding." But do all men interrupt all women?[14] And when they do, is it "natural" male behavior or a sense of entitlement that's operating? Where is the rigorous approach that would bolster her theory?

Critics are quick to point out that most studies on gender and communication involve college students who don't know each other and meet in artificial laboratory settings, usually for a brief encounter. In the dating years, both men and women are apt to play out traditional gender roles to please potential partners. Mature men and women operate by a different set of rules. When you're talking to your husband of five years, are you worrying that he'll see you as unfeminine if you voice an opinion counter to his?[15] A college professor we know enjoys getting into lively debates with her husband: "We're both political junkies and we don't agree on everything. We both give as good as we get and we come away respecting each other's point of view—and we both usually learn something." Communication between two people is a fluid and evolving phenomenon, not the defined role-playing Tannen has taught millions to believe.

In her scholarly publications as a linguist, Tannen emphasizes the importance of a multitude of social factors in male–female interactions. In her popular books, however, she treats sex as the only explanation for differences in speech styles. But no one can honestly believe, for example, that a buttoned-down twenty-something male investment banker has the same communication style as a fifty-year-old Italian American firefighter. Class, race, age, ethnicity—all these factors and many more influence how people communicate.[16]

Most significantly, of all these factors that influence speech between the sexes, power is perhaps the most important. Men and women with less power are more deferential and timid than those of either sex with more power. A widely cited study bears this out. Psychologist Sara Snodgrass of Florida Atlantic University created mixed-sex pairs (in a laboratory setting) to do certain jobs, assigning one member to be the leader and the other to be the subordinate.[17] Her intention was to create a power differential; the superior had the power and the subordinate did not. What did she find? The person in the subordinate position, male or female, was more sensitive to the leader's nonverbal signals than the leader was to the subordinate's. It's not hard to find examples of this power differential in real life. Both men and women quickly learn to read the boss's moods, wishes, and whims for their own advantage and chance for advancement. Men are no less sensitive to who has the power than women. Do you suppose Supreme Court Justice Ruth Bader Ginsburg is regularly interrupted by her male clerks? Do male students constantly interrupt their female professors? Of course not. But this is a topic that Tannen treats only tangentially.

Other researchers come to conclusions that differ from Tannen's. In a review of more than 300 studies, psychologist Elizabeth Aries of Amherst College found that men often interrupt women in conversation.[18] But when traditional power relationships are reversed—in couples where the woman is the higher earner or in situations with female superiors and male subordinates—speech patterns also undergo a reversal. The person with less power, female or male, interrupts less and works harder to keep the conversation going. Those with more power, male or female, are likely to take control of the conversation. It's impossible to see this dynamic if we are blinded by the notion that something buried deep in women's psyches chains them to the speech styles of the powerless.

The interplay of power, gender, and communication is far more than an academic discussion. It influences the everyday lives of Jane, Bette, and Charles—and all of us. The powerless feel they must place the needs of the powerful above their own. Of course, not everyone is either always powerful or always powerless. Power can shift, based on the situation. A man who has more power than his female colleague one day may find that she has been promoted and the next day he's reporting to her. He will soon find himself addressing her in a very different way—and vice versa. As we noted in our discussion of Carol Gilligan, the powerful person feels entitled to get what he or she wants—and usually does. We are all surprisingly flexible in our speech, speaking differently in different situations. We don't talk to our kids the same way we talk to our bosses. That commonsense observation is supported by a study in which women were told they were going to be judged on their leadership ability. In this case, they spoke up as much as the men. But when women were told that they were going to meet attractive men who preferred women who let men take the lead, they altered their behavior to be more stereotypically feminine.[19] We're aware of what others expect from us regarding appropriate sex-role behavior and we tend to react accordingly.

Different Power, Not Different Planets

Riding an Amtrak train to Washington, one of us (CR) found herself sitting next to a man who identified himself as a marriage counselor. He said that he consulted John Gray's *Men Are from Mars, Women Are from Venus* for advice, and often recommended the book to his clients. Caryl asked him if he knew that when researchers at the University of Colorado reviewed the best-selling advice books in 2001 to see how they dovetailed with the latest findings in the behavioral sciences, Gray's book was rated one of the worst.[20] The counselor on the train shrugged off this information. "I think the book is very helpful for couples," he insisted.

As we'll soon see, the opposite is true. Gray flattens out complex ideas into trite, unscientific prose. These easily swallowed sound bites, despite their harm, have come to dominate the popular imagination. The scholarly writings of Carol Gilligan and Deborah Tannen allow nuance into their theorizing, but the Mars and Venus books are a one-size-fits-all approach to gender relations. It's frightening to think about the impact of his huge best-sellers when you examine who John Gray is and what he has to say. At last count, he had sold 15 million books, outstripped only by the Bible. He had a two-hour special on ABC and his Mars and Venus institutes around the world are a merchandising phenomenon. He is the only author in history to sell out Carnegie Hall. Gray got his doctoral degree from Columbia Pacific University, a correspondence school that, according to the *San Francisco Chronicle,* has since been shut down by the California State Department of Consumer Affairs. Investigators charged that the faculty was virtually nonexistent, the course work "laughable," and degree requirements routinely ignored.[21]

We might overlook these dubious credentials if the books really helped the sexes communicate. But what does Gray have to say once he hooks us with those attention-grabbing titles? Men, he says, are naturally programmed to go into their "caves" and not communicate with other people. Women must never try to talk to men when they withdraw in this fashion but must honor their behavior. A woman must not offer help to a man because it makes him feel weak and incompetent. A woman must never criticize a man or try to change his behavior. She should never be angry; she must wait until she is "loving and centered" to talk to him. Only when she is loving and forgiving can she share her feelings. If a man pulls away from her, "he is just fulfilling a valid need to take care of himself for a while."[22]

Gray cites the case of "Bill," who asks his wife, "Mary," to make a phone call for him while he is sitting on the couch watching TV.[23] Mary "reacts with a frustrated and helpless tone of voice. She says, 'I can't right now, I already have too much to do, I have to change the baby's diaper, I have to clean up this mess, balance the checkbook, finish the wash, and tonight we are going out to a movie. I have too much to do. I just can't do it all!'"[24]

Bill goes back to watching TV and disconnects from her feelings. Bill, says Gray, is angry at her for making him feel like a failure. He retreats to his cave, "just taking care of himself." If Mary realized this, Gray suggests, she would smile at his request and say sweetly that she's running behind. As for Bill, all he has to do, Gray suggests, is say admiringly to Mary, "I just don't know how you do it!" Gray cautions, "This backfires, of course, if it is not done with sincerity." No argument there; that line might just get Bill a damp diaper in the face—sincere or not.

Gray does *not* suggest that Bill might (1) change the baby's diaper, (2) help clean up the house, (3) balance the checkbook, or (4) help with the wash. Who has the power in this marriage—and isn't this really the issue? Gray's scenario puts women in a tight bind while requiring little from men.

"For all practical purposes," he advises, "I strongly recommend that couples not argue."[25] A woman mustn't, for example, ask a man to change the awful purple shirt he is putting on for an important event at her company. If she does and he gets annoyed, she should apologize and say, "I'm sorry. I don't mean to tell you how to dress." Gray adds, "The biggest problems in relationships occur when a woman shares her upset feelings and, as a result, a man feels unloved." She can't be too needy because this "pushes men away and makes them feel rejected and unappreciated."[26]

Men, on the other hand, are advised to listen more, respect their partner's feelings, and send flowers. Gray's first book offers seven pages of advice to women and two pages to men. In Gray's universe, the woman tends the relationship. "Instead of being goal oriented [women] are relationship oriented. They are more concerned with expressing their goodness, love and caring." Men are goal oriented, only interested in results. They see life completely in terms of competition: "I win, you lose."[27]

Gray's prescriptions leave a woman with only one solution to problems of communication with a man. She has to be the caring, sacrificing, ethereal "Venusian," completely tuned in to the wants and needs of others while denying her own. A Venusian can't get angry. She can't criticize. She can't offer to help if he has a problem. She can't ask him to change his behavior. When he withdraws, she can't object. And if she isn't feeling "loving," she can't even talk to him.

One must wonder why millions of women bought into a book that puts them at such a disadvantage, and why the book became phenomenally popular when it did. Just as women were moving out of the house in huge numbers to take on full-time employment, they were presented with a book that argued for the preservation of the most traditional gender roles at home, saying, in effect, that those roles were innate. Why would women want to believe that? Perhaps because it was simply easier than trying to change the power base at home. Millions of working women were going home to find another day of work ahead of them—the famous second shift. No one else was volunteering to take on that traditional female job shift: Who wants to work all day and then go home to be the janitor? So women had—and often still have—two choices. They can either fight it out—begging, screaming, pleading, to get husband and/or children to pick up their dirty laundry—or they can take the seemingly easier route of doing it themselves. In this way they help perpetuate traditional gender roles in the home.

How did women rationalize their powerlessness, deal with the underlying anger they felt at having to "do it all," and end the countless arguments about who's doing what in the home? They told themselves, courtesy of John Gray, that those gendered roles were innate. It's not that a guy is refusing to do the child care, laundry, cooking, and emoting; he's just not designed to do it. Women are designed to do it. In the short term, such rationalizations may help women feel less angry at their powerlessness, but as a long-term strategy they leave women in an untenable position.

As for men, retreating into "caves" to avoid connection is plain old passive aggression, which any psychologist can tell you always creates tensions. "Martians," says Gray, "tend to silently pull away and think about what's bothering them. . . . A man gets close but then inevitably needs to pull away." Of course, women pull away as often as men. Whether it is called the "silent treatment" or "withdrawing into a cave," it is destructive behavior.

Gray's prescription for relationships, say the Colorado University researchers, amounts to "leave him alone while the wife supervises the kids' homework, cooks dinner and turns to her girlfriends for emotional support. That's the very advice that gets people into trouble, not out of it."[28] A woman who takes Gray's counsel at face value may be at serious risk for high stress. Unable to express her anger openly, to ask for what she really needs, always on edge because she must sense a man's every whim and need, she is likely to turn her anger inward. Repressed anger leads to depression and lack of sexual desire. An angry, depressed woman who's rarely in the mood for sex is hardly an ideal mate.

Here on Earth

For a more textured and realistic analysis, let's picture communication as a dynamic process between people who are alike deep down, with similar feelings, abilities, and capacities. In this scenario, both sexes are sometimes goal-oriented, sometimes tuned in to feelings, sometimes needing solitude, sometimes needing company, and sometimes angry. This is what research tells us that real people are like. If we recognize power, not sex, as being at the root of male–female communication difficulties, then solutions to many seemingly intractable problems become possible. For example, anger is as natural for women as for men. A woman who feels powerful doesn't have to accept withdrawal or hostile behavior from her male partner as natural. It would be harmful for both if she simply gritted her teeth and kept her anger under wraps, only to have it explode sooner or later. By then, there might be no chance to repair the relationship. If she regards her partner as someone who is capable of listening and modifying his behavior, however, they will have a chance to improve the relationship for both of them.

Bob and Marcia, both lawyers in their late thirties, decided to share an office in their suburban home. Theirs was generally an egalitarian marriage, but in this case, Bob stepped in and tried to make all the decisions. If Marcia suggested certain types of furniture or room arrangements, he'd talk her out of it to get things done his way. "It's creating a lot of tension between us," Marcia explained. But once Bob realized that Marcia had a good reason for the decisions she was making, he began asking her why she wanted something, instead of just charging ahead. For example, Marcia wanted to buy a convertible couch so her favorite sister and young niece and nephew could stay over. Bob thought this was ridiculous because there were two hotels and a bed and breakfast nearby. Bob wanted a computer table in the office instead of a couch. But Marcia explained how important it was for her to be able to tuck her niece and nephew in bed at night and chat with them in the morning. Once Bob understood, he agreed. In other cases, Bob argued for his choice and Marcia agreed. Both trusted the other to reciprocate each time they made a compromise.

If Bob had been influenced by John Gray's writings, however, he would have learned to see women as creatures incapable of action and rational thought, who only want to talk endlessly about their feelings. A man who internalizes this message will simply tune his partner out because he's convinced he can never explain himself to her. Now and then he might bring home a bouquet of flowers to placate her, but the couple won't really communicate. How can they if they believe that men are no good at expressing feelings and can't be rational? The couple will drift apart.

Bob understood that his wife *can* share his thoughts and feelings. He found out that if he tries to explain himself, he'll probably do fine and she will listen. Indeed, some men (and some women) do have problems expressing their emotions. But there's no evidence that they can't change—with encouragement. If they accept Gray, however, they'll just give up. It's their "nature" to be inexpressive. If it bothers their partners, that's their problem. But if men and women can discount Gray and see each other as more alike than different, both sexes benefit. Understanding the role that power plays in communication can also help them sort things out. *She* can recognize her own sources of power, and if she's using a "powerless" speech style, she can change it. *He* can question his automatic assumption of greater power, recognize the consequences of his "powerful" speech style, and modify his behavior. Charles, for example, may destroy his marriage if he continues to dominate conversations with Bette. He has more to gain than to lose by changing. If Jane can't move beyond the idea that there's nothing she can do at work in the face of natural "male" behavior and speech, she will remain miserable. If she understands the true cause of the problem, she can figure out how to change the power balance in her situation and get the recognition she deserves.

Often people, especially women, have more power than they realize. If Jane focused on the successful work she's done on several high-visibility cases and on the excellent performance reviews she received from senior partners, she'd come to staff meetings with a more realistic sense of her own worth and personal power. She'd realize that she was more powerful than some of the men around the table, and she'd feel entitled to speak her mind in a way that others would hear. A little power goes a long way.

But turning knowledge into behavior is not easy. And sometimes it's risky. Owning one's power may be especially difficult for women, who in our culture have typically occupied low-power positions. Jane may feel uncomfortable flexing her newly acquired "conversational muscles." And her male colleagues may not be pleased by her show of power. With their previously unchallenged supremacy threatened, they may strike back. Hard as it may be for Jane to act powerfully in mixed-sex settings, it is certainly an improvement over staying silent and seething with resentment.

Women are often punished when they step out of low-power behavior. When First Lady Hillary Clinton talked like the high-powered corporate lawyer she was, her approval ratings plummeted. When she talked about kids or baking cookies, her ratings soared. The women managers who were sent off to the Bully Broads seminars by their companies ran into the same issue (see Chapter 2).[29] In a group session, a woman who runs Asian operations for an executive search firm said to a facilitator, "I'm not a bully; I'm not obnoxious; I'm not unreasonable." She chopped one hand in the air for emphasis. "Where'd you get that gesture?" the facilitator asked, disapprovingly.

As more women become bosses, certain language patterns will no longer be for males only. Women won't find themselves criticized for behavior that is acceptable for a male manager. When that time comes, "Can we talk?" will not be a loaded question for either sex. Both sexes will speak up in ways that fit the situation they are in without worrying about being misinterpreted. But what about the other consequences—for both sexes—when women are in charge?

The End of Men?

Women are, at long last, getting a secure foothold on the ledge of public and economic power. The Labor Department reported in 2000 that 45 percent of all American managers are women,[30] and women are performing so well on the job that *Business Week* headlined in 2000: "As Leaders, Women Rule."[31] A 2003 *Fortune* magazine cover heralded "The 50 Most Powerful Women in America," including women in government, business, politics, and entertainment.[32] The same issue spotlighted the fifty most powerful women on the international scene. Women are rapidly closing the MD and PhD gap and are on the verge of making up the majority of law students.[33] Will they be miserable because they have exchanged their old protections for an uncertain future? Will men become the "second sex," unmanned and unable to cope with their diminished status? That's precisely the argument that many influential writers and scholars are making today. The biggest—and most significant—gender difference, they say, is that men are losing power while women are gaining it.

In the past, there were significant gender differences in the kinds of power men and women wielded. Men controlled the public arena, while women's only sphere of control was the home. Even there, they had limited power because their husbands often had the last word. Even the brightest, most competent women were generally barred from the halls of power.

As we've noted, new research suggests that in prehistory women were not the second sex; rather, our earliest male and female ancestors were much more alike than different and shared power fairly equally. Male dominance only emerged after a long period during which settled agriculture replaced nomadic ways of life. As simpler, relatively egalitarian societies gave way to more complex social structures, some men gained power over most other men and nearly all women.

With this change, humans began to understand the concept of paternity and children became equated with wealth. Women's ability to bear children became a valuable resource. Plow agriculture needed laborers; the more hands to furrow and till, the greater the wealth. Women's reproductive labor became a commodity, and the concept of private property—unknown to nomads—emerged as a hallmark of civilization. Women were denied access to education, which limited their major roles in society to the domestic sphere—marriage and childbearing. When reliable methods for limiting the number of births became available in the twentieth century, women often were barred from using them.

In 1965—when the U.S. Supreme court struck down prohibitions on contraception—the nation was a very different place than it is today.

There were no female Supreme Court justices, no female national news anchors, no female police chiefs, no female generals, no female professional basketball players, two women in the Senate. There were no female marathoners (women were not even allowed to run marathons), no female heads of Fortune 500 companies, no female presidents of major universities, no women flying military jets, no female FBI agents. A married woman could not get a loan without her husband's permission, and women had to leave their jobs as elementary school teachers when they became pregnant. It would have been hard then to imagine the United States of the twenty-first century, where women fill more college seats than men, where some women can get jobs that earn them what men routinely earn, where women can get Harvard or Yale MBAs—or be admitted to any elite professional school.

Today large numbers of women no longer have to rely solely on men for their economic well-being. The balance of power between men and women, always a complex and subtle dance, has become more nearly a waltz of equals. To many, this sounds like a bright new world for both men and women, but the media paint it as pure disaster. The concerns are never couched in direct appeals for a return to male dominance. They are expressed in code words like family values, patriotism (after 9/11, how can women be so selfish as to advocate for their own rights?), innocent children, self-absorbed mothers, the evils of day care, the high divorce rate—and recently, the notion that *men* are really the ones who need help.

This last argument clangs through the popular media: As women gain power, men are losing it. They are dropping out of school, not getting the good job, falling prey to learning disorders and school violence. Some observers respond with apocalyptic dismay at the changing picture. They see *The Decline of Males,* as anthropologist Lionel Tiger puts it;[34] they see a *Mismatch* between men and women, as Queens College professor Andrew Hacker argues in his book: Women's growing economic power and unwillingness to defer to men are disrupting the old stability.[35] In Y: *The Descent of Men*, British science writer Steve Jones calls men an endangered species in the approaching age of female supremacy.[36]

This theme is being sounded in publications around the world. "The Descent of Man," headlines the *Weekly Standard*, decreeing, "The decline of men . . . stands as the most stunning sociological fact of our day."[37] *Business Week* says, "From Kindergarten to Grad School, Boys Are Becoming the Second Sex."[38] The *Singapore Straits Times* chimes in: "Women are taking over the workplace in the developing world and men are increasingly being marginalized."[39] *USA Today* headlines: "Male Students Lag [Behind] Females, But Few Educators Are Paying Attention."[40] *Adweek* says, "The post-feminist man is a henpecked wuss. How did that happen?"[41] "On campus, men are vanishing," says the *Washington Post*.[42] The *Boston Globe* opens a story with a vignette of two girls dancing the samba with each other at a Boston University ballroom dance club.[43] "There just aren't enough guys to go around," says one coed. "They're dropping off like flies, wherever you go on campus." One reporter writes that if present trends continue, "the graduation line in 2068 will be all females."[44] This sense of impending doom is peculiarly American. Historian James Oliver Robertson notes that we Americans frequently feel that our world is falling apart.[45] We fear that we have strayed from a glorious past filled with heroes and triumphs. In the present, by contrast, we seem to be setting sail into dark and churning waters.

This alarmist vision exaggerates both the gains made by females and the losses suffered by males, and sees the past as much more tranquil and happy than it really was for men. It implies that these problems are unique and brand-new. But news of a "male crisis" was just as big in 1880 as it is today. "The idea of what men are and what women are is always changing," says Notre Dame historian Gail Bederman, the author of *Manliness and Civilization*.[46] So, she says, "there's always a crisis." Indeed, we have fretted as a society about American men for a very long time. Before the Civil War, some 80 percent of men were self-employed farmers, tradesmen, and merchants. A scant twenty-five years after the war, when the industrial revolution had transformed the economic landscape, only one-third of men were their own bosses.[47] At the same time, the closing of the frontier dimmed the old American dream of heading west to the wilderness, and critics worried that the self-reliant, adventurous Anglo-Saxon male was in decline.

Henry James voiced this concern for the loss of male power in his 1885 novel *The Bostonians*, through the character of Basil Ransom, who rants, "The whole generation is womanized; the masculine tone is passing out of the world . . . it's a feminine, nervous, hysterical, chattering age."[48] He worries that "the masculine character, the ability to dare and endure, to know and yet not fear reality, to look the world in the face and take it for what it is" is fast vanishing.

The Boy Scouts were founded in 1911 largely because of worry about the "feminization" of young boys who spent their days in the female world of school. The same worry prompted prominent educator G. Stanley Hall to claim that little boys had to go through all the phases of savagery in childhood to become manly men. "All that rot they teach to children about the little raindrop fairies . . . must go. . . . We shall go back to teaching children the old bloody stories."[49] Masculinity, it seems, was always in need of bucking up. The Great Depression dealt a body blow to American manhood. In 1932 some 12 million men were unemployed, often living in shantytowns known as Hoovervilles. Men were seized by "panic, utter hopelessness about the future, an inability to initiate or sustain any activity."[50] In the 1950s, critics worried that the once independent American male was becoming the conformist, sheep-like *Organization Man* in his gray flannel suit, and pundits blamed overprotective mothers for producing "wimpy" sons who broke under brainwashing in the Korean War.[51] It would appear that reports of the death of masculinity have been greatly exaggerated.

The Myth of the Disappearing Daddy

Lionel Tiger (the Rutgers anthropologist noted for his work on male bonding) argues that the beginning of the end for men occurred in the 1970s, when women gained control of reproduction with the widespread use of the contraceptive pill. The decline of men, he says, "has everything to do with their being alienated from the means of reproduction."[52] Men, he says, are withdrawing from family responsibilities, abandoning their roles as fathers at an alarming rate, with dire consequences for women.

And modern females, he says, pine for the good old days when they enjoyed the "classic pace" of their traditional roles and the predictability of their life course. "Youth, growing up, marriage, children . . . bustle, grandchildren, seniority, pop off, the end." Such blissful lives were to be envied. "No independent initiatives, no bravado, no separate bank accounts . . . no disruptions of the universe."[53] Why is it that well-paid male intellectuals long for the traditional life for women, but they never seem the least bit nostalgic for the life of a Russian serf or a Dust Bowl wheat farmer for themselves?

Tiger claims that men were better fathers before reliable birth control but are rapidly becoming disengaged from their children. Men in the prepill past, however, were hardly models of involved fatherhood. The absence of effective birth control often meant that men sired children they didn't want and didn't—or couldn't—support. In post–Revolutionary War Concord, Massachusetts, for example, one-third of births occurred out of wedlock.[54] Some of those fathers married and supported the mothers of their children. Many others did not. A study of illegitimacy in North Carolina found that out-of-wedlock births for white women numbered the same in 1850 as they did in 1970 (when the pill was widely available).[55] Desertion of children has been a common practice for men throughout American history; the men who followed Horace Greeley's advice to "Go west, young man!" often left entire families behind. Historian Stephanie Coontz notes that even in two-parent families, emotional absence has been the norm—with employed fathers spending only two hours per week with their children in the prepill days that Tiger admires.[56] One study found that fathers in intact families in the 1950s spent less time with their children than did divorced fathers in the 1970s.[57]

Many middle- and upper-class fathers today, however, are intensely involved with their children. Most studies show that men now spend *considerably* more time with their children than they did twenty-five years ago.[58] Kids themselves report being close to their fathers, says

Ellen Galinsky of the Family and Work Institute.[59] In a 2000 study, a representative sample of about 1,000 third through twelfth graders, almost three in four children, said that their fathers rarely or never put their jobs before their families, and the children gave their fathers high marks as parents. One father, "Ray," a manager in a retail store and the father of four children, says, "When I look at the level of satisfaction that I get from being a father versus being a manager, I get far more satisfaction from being a father."[60] Dean, a park worker, says, "When Joey was born, I could have taken a promotion which would have been a pretty good amount of money, but would have changed my lifestyle a whole bunch because of the hours. I decided I wanted to spend time seeing my kid grow up."[61]

Are men really losing power, as Tiger suggests? In fact, traditional men who get their total sense of identity from being the sole breadwinner are in a precarious position. Their power base is shaky in an uncertain economy. But men who can be flexible, like the involved fathers above, actually gain power. They profit from both their wives' earning power and their own intense involvement with their children. For them, it's a win-win situation. This is a very clear illustration of how clinging to gender stereotypes can be extremely harmful to men and their families, while letting go of them benefits everybody.

The Myth of the Male Dropout

Those who fear the end of men may bemoan the fact that more women than men are now in college classrooms, but where are those male dropouts going? Not to prison, not to dope dealing, not to flipping burgers at McDonald's. During the late 1990s, many young men were dropping out to take jobs in the red-hot computer and dot-com sectors. Furthermore, the numbers are deceptive. Females may, for the first time, outnumber males in college classrooms, but female presence increases as the status of the college decreases. Female students do not dominate in the Ivy League. And in the academic majors that lead to the highest-paying jobs, males still dominate. They make up 60 percent of computer science and business majors, about 70 percent of physics majors, and more than 80 percent of engineering students.[62]

Compared to girls, boys have more reading problems and learning difficulties, drop out of school more often, and have more problems with violence. But this is nothing new. The same patterns appeared in the classrooms of the 1950s (*1,000,000 Delinquents* was the title of a 1950s book on boys' problems, referring to the number of boys in the criminal justice system).[63] Despite these historic problems, male power did not decline in those years. And just because women perform well in school, it doesn't follow that they will automatically rise in the work world. The glass ceiling is still firmly in place, even for high-achieving women. At the current rate of progress, it will take roughly forty years before women occupy even half of all corporate officer jobs.[64]

Although males drop out of high school more often than girls (a trend that is most pronounced among African American, Latino, and working-class white males), privileged upper-middle-class males overall do well scholastically. Poor and working-class males need help—especially when the manufacturing jobs that these men traditionally occupied are fast vanishing. This is not an issue of gender; rather, it's one of social class. On average, boys have always had greater problems than girls with reading, but their disadvantage may be more damaging in an Information Age that places heightened importance on verbal skills. No one doubts that certain boys need special attention in these areas; that's far different from saying that men are losing ground to women. The alarmists see what's happening with boys and girls as a zero-sum game; if girls advance, boys lose. Jacqueline E. Woods, executive director of the American Association of University Women, wrote in *USA Today* that "the flames of a gender war are being unnecessarily fanned, implying that educational achievement is a zero-sum game and that girls' achievements have come at the expense of boys." The message to girls and women, she says, is clear. "You are taking more than your fair share. You are too successful, you have come too far, and boys are paying the price for your accomplishments. This is not the case. Worse, the implicit solution sounds disturbingly close to advocating rolling back gains for girls to address our concerns about boys."[65] Setting up the issue as a war between the sexes will harm everyone. Gains made by girls seem so stunning mainly because they started so far behind. The idea that girls will continue to rocket ahead of boys is probably unrealistic. Girls may continue to advance but at a slower pace.

Interestingly, kids themselves don't think that girls are winning all the marbles. As cited by American University professor David Sadker, "When more than a thousand Michigan elementary students were asked to describe what the world would be like if they were born a member of the opposite sex, more than forty percent of the girls saw positive advantages to being a boy: better jobs, more money and definitely more respect. Ninety-five percent of the boys saw no advantage to being a female."[66] In her book *Stiffed* Susan Faludi notes, "There's a lot of blaming and confusion over women's meager gains and the so-called feminization of culture. It may appear to men on the down escalator that women have the upper hand."[67] But, she notes, in the new service economy, many women "are still relegated to jobs that don't pay a decent wage. Men are not declining while women rise; the new economy makes it tough for workers of both sexes."

Lionel Tiger, for one, wildly exaggerates women's progress. "There are no effective national entities comparable to the National Organization for Women that reflect the interests of men. Meanwhile, well-schooled graduates of activist programs of women's studies migrate onto the staffs of politicians and other decision makers, which they will become in due course."[68] Graduates of women's studies programs will be delighted to hear of their success. If only men had such an organization, they'd run most of the Fortune 500 companies, hold most elected political posts and judgeships, be presidents of most universities, and earn 40 percent more than most women. Wait a minute—they already do.

The Myth of the Disappearing Husband

A major consequence of the notion of the decline of men and its corollary, the supposed war between the sexes, is the idea that women will find no men to marry. Andrew Hacker writes: "As women are becoming more assertive, they are finding that all too many men lack the qualities they desire in dates and mates." He concludes that "there is a greater divide between the sexes than at any time in living memory. The result will be a greater separation of women and men, with tensions and re-criminations afflicting beings once thought to be more naturally companionable."[69] But we've seen that men are now seeking out educated women to marry, and, except for the most traditional among them, don't have a problem with their wives earning more than they do. The marriage rate remains high—and most men and women who divorce eventually remarry.

Another fear: Won't all those "assertive" women Hacker writes about be too tired for sex? Isn't their ambition going to lead to *Sexual Suicide*, as critic George Gilder writes in the book of that name?[70] In a word, no. Fatigue does depress sexual desire—but working women are no more tired than homemakers. Janet Hyde's study of 500 couples bears this out.[71] These couples had just had a baby and were under a great deal of time pressure; if ever sex would suffer, it should be among these couples. It didn't suffer, even when one or both partners worked forty-five or more hours per week. The strongest finding was that fatigue depressed sexual expression of any kind; homemakers were no less fatigued than working women. The sexual satisfaction of men is unrelated to whether their wives are at home, working part-time, or working more than forty-five hours a week.

Hacker predicts that the problems encountered by black men and black women provide a paradigm of what will happen to everybody else. Black women often complain that there aren't enough men of their race with well-paying, stable jobs to make them good marriage material. But white men don't face the historic racial, social, and economic problems that keep so many black men in the underclass. Making the very real plight of black men a prototype for the U.S. population as a whole is illogical and unsubstantiated. We argue, on the contrary, that in the present economy women's new earning power is a boon to marriage rather than an impediment. Among the main beneficiaries of women's new earning power are the men they marry or live with—and their children.

Having two incomes in the lifeboat enables most couples to stay afloat, and men understand this. They are responding by spending more time with their kids while their wives work and are doing more of the housework. Their marriages are happier when they do, research shows, giving them a double benefit: a better relationship with their spouse and access to the wife's income for family necessities as well as extras.[72] Two incomes in a family may enable a man to go back to school to get a better job that could lead to even more income. Moreover, if a man gets laid off in this uncertain job market, his partner's income and benefits can keep the wolf from the door.

One manager in the human resources field lost a high-paying job during his company's retrenchment in the late 1990s, but the salary his wife earned as a teacher kept the family from financial ruin. He worked a series of minimum-wage jobs in retail until he found a good consulting position. Throughout this disruption, their daughter didn't have to drop out of college. Meanwhile, Hank, a medical technician, counts on his wife, a hospital administrator, to buffer him from the insecure job market. "She's my right arm. If I were to lose my job, I know I'd be supported. 'Cause sometimes I feel like, 'I quit' and she says, 'Okay, do what you want.' And the same thing with her if she said, 'I can't handle this anymore.' I see my mother was stuck, my father was stuck. I have the support they didn't have."[73]

Such stories are becoming more and more typical. For men, since the suicide rate closely shadows the unemployment rate, a wife's salary could literally be a lifesaver. (Imagine the different ending *Death of a Salesman* might have had if Willy Loman's wife had held a good job?) A likely model for the future of men and women is not the disadvantaged, single-parent black family, but today's hardworking dual-earner couples of all races. Our major study of such couples found them to be doing well—happy, healthy, and satisfied with their lives, though certainly busy juggling their many roles.[74]

Today, young men and women tend to marry a bit later and look for a "soul mate" to wed. As one man in his thirties, a police officer, says of his artist wife, "She'll understand my dumb jokes, and I'll understand hers. We'll be in a room full of twenty or thirty people and we'll both crack up, because we both thought of the same thing at the same time. Everyone else will turn to us and say, 'what a couple of weirdos.'"[75] Another man says of his wife, "We're each other's best friends and get a lot of pleasure learning things together, changing together. We're good together. We try to spend as much time as we can together."[76]

The intricate and ongoing negotiations required for a husband and wife each to hold down a job, while both also manage the kids and the house, lead to the creation of a complex relationship that is not easily abandoned or re-created. One couple—she's a bank executive and he's a public relations specialist—remembers coming home from the hospital with their first child, when panic set in. "There was this feeling of 'Now his real parents will come along and pick him up and they'll know what to do,'" the husband said, laughing. Now they successfully juggle two jobs and two kids, and they are closer than ever. "I think we're better lovers than we ever have been, because we're such good friends," the wife says. She adds, however, that there's more quality than quantity, because "who's got the time and energy?"[77]

Women's gains will not bring about an inevitable war between the sexes. The divorce rate is no higher among dual-earner couples than in the traditional family—in fact, it's lower.[78] As one couple puts it, the costs of switching are simply too high. Looking at the data, Berkeley sociologist Valerie Kincade Oppenheimer concludes that income equality between husbands and wives is *not* synonymous with unstable marriages, but rather with couples staying together.[79] As we saw earlier, the divorce rate is higher among women who have no earnings—housewives often have no power. A man who wants to leave can do so, knowing that he may not lose a lot economically. Research shows that after a divorce in a traditional family, the wife's standard of living declines far more dramatically than does the husband's.[80]

But if the alarmist message spreads that women have gone too far and have acquired too much power, both the American economy and women themselves will suffer. The effort to put systems in place to support working women (paid family medical leave, flexible work schedules, paid paternity leave, etc.) could stall completely—and that will mean a big downturn for the U.S. economy. The great American economic boom of the 1990s, says Professor Richard B. Freeman of the National Bureau of Economic Research at Harvard University, was "not a story of male employment but of the large increase in female employment."[81] And, he notes, the employment of married women with children was a major reason why the United States outstripped the European Union economically in the 1990s.

Despite these gains, employed women with children still suffer a "mommy gap" of about 20 percent in wages—behind both men and childless women.[82] Efforts should be underway to close this gap, which would be an enormous boon to the American economy. Instead, we see a steady chip away at women's gains. Title IX, which gave young women equal funding in sports, is under attack; there's a move in Congress to restrict women's roles in the military; and women's reproductive rights are already being rolled back on many fronts.

Underlying many of the arguments about men, women, and power that we've just reviewed is the notion that women are supposed to be caring, selfless "Venusians" who are by nature uninterested in and unsuited for power. The Martians are the ones who are programmed to achieve and to protect and care for the "weaker sex." By this logic, any change in this equation is turning nature on its head, and all manner of terrible events will follow. But, as we've shown, the problems *really* occur when women and men hold onto outmoded ideas. In their personal lives and (as we'll discover in the next section), in their careers as well, both sexes benefit when they reject rather than embrace the gender-difference models.

part two

Work

Man (and Woman) the Hunter

HE COMES STRIDING OUT of the fog of prehistory, cobwebs of myth clinging to his broad shoulders. Alert, muscular, sharp-eyed, he is Man the Hunter, and he carries not only his sharp-pointed spear but the destiny of his species. With his long-legged stride he steps decisively over the divide that separates prehuman from *Homo sapiens*—us.

This is another chapter in the evolutionary narrative that Ultra Darwinists use to tell the story of our species: Males are the aggressive sex and females the docile sex. We have already seen how they present this image in the mating game. The chapters in Part II explain how they present it in the world of work, where it is just as unfounded and just as damaging. As our ancestors moved from the forest to the grassy savanna, their diet changed from berries, nuts, and roots to meat, say the Darwinists. And meat-eating males were responsible for the development of our capacity to stand upright, make tools for hunting, develop speech to facilitate the group hunt, and bring back provisions to women and children. Males skilled at warfare and hunting came quickly to dominate the environment around them. Hunting in particular, they say, equipped males with a distinct advantage that still plays out in the workplace today, giving men an edge in jobs from piloting airliners through the sky to governing a state.

Nothing illustrates this narrative better than the dramatic opening of the film *2001: A Space Odyssey* (1968), set on a stark primeval plain, with a group of apes milling about. When three giant, mysterious slabs suddenly appear on the plain (the gift of an extraterrestrial culture, perhaps), the apes' movements become purposeful. One picks up the jawbone of a carcass from the ground and begins to break the other bones around him with what is symbolically the first weapon. Faster and more furiously he wields the weapon, finally, in triumph, hurling it high into the air. In a famous sequence, the bone transmutes into a spaceship, silently circling the earth. The history of mankind is encapsulated in an instant, and it is the story of males advancing the species through their hunting and their aggressiveness. In this drama, woman is nowhere to be found.

Man the Hunter has become firmly lodged in our imagination. Nearly every popular new book and article about gender differences takes us back to the primordial landscape in which fierce warriors whacked their way through the veldt. Best-selling author Michael Gurian states flatly that because women didn't hunt, their brains do not equip them to be engineers or scientists.[1] In *Why Men Don't Listen and Women Can't Read Maps*, an international best-seller, Barbara and Alan Pease declare, "Once upon a time, a long long time ago, men and women lived happily together and worked in harmony. The man would venture out each day into a hostile and dangerous world to risk his life as a hunter to bring food back to his woman and their children. He developed long distance navigational skills and excellent marksmanship skills."[2] Not having hunted, women can't read maps, can't parallel park, and can't play video games, say the authors. Occupations that women should not enter, because "their brain bias is not suited to these areas," include flight engineer, engineer, air traffic controller, architect, flight deck officer, actuary, accountant. "While men play chess, women dance and decorate."

Countless media stories echo this notion. In the *Washington Post*, a review of a Discovery Channel show refers to a past "idyllic arrangement—men out hunting, women in charge of the home and children" and adds, "Women have tried to compete with men, but we should relish our differences—if we accept them, it's the best of all possible worlds."[3] A writer in the *Financial Times of London* says, "It may be that we will see the traditional division of labor mirrored in the market-place: female managers keeping the home fires burning at headquarters while intrepid male managers travel, hunting and gathering in the jungles of global business."[4] It's a short hop from such media presentations to public policy. Former House speaker Newt Gingrich argued that men are better suited to military service because they are "programmed to hunt giraffe."[5]

How did Gingrich, and so many others, come to believe this idea? Ironically, the saga of Man the Hunter first emerged in the 1950s in a postwar world gripped by the problem of the fate of modern civilization and facing the struggles against racism that were beginning to mark the American landscape. Man the Hunter, who emerged in Africa, seemed to embody an antiracist, universal message to a world that had just undergone a cataclysm among nation-states. In 1950, UNESCO issued a statement proclaiming that "every man is his brother's keeper."[6] Man the Hunter contained a powerful antiracist message, but a darker message also ran through the story and has left a lasting effect. Professor Donna Haraway of the University of California–Santa Cruz, author of *Primate Visions*, argues that it was "unintentional and therefore particularly powerful scientific sexism."[7]

In that era women's only legitimate function was decreed to be wife and mother, and women who wished to venture beyond this limited turf were told they were displaying "penis envy." Consequently it is not surprising that almost all scientific interest in our female ancestors focused on the pair bond and motherhood. (Female–female conflict was dismissed as mere bickering tied to sex, not war or species making.)[8] During the 1960s and 1970s, the culture of Man the Hunter and his male-centered universe was vigorously promoted through a series of books: Robert Ardrey, *The Hunting Hypothesis;*[9] Desmond Morris, *The Naked Ape;*[10] and Lionel Tiger, *Men in Groups.*[11] Ironically, these books held sway just as the women's movement was having its maximum impact on society. As Haraway points out, the hunter books "appeared just in time to slay dragons released by the women's liberation movement." Although dated, the ideas in these books are still widely disseminated. "U.S. libraries continue to teach young people the lessons of male agency "through man the hunter in their Life Nature Library book, *The Primates.*"

If female activity was all but ignored, the importance of activities thought to be male, such as hunting, was glorified and credited with giving us our very humanness—while at the same time giving modern-day men an advantage in the professions. In a staggering leap from the Stone Age to the Information Age, Harvard sociobiologist E. O. Wilson states that because men hunted and women didn't, "even with equal education for men and women and equal access to all professions, men are likely to remain disproportionately represented in political life, business and science."[12] Tiger and Fox write in *The Imperial Animal* that because men controlled hunting and wanted to keep women out of it, "women will be unlikely to make effective inroads into the centers of economic power."[13]

The real-life repercussions of these speculative theories constrain women's choices in arbitrary ways. The president of one large company said during a radio interview that he keeps in mind the ideas he has picked up about male–female differences when making decisions on hiring, firing, and employee policy. How often might he—like the Sears executives mentioned earlier who didn't want to promote women—have decided that women were not assertive enough for the top jobs in his firm and belonged in lower-ranking positions? Obviously such thinking would have a huge impact on women's upward mobility in the workplace. When we spoke to George, 42, a high-level supervisor at a biotech firm, he peppered his speech with military language such as *we're gonna stalk our prey, let's get 'em in the crosshairs, we've got only one shot at the target.* His language codifies a belief he holds strongly: Women don't belong in the competitive arena of the boardroom. When it comes to hiring and promoting, George favors those he sees as aggressive males. For him and many male managers like him, corporate leadership is a battle, a duel, to be fought by men who are up to the challenge.

The Man the Hunter legend includes vivid domestic scenes of women and children huddled by the campfire, waiting patiently for the hunter males to return home to provide food and protection. More likely, "home" was wherever roaming bands hung their figurative hats for the moment. Anthropologist Richard Potts, director of the Human Origins Program of the Smithsonian National Museum of Natural History, examined the assemblages of bones, tools, and rocks on which the "home base" theories were built.[14] He argued that early humans did not dwell in one place for long periods of time, since the remains of large carnivores were found along with the human remains; obviously humans would not have sought out the presence of these other carnivores. Rather, Potts saw the sites as places where early humans stopped for a time and stored caches of tools and weapons. Primatologist Linda Fedigan of the University of Alberta thinks that Potts's work should overturn the old ideas: "If there is not evidence for home bases where the sick and dependent waited for the well and productive, then we can perhaps finally free our minds of the image of dawn-age women and children waiting at campsites for the return of the provisioners."[15]

As for early males, the heroic yarn has it that big-game hunting arose early and launched man on his way to dominating all other species. One basis for this story line, however, turns out not to have been true. In the 1950s, Australian paleontologist Raymond Dart discovered a group of fossils in a South African cave; one was the skull of an early human that bore the marks of what looked like a blow from a weapon.[16] According to Dart, this proved that warfare was part of the legacy of early man, fueling the mythic (and violent) saga of *Homo sapiens*.

Later, researchers studied the fossils that Dart had examined, this time with the aid of an electron microscope. They determined that this early man had not been a warrior's victim but a carnivore's lunch: The injury exactly matched a leopard's bite pattern. Of course, agile but relatively weak humans scavenging for food, with men and women cooperating to outwit much larger predators, using brain instead of brawn to survive, makes for a less dramatic story than Man the Hunter. But the former is more likely the true picture of our prehuman ancestors. Anthropologist Robin Compton of Liverpool University says, "E. O. Wilson's model of the development of male dominance as a genetic adaptation to the hunting life represents an unacceptable distortion of the available data—or at best, pure speculation."[17] Noted paleontologist Richard Leakey adds, "There is absolutely no evidence that we became human through hunting. Up until recent times, there's no record at all of human aggression. If you can't find it in the prehistoric record, why claim it's there?"[18]

In evolutionary code, the earlier a behavior shows up, the more fundamental it is to human nature.[19] In other words, big-game hunting, arriving relatively late on the scene, could not have hardwired abilities into men's brains. So much for claims that men can park their cars or guide aircraft into New York airspace better than women can because of their ancient hunting prowess.

One intriguing illustration of this common misinterpretation is the saga of the Ice Age hunters. You have no doubt seen—in a history book or a museum exhibit or an old issue of *National Geographic*—an artist's rendering of fur-clad male hunters poised to hurl their spears at a gigantic woolly mammoth. To University of Illinois archaeologist Olga Soffer, this picture seemed off-kilter.[20] There was no evidence from Africa or Asia that hunting bands went after these huge, dangerous elephants until about the fifth century B.C., some 8,000 years after the Ice Age. Only with the coming of the Iron Age, with its heavier, more lethal weapons, might such a picture have been possible.

Soffer journeyed to Paleolithic sites in Russia and eastern Europe to look at newly discovered fossil remains. Most of the elephant carcasses she saw belonged to smaller females and juveniles, not adult males. Instead of taking on a 6,000-pound creature with sharp tusks, early hunters had more realistically set their sights on dead or dying juveniles and a few adult females. "If one of these Upper Paleolithic guys killed a mammoth, and occasionally they did," Soffer muses, "they probably didn't stop talking about it for years."

As we piece together a new, more accurate picture, the legend of the he-man dissolves and makes way for a portrait of prehistoric males and females, and even children, working together to survive. This is still a portrait in the making, however. Much remains to be discovered about our early ancestors and how they lived. Before the electron microscope, carbon dating, and DNA technology, much of what we now know was impossible to fathom. Who knows what future technologies and discoveries will teach us?

Woman the Hunter

New research has supplied us with a character from our early history who has received scant attention: Woman the Hunter. You won't see any pictures of her in textbooks or natural history museums, but dramatic new finds from the Ice Age have uncovered her tracks. They were hard to spot because nets were her tool of choice in the small-game hunting she appears to have engaged in extensively. (The large, hard weapons males would have used survived for eons.) Soffer, working at a Paleolithic site in the Czech Republic, came across a series of crisscrossed lines preserved in clay, which she speculated were the remains of woven fibers from 25,000 years ago. After looking at 8,400 more clay fragments from sites in the area, she found the remains of what seemed to be a mesh net—a likely tool of the communal hunt. When her colleagues David Hyland and James Adovasio used a zoom stereo microscope to examine the impressions in the clay, they found evidence of weaver's knots, a technique used to make strong nets for fishing or hunting.[21]

The researchers speculate that the nets were used to capture Ice Age hares, whose remains are plentiful in the Upper Paleolithic site. Many such sites are strewn with the bones of small animals and birds, and some of the bone tools found resemble net spacers (used for tying nets). "This is not the image we've always had of Upper Paleolithic macho guys out killing animals up close and personal," Soffer says. "Net hunting is communal, and it involves the labor of children and women." This we can surmise by observing gatherer tribes of today, many of whom work together in groups and use nets more than weapons like bows and arrows to supply food.[22] The Mbuti in the Congo, for example, report that they catch 50 percent of the game for which they set their nets, undoubtedly a larger percentage of kills than hunters experience as they track large prey through their natural habitat. Weavers in North America have made nets that can capture 1,000-pound elk and bighorn sheep, demonstrating that even large game can be the object of net hunting.

Evidence is accumulating that women provided critical food supplies throughout our early history, not only by foraging but through hunting, trapping, organizing communal hunts, and sometimes hunting with what were once thought to be male-only tools. Inuit women carried bows and arrows, especially blunt arrows designed for hunting birds.[23] Wouldn't taking aim at a bird in flight and hitting it with an arrow or hunting agile Ice Age hares with a net have sharpened women's skills at dealing with distance and space? Wouldn't the sex that spent centuries hunting small game have developed a brain that would make it possible to park a Chrysler? It wasn't only men whose brains were wired over centuries by the skill and discipline of hunting. The icon of Man the Hunter is being toppled by the weight of new knowledge about women's capacity for aggressive behavior.

Woman the Aggressor

Aggression is a highly charged issue; myth and emotion often take the place of data when it is considered. The stereotype paints men as the more violent, angry sex, while women are peaceful. But results from three major analyses of approximately 300 studies show that there isn't much difference in the rate at which the sexes experience anger.[24]

Aggression, as opposed to anger, conveys an intent to hurt or harm and can be expressed physically, verbally, or by withdrawing. There is general agreement that men exhibit higher levels of physical aggression than women, but the differences are small to moderate.[25] After a thorough review of the literature on who initiates violence in couples, Murray Straus of the University of New Hampshire reports: "It is painful to have to recognize the high rate of domestic assaults by women. All six major studies which have investigated this topic found that women initiate violence in a large proportion of the cases."[26] For example, of the 495 couples in a 1985

National Family Violence Survey for whom one or more incidents of assault were reported by a woman respondent, the man was the only violent partner in 25.9 percent of the cases, the woman was the only one to be violent in 25.5 percent of the cases, and both were violent in 48.6 percent of the cases.[27] Of 446 women who reported being involved in violent relationships, their partners struck the first blow in 42 percent of the cases. They hit first in 53 percent of the cases and they could not remember who hit first in the remaining 3 percent. However, men are far more likely to kill or seriously injure their partners when they become violent. (Therefore, these statistics should not be used to downplay the seriousness of violence against women.) As with most behavior, there is far more variation among men as a group and women as a group than there is between the two. For women, the power of situation cuts both ways. On the one hand, there are many more social constraints against female aggression. Add to these Gilligan's idea that women are naturally caring and relational, which could put an internal constraint on women's aggression. On the other hand, violent women are perhaps aware that society and the legal system hold them less accountable than men, since the gender stereotypes *always* cast women as the victim.

Whether men or women behave in an aggressive manner depends on a multitude of factors. One is the level of provocation. If someone slaps you playfully on the wrist, you won't react the same way you would if you had been slapped hard on the face. Another factor is whether the called-for response seems physical or verbal. If somebody calls you a name, you'll probably reply in kind; if someone shoves you against the wall, you're likely to shove back.

Fear of danger from retaliation is also important. You're more likely to be aggressive with someone nearly your size. If the offender is a 250-pound fullback, you'll think twice before taking him on. Likewise, the gender of the target may come into play. Some men will hesitate to strike a woman. Some women will hit a man, thinking they can't do him much harm.

A final factor is degree of anonymity: Being observed changes women's behavior—but not men's. Women often get the message that they are supposed to heal, not hurt, and when they behave aggressively they may fear they will be punished more severely than their brothers. After all, "boys will be boys." But what happens when women think nobody's watching? A study conducted by two Princeton psychologists sheds some surprising light on this question.[28]

They asked a random sample of eighty-four men and women to play a video game in which they would drop bombs on an opponent and would be bombed in turn. Study participants were told they had been matched with someone at another terminal in the room but would never know who that person was. The researchers knew the identities of only half the group. In the unknown group, both gender and names were hidden; in the known group, participants wore name tags and were visible to the experimenters.

The results were revealing. When their identity was known, males dropped significantly more bombs than did females. But when names were unknown, females dropped more bombs than males. Granted anonymity, women were significantly more aggressive than men. Indeed, they bombed their opponents back to the Stone Age—a most unladylike way to behave.[29] As you can see in Figure 6.1, men didn't behave much differently whether they were watched or not—because there are few social constraints on men's macho behavior.

After the game, participants were asked to report their own aggressiveness and the number of bombs they dropped. The men accurately described themselves as aggressive. But the women reported themselves as having behaved less aggressively than they had. If the study had only accepted the women's self-reports, it would have reflected the common wisdom that women are naturally less aggressive than men. But a treasure trove of new human and primate data is refocusing that picture.

Girls Will Be Girls

In the past, most primate research was conducted on a few species in captivity—which told us little about what those species would do in a natural setting. But new field research is changing this picture. Because we

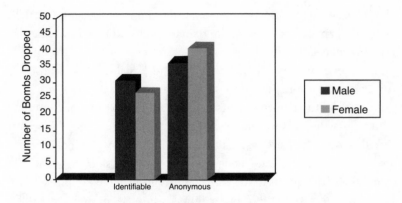

Adapted from J. R. Lightdale & D. A. Prentice, "Rethinking sex differences in aggression: Aggressive behavior in the absence of social roles." *Personality and Social Psychology Bulletin* 20 (1994): 34–44.

FIGURE 6.1   Effects of Anonymity and Subject Sex on Number of Bombs Dropped

assume that males are the violent sex, when females engage in aggression, we tend to see it as unnatural, says psychologist Charles T. Snowdon.[30] But, he explains, aggression in males—whether male–female aggression or male–male aggression—is complex and not as widespread as we believe.

Snowdon says that the size difference, or sexual dimorphism, in many species is what determines male–female aggression. Among primate species with little sexual dimorphism—marmosets, tamarins, woolly spider monkeys, lemurs—there seems to be little or no aggression between the sexes. Given the limited degree of sexual dimorphism in humans, with males only 5–10 percent larger, on average, than females, he suggests that male–female physical aggression should be minimal.

It's also accepted wisdom that male hormones lead to "blood lust" among males of all species. But both males and females secrete testosterone from the adrenal glands, and progesterone can be metabolized into testosterone; "thus, at the level of the hormones, there is no need to conclude that males are 'naturally' more aggressive than females." (More on this issue in Chapter 8.) Snowdon observes that among chimpanzees, males are aggressive more often than females, but their aggression appears to be no more than a ritual, and they rely on a variety of reconciliation mechanisms to restore peace after a flare-up. Female violence is typically more severe, and females are less prone to forgive and forget. Snowdon says we assume that males are programmed by their hormones to behave aggressively toward females with whom they wish to mate. But primate behavior doesn't support this idea. Among macaques, male success is greater when females initiate the mating and use such cues as head bobs and sidelong glances to signal their willingness to the male. Male rhesus monkeys pursue preferred partners and ignore other females in heat, even when the favored female is not ovulating. Among brown capuchin monkeys, the females make overtures to the males to persuade them to mate, and male muriqui monkeys wait patiently in line to mate with a receptive female. Snowdon concludes, "Not only are male mammals not sex machines pumped up by their hormones, but they often do not initiate sexual activity but wait to be actively solicited by females."

Snowdon and others find no consistent pattern of aggression within or between sexes, challenging the notion of ever present male competition. But countless nature documentaries and magazine photographs feature images of male rams butting heads, elk locking horns in a fight to the death, grizzlies clawing at each other in battles over turf or mates. Male animals are rarely presented hunting together, grazing peacefully side by side, or sharing food after a kill. But cooperation is as much a part of male existence as is aggression.

Female aggression is a part of evolution as well. Sarah Blaffer Hrdy writes, in *The Woman That Never Evolved*, that females seek dominance to protect their genetic legacy just as men do.[31] She debunks myths that exaggerate "woman's natural innocence from lust for power, her cooperativeness and solidarity with other women." Females in many species compete as avidly as males, she reports. UCLA psychologist Shelley Taylor emphasizes female bonding rather than aggression.[32] Taylor rightly points out that "tending and befriending" play a much larger part in the daily life of most women *and* men than aggression.

However, she's on shaky ground when she says that while the "fight or flight" response to stress is hardwired into males, females instead calm their young and befriend other females in times of stress. She makes an evolutionary argument for this behavior. Is this a strategy that would have worked back in the Pleistocene? Sometimes, perhaps. But would the first instinct of a vulnerable female be to link up with other vulnerable females? On occasion, bands of females can keep aggressors at bay, but a better strategy would be to bond with powerful males, which they do. Female primates often seek to mate with aggressive males to deter them from killing their offspring. At other times, females choose to fight. Everyone knows to stay far away from a mama bear with cubs. Even small females will attack larger intruders; anyone who has been chased by a snapping mother goose can attest to that.

And there's another important question. Do women in fact tend and befriend more than men? Gender stereotypes suggest they do, but who says males don't tend and befriend? Male baboons regularly care for infants not their own, and, as we've noted, there is a wide range of male fathering behavior across many species—including our own. Many males, faced with other powerful males, neither flee nor fight—they curry favor with displays of submission. And the "male bonding" that is easily recognizable among sports teams, fraternities, army buddies, and drinking buddies is sometimes seen in primates. For example, males isolated from their social group tend to suffer from a range of physical and emotional problems.

Certainly there are situations in which female competition rather than befriending is typical. There has been a lot of press in recent years about "mean" girls in their early teens, as well as all-female gangs and cliques that ostracize other girls. Psychologist Phyllis Chesler has examined centuries of female-on-female cruelty in *Woman's Inhumanity to Woman* and reports that "we've been so much focused on male violence—which is so dangerous and affects other men and women, of course—that we haven't paid attention to aggression in females. Women's aggression is indirect. It's shunning, taunting or ostracizing, which traditionally is seen as a lesser form of violence, but it's equally dominating and cruel."[33] Aggression can be added to the list of human behaviors and traits that one sex hasn't cornered the market on, as evidenced by the fossil record, primate research, and data on humans.

Sticks and Stones

Children may chant, "Sticks and stones can break my bones but names will never hurt me," but that's far from the truth. Overall, males have the advantage in the "sticks and stones" domain, but females and males vie for first place in the "names can hurt" arena. In one study, 459 third-through sixth-grade children (9–12 years of age) were asked what most boys do when they are mad at someone and what most girls do when they are mad at someone. They cited verbal insults as one of the most typical behaviors in both mixed- and same-sex interactions.[34] Boys sometimes punch and fight, but the unkindest cut of words appears to be the most common means of aggression for both sexes.

Girls tend toward verbal threat, or "relational aggression," which hurts others by excluding them from social relationships.[35] A University of Minnesota study of 496 third, fourth, fifth, and sixth graders found that a significant number of girls had been "relationally victimized" in this way. Anyone who has spent time with young girls has seen them act out this form of aggression by name-calling, stigmatizing others as losers or keeping them out of groups, rebuffing offers of friendship, and mockery, all of which can hurt more than sticks and stones. "We make each other miserable," says one Maryland teenager.[36] The Internet has given girls' aggression another outlet, a place where they can post nasty messages about others. One teen's best friend chose to tell her she hated her online. "You're conceited," the friend wrote.[37]

As they mature, girls and women nowadays are taking on more physically risky and previously off-limits aggressive behavior. In Las Vegas in 2003, a group of teen boys and girls videotaped their brutal fights—possibly inspired by the movie *Fight Club* or reality TV shows.[38] In one graphic sequence, two girls slug each other with all the brutality displayed by males. And in a high school hazing incident, also videotaped, that occurred in Illinois around the same time, senior girls beat junior girls and showered them with filth—mud and excrement.[39]

Women ride motorcycles, play rugby, speak out in public meetings, travel alone, and, as policewomen, wrestle felons to the ground. What some have called the "feminization of crime" is occurring as women engage in substantially more criminal behavior than in the past. Young girls are joining gangs and engaging in more assaultive behavior. From 1990 to 1999, arrest records for U.S. girls rose by a whopping 57 percent.[40] In New York City, arrests of girls for violent crime jumped 58 percent between 1987 and 1997.[41] "We used to marvel when one girl was referred to us," says Nina Jody, chief prosecutor for Manhattan Family Court.[42] "Now it's like ladies day around here. There are many days when half the cases are girls. In the last two years, girls have become the main actors in assaults, robberies and even gang assaults. They are out on the street at 2:00 A.M., riding the subways, doing everything boys are doing." A San Francisco girl gang roamed the city in 2003, assaulting people and snatching an infant from the arms of a woman they then proceeded to beat.[43] A fourteen-year-old girl walked into her parochial school in Pennsylvania in 2001 and shot a classmate in the shoulder.[44] One fifteen-year-old in a high-security prison for girls says, "This girl made fun of my hair, she kept touching it. So I put razor blades in my pigtails. She don't make fun of me no more."[45] These actions were all taken by members of the sex that is supposedly caring and relational by nature. What we are seeing is that as constraints on female behavior loosen, behavior also changes.

Statistics from across the globe show a marked rise in violent criminal actions by women, though they serve much less time in jail than men do. Males remain well ahead of females in violent crime; but when a broader range of aggressive behavior is considered, there is no longer a huge gender difference. In a Finnish study of adolescent aggression (including relational aggression), the researchers say: "The claim that human males are more aggressive than females . . . appears . . . to be false, and a consequence of narrow definitions and operationalizations of aggression in previous research, with a predominant emphasis on physical aggression."[46] Taking a cross-cultural perspective also sheds light on this issue. The U.S. culture is, relatively speaking, violent. Although overall women are less aggressive than men, American women are more aggressive, on average, than men in more pacific cultures (e.g., Japan).

What about the special type of aggression called for during wartime and historically associated with men only?

It's War

When he served as ambassador to Bahrain, the late David Ransom invited a group of Bahraini businessmen aboard an aircraft carrier involved in operations in the gulf.[47] The businessmen came aboard by helicopter. Because the ship was moving, when it was time to return them to Bahrain, the choppers did not have adequate range. The businessmen climbed aboard a supply plane and held on to their seats as the plane was catapulted from the carrier. Once they landed, the ambassador told his guests that it would be courteous to thank the pilot. They lined up as the flier climbed down from the cockpit. The surprise on the men's faces was evident as the pilot pulled off a flight helmet to reveal a mane of blond hair and earrings. "Hi guys, I hope you enjoyed the ride," she said.

The long-standing taboo on women in the military is crumbling, thanks to a range of new social and economic forces. This taboo had little to do with size or strength; some women have always been taller and stronger than some men. Nor did the fact that women bear children mean they could not kill if circumstances required. In 1998, ancient grave sites near the Kazakhstan border in Russia were found to contain the skeletal remains of women buried with daggers, swords, and tools for sharpening metal.[48] One of the female skeletons had a bent arrowhead lodged in her body, suggesting that she had been killed in battle. The idea that parts of ancient eastern Europe were patrolled by groups of armed women was given credibility by the findings of Russian archaeologists. They investigated 2,400-year-old burial mounds and found that five of twenty-one graves contained the bodies of young women with weapons.[49]

Rather than women's weakness, we believe, the fragility of the human infant and the extended human childhood lay at the root of the historical taboo on women in combat. A single male could produce enough sperm to repopulate a tribe. But it took one female years to bear and nurse each child. Women simply could not be spared for combat. When parents could expect only half of their children to make it to adulthood, large families helped ensure the survival of the tribe and the species.

In the developed world, modern medicine and a plummeting infant mortality rate put less pressure on women to reproduce. As a result, age-old restrictions on women's behavior are fading away. It's not surprising that increasing numbers of women have moved into almost all areas of military service, including combat. Put bluntly, women are now just as expendable as men and just as free to take part in risky behaviors. With the prospect of a world war between superpowers receding, the military needs a highly trained, technologically sophisticated force, not hordes of foot soldiers. The nation's warrior elite increasingly will be a group of men and women who share the same military culture and attitudes.

When army officer-turned-journalist David Hackworth interviewed a woman pilot who flies the army's Apache helicopter, he asked her if she could kill in the line of duty.[50] She replied, "I accept responsibility that I might shed blood or I may shed the blood of others." Hackworth noted that she expressed less bravado than male flying aces of the past, but her resolve was clear. In his words, "I have no doubt she'd shoot to kill and win." A former air force officer who served in the Gulf War, Debra Dickerson, writes, "I'm not bloodthirsty. I can't watch horror movies, people yelling at each other or a hypodermic needle piercing flesh. You cry, I cry. You puke, I puke. I'll walk away from a fight so fast you'd get dizzy."[51] None of this kept her from going to war. "For whatever reasons, Iraq was shooting at America. America is where my mama lives. . . . I wanted to help keep my team, my friends and all those anonymous captains just like me alive and in one piece. To do that, I had to be in the game."

Throughout history there have been more female warriors like Dickerson than our portrait of the "weaker sex" would let us admit. In the first century, the warrior queen Boadicea led her tribal warriors in what is now Britain against the Roman invasion. In the recent civil war in Eritrea, which began in 1998, some 35 percent of the combat soldiers were women who endured years of harsh battlefield conditions and fierce fighting. In Operation Desert Storm and in the 2003 U.S. invasion of Iraq, women served with courage. There has perhaps been undue alarm about women warriors because the myths of the recent historical past exaggerate women's gentleness and frailty, which does not reflect the historical record. In fact, government officials were surprised that there was no expression of national outrage at the female casualties in the Gulf War and later in Iraq.

Women used to serve in female-only units such as the WAVES or the WACS. Not until the door was opened to a sexually integrated military in the mid-1970s did large numbers of women stream through. Today more than 70,000 female soldiers comprise about 15 percent of the army, 13 percent of the navy, 19 percent of the air force, and 6 percent of the marines. And the proportion of jobs open to them ranges from 91 percent in the army to 99 percent in the high-tech air force. Men and women serve together on navy ships such as the aircraft carrier USS *Eisenhower,* and in 1999, in military action over Iraq, a female pilot fired a missile in a combat situation for the first time. Such activity has since become routine.

Newsweek describes a female pilot assigned to the aircraft carrier USS *Carl Vinson* who says, "I wake up, I breathe, I hit the head, then I walk (suit up)."[52] When her F-14 Tomcat is airborne, she says, fear vanishes. On her first combat mission, 15,000 feet over the mountains of Afghanistan, she zeroes in her target, two antiaircraft batteries. The puffs of smoke coming from the terrain below tell her she's hit the mark. On the flight home, she's smiling most of the way. "I was smiling at the fact that I had done my thing for my country," says the twenty-six-year-old pilot (identified only by her first name, Ashley, due to Pentagon regulations). Another female pilot, "Charlie," says that not too long ago, female pilots were news. "Now people talk about you and you're the fighter pilot—not the female fighter pilot, just the fighter pilot. We're starting to be just one of the guys."

Just as women are finding more opportunities to prove themselves, conservatives in Congress are exerting pressure to roll back women's gains. Some argue that women reduce the combat effectiveness of American forces. But do they? The example of air force Captain Kim Campbell, known as "Killer Chick" to her fellow fliers, suggests that the answer is no. Campbell was flying her A-10 Warthog aircraft when she began taking fire in the skies over Iraq in April 2003. On Campbell's final pass her jet took a crippling hit, most likely from a surface-to-air missile, which disabled the plane's controls and put the pilot to the test. "I heard a loud explosion," Campbell said. "There was no doubt I had been hit, but I was surprised they actually got me. Part of you feels invincible up there." Immediately warning lights flashed in the cockpit, and the plane rolled left and began to dive. Campbell was losing control. The hit damaged one of the A-10's two engines and destroyed its hydraulic system, disabling the plane's stabilizer and flight controls. Campbell said at the time she realized she had two choices: either try to land the damaged jet or eject over Baghdad. Parachuting out over hostile territory was not an attractive option, she said. So she put the jet into manual-control mode and began to climb. After flying 100 miles in a craft riddled with hundreds of holes, she made "one of the best landings of my life." The next morning, she was back in the air. "I had a job to do," Campbell said with a confident smile. "The war was still going on."[53]

Military sociologists David R. Segal and Mady Segal of the Center for Research on Military Organizations received a $1 million grant from the U.S. Army to find out what conditions will make an increased military role for women likely. In a major review of the literature, Segal concluded that the level of threat, along with society's ideas about gender, combine to predict the patterns of women's service.[54] Such service is likely to increase under the following conditions.

1. High threat exists. "If the very existence of the society is immi-
   nently threatened many women are involved in military operations, including as combatants," Segal says. For example, many
   women fought in Liberia's recent civil war. Segal says that even in
   historical eras when women were forbidden to fight, if the whole
   society was swept up in war—as in the American Civil War—
   some women disguised themselves as men in order to fight. Afterward, however, society often develops a "cultural amnesia"
   about women's participation.
2. Low threat, but cultural values support gender equality. Examples
   here include Canada and Sweden, which allow women to volunteer for combat jobs. The United States is moving into this category, as the "battlefield" expands to include an armada of support
   personnel.
3. Later age at marriage and fewer children, combined with growing
   acceptance of nontraditional family forms. These conditions reflect social and demographic changes, not genetic, biological, or
   early socialization changes.
4. Technological change. As Segal notes, "the substitution of brain-
   power for brawn" makes it more possible for women to be combatants.[55] Computer technology, the miniaturization of weapons,
   and the development of air power are all part of that movement.
   Also, military jobs have become much more specialized, requiring
   higher levels of technical skills than in the past.

Despite the objections of some conservatives, despite thorny issues
such as young mothers serving, female casualties, and problems with
sexual harassment, chances are that women's roles, including combat
roles, will expand. Mady Segal says that women's successful performance in the Gulf War led directly to the repeal of a 1948 law barring
women from combat aircraft and contributed to the admission of
women to naval combat ships. With the War on Terrorism, U.S. forces
have been stretched thin, and women will be needed to serve more
than ever.

Many of the arguments against female service are fading as women's presence grows. One argument was that women would erode unit cohesion, reducing the effectiveness of fighting groups. Lionel Tiger says in *The Decline of Males* that male bonding is essential to combat soldiers, and the presence of females would probably destroy such bonds.[56] But a 1997 RAND corporation study sponsored by the Department of Defense dispelled that fear:

> Gender differences alone did not appear to erode cohesion. Cohesion was reported high in units where people believed the command emphasized unity and the importance and necessity of all members and divisions in accomplishing the mission. . . . Women and men can bond to form effective units in any job field or situation as long as the women feel they will be treated equally and the men perceive that the women will not receive special treatment.

The token woman may still have a hard time. But as women reach a critical mass, they will be more readily accepted, the RAND study explains: "Once women comprise more than 20 percent of a unit or class, they are judged as individuals and not as representatives of their gender. Successful women cadets in the group become fellow cadets, not female cadets. Overall unit acceptance soon follows."[57] Former army secretary Togo D. West Jr. said in 1996, "There is no turning back. Women are here to stay if we are going to have a successful Army. We are going to have to pull from the widest available pool of talent."[58]

West's sentiments apply equally to much of the rest of society. Gender boundaries are becoming blurred in arenas such as law enforcement, medicine, the media—almost everywhere. Indeed, the very notion of male and female preserves has begun to erode. Just as the behavior of men and women as individuals is becoming more similar, so too are their occupational choices—although the flow is more one way than the other. More women are going into traditionally male occupations than vice versa. The reason is obvious. Study after study shows that female-dominated occupations command less pay and prestige than male jobs. There is no denying that women who enter male-dominated fields still encounter roadblocks—glass walls, glass ceilings, sexual harassment, discrimination, old boy networks, and the like. While the road isn't smooth, women are making gains. As we see with the military, it is not women's abilities that are the issue, but a host of cultural and political factors. These obstacles, one way or another, reflect the stereotypes created by myths of gender differences. But once again, situation will make the difference. With U.S. forces now serving around the world in the face of new global threats, and with a desperate need for technologically savvy forces, women will continue to be a major presence in the armed forces.

Do the Math

WHEN YOUR DAUGHTER was nine, she revamped her Barbie town house. Today, at fifteen, she doodles pictures of dream houses all over her school notebooks and often puts down her copy of *Elle Girl* to borrow your *Architectural Digest*. She'd like to be an architect, but you worry that she may be heading into a field in which she can't succeed. Perhaps you watched an ABC-TV special called *Boys and Girls Are Different* and heard host John Stossel suggest that girls should probably not choose architecture as a profession.[1] Or you may have read the 2002 best-seller *The Blank Slate*, by Steven Pinker, which cites a study of gifted students in which the majority of boys chose engineering, while the girls—who were equally talented at math—chose medicine or history or journalism as more interesting and challenging.[2] The girls, he says, weren't steered away from math—they just liked the other stuff better. Perhaps your daughter's teacher told you about a book she read called *Boys and Girls Learn Differently,* which explains that girls' brains are not wired for mathematics—especially the ability to imagine objects in space.[3] And isn't that what architecture is all about?

You may worry if someone gives you a copy of *Building Design* magazine and you see an article suggesting a biological explanation for men's greater success in architecture.[4] It cites a study comparing how long thirty-six-hour-old baby boys and girls look at either a mechanical mobile or a human face. The boy babies spent more time than the girls watching the mobile. Based on these results, the magazine says, boys are more naturally suited to architecture than are girls. You may also remember reading some years back that only men have a "math gene," which makes them inherently better at calculus, engineering, architecture, and physics. You gently try to steer your daughter away from architecture and suggest that teaching or public relations might be a better fit for her abilities. You may just have unwittingly deprived the world of the next Maya Lin, the brilliant architect who designed the Vietnam Memorial in Washington, D.C., or Zaha Hadid, the first woman to ever have won the world's most prestigious architectural award, The Pritzker Prize (2004).

Male superiority in math-related subjects is often taken as fact in conversations between parents, teachers, counselors, and others. Mathematics requires a rational problem-solving ability, and boys, with their "innate" capacity for logical, nonemotional thinking, excel in it. Many girls who are talented in math, like your daughter, find the cultural messages too tough to fight. Science writer K. C. Cole tells of a friend who won a Bronx-wide math competition in second grade.[5] Her girlfriends asserted that no boy would like her if she was good at math, but she persisted. Ten years later she entered Harvard as a science major— but switched to English in her second year because she found that women in science were considered freaks.

We know that there is no gene for math, just as there is no gene for religious faith, writing ability, or any other complex trait. The belief that girls lack math ability has been around for a long time, but scientists first suggested an actual genetic basis for this deficiency in the early 1980s. A team of scientists from Johns Hopkins University examined the math SAT tests of 9,927 gifted seventh and eighth graders.[6] The boys outperformed the girls on the test, which prompted the researchers to draw a startling conclusion. Since the children shared the same classrooms, their experiences must have been the same. Therefore the difference could not be due to environmental factors; it had to be genetic. The researchers suggested that perhaps girls shouldn't even *try* to succeed at math. Their plight was compared to that of a short boy thinking he could make the basketball team.

The influential journal *Science* published the study under the headline "Math and Sex: Are Girls Born with Less Ability?"[7] The mainstream media picked up the cry. The *New York Times* asked, "Are Boys Better at Math?"[8] *Time* looked at "The Gender Factor in Math."[9] The study became a major national story, and many parents worried that their daughters would not be able to compete with their male peers in math. Sadly, some even started to look at their daughters differently. One longitudinal study about ten years later reported that mothers who knew about the articles lowered their expectations of their daughters' math capabilities.[10] One mother remembers breathing a sigh of relief when her daughter nearly flunked chemistry; she was glad that her daughter wouldn't have to compete in that arena. She herself had performed well in math and science on her college boards but thought that her scores were a fluke.

The "math gene" is another wave in the sea of flawed ideas about gender that has been flooding the mass media and the popular imagination. Not long after the first headlines appeared, one of the first talking Barbie dolls burbled "Math class is hard!"[11] Lost in the maelstrom was the quieter voice of reason. "Just because seventh-grade boys sat the same number of hours in the same classroom doesn't mean they got the same mathematical education," noted Alice Schaffer of Wellesley College, chair of the Women in Math Committee of the American Mathematical Society.[12] Indeed, as it turned out, the kids who took the test showed marked differences in their attitudes about—and experiences with—math. When another Hopkins scientist interviewed the same group of students, she found that the parents of gifted boys picked up on their sons' talents at an early age, bought them math books, and talked with them about their future careers.[13] Parents of gifted girls took little notice of their daughters' ability. Worse, nearly half the girls interested in math careers were actively discouraged from taking advanced math courses. One high school guidance counselor told a visiting math professor, "I'll be honest with you. I don't encourage girls to go into mathematics. They wouldn't be good at it, and in any case, what would they do with it?"[14]

By the time girls get to high school, their attitudes about their math ability and future careers may have been damaged beyond repair. It's critical to understand how small differences accumulate over time. Take two first graders: a boy and a girl. The boy is a tiny bit better in math, but teachers give him more attention and his parents buy him more computer games. By high school, he has a more positive attitude toward math and more confidence than the girl. By the time they approach college, these cumulative effects may show up in dramatically different test scores that could have a major impact on their career choices.

Furthermore, the data that fuel the math gene arguments are almost all based on white males and females. The few studies of other groups paint a different picture. Among Latinos, no gender difference is discerned; among African Americans and Asian Americans, there is a small difference favoring females.[15] Why wasn't it called a white male math gene? And Asian males consistently outscored Caucasian males. Why didn't anyone propose an Asian math gene? Here is another example of the dismal history of using "statistics" to support politically motivated theories of one kind or another. The "bell curve" debate, as noted earlier, simplified the issue of race and intelligence.[16] The authors ignored the many social and educational advantages that whites enjoy compared to their black counterparts. When race differences in test scores surfaced, they concluded—naively or cynically—that these differences reflected unchanging genetic factors.

As for the SAT exams, they are designed to predict math grades for college freshmen—which they don't do very well. Debate about gender bias in the tests spurred efforts that are now underway to correct it, but it is still a work in progress. If the tests were valid, then women should do less well than men in their first-year math courses. The reality is different. Women do as well as men, even though their average math SAT scores were not as high.[17] How boys or girls do in math depends on the content and structure of the test. Diane Halpern of Claremont McKenna College, president of the American Psychological Association, notes that the usual male advantage in the math GRE (the test most students take to get into graduate school) can go up or down depending on how the problems are presented and what skills are required to solve them.[18] Overall, Halpern says, while boys score higher on tests of mathematics, girls achieve higher grades in math classes. One Pennsylvania high school senior, in the top 10 percent of her class and a member of the National Honor Society, scored lower on her SAT test than did many of the boys in her class who had much lower academic rank.[19] She went on to graduate magna cum laude from the University of Pittsburgh. The test, she said, "didn't really predict how I did, that's for sure." Some people believe that the SAT resembles a fast-paced game, like a computer game, that puts a premium on strategic guesswork. Boys tend to perform better in that situation. But when girls get coaching on how to take the test, their scores improve.[20]

The Bigger Picture

To explain why the media headlines don't tell the more complex story of what's happening with boys, girls, and math, we have to take a peek under the hood, so to speak, at the mechanics of research. How gender differences in tests are interpreted is crucial. If you accept the status quo as the inevitable consequence of an evolutionary script, you will probably not consider that factors such as deficiencies in schools, lack of parental encouragement, meager training and practice, and the impact of rigid gender roles also play a role.

Most researchers examining gender differences in math rely on reports of group "mean" differences: They test groups of boys and girls and may find that, on average, boys outperform girls. (Say, for example, that the average score for boys is 104 and for girls, 97.) Analysis may find that this difference is statistically significant, meaning that it is unlikely to be due to chance. The result? Headlines such as "Boys Outscore Girls in Math," suggesting that the gulf in scores is wide and important. The reporter who wrote the story, who is probably not sophisticated about the mysteries of statistics, fails to ask the key question: What does that difference mean? Is it large, or is it so small as to be basically meaningless, though statistically significant? Remember, the key issue is not the size of the difference in the average scores of the boys and girls. What counts is how that difference relates to the *range* of scores in each group.[21]

Since numbers can lie, or at least mislead, we need to look at studies that take this more sophisticated approach into account. For that reason, we rely heavily on major reviews, large-scale studies with representative samples, and meta-analyses, which combine results from many studies.

Psychologist Janet Hyde of the University of Wisconsin conducted a large meta-analysis, combining 254 studies of math performance among 3,985,682 students.[22] She compared the effect sizes of boys' and girls' scores. The results, shown in the Figure 7.1, demonstrate that the differences between the sexes are slight indeed, and there is a huge overlap. In 51 percent of the studies examined, males outperformed females; in 43 percent, females outperformed males; and in 5 percent, there was no gender difference. Hardly evidence of a big gender gap in math.

In a 2001 study, sociologists Erin Leahey and Guang Guo at the University of North Carolina–Chapel Hill followed 20,000 four- to eighteen-year-olds to track the development of specific math abilities—including such "typically" male talents as reasoning skills and geometry. As you can see in Figure 7.2, they found that the trajectories of male and female math scores are nearly identical across the age range.

This finding astonished the researchers, who said, "based on prior literature . . . we expected large gender difference to emerge as early as junior high school, but our results do not confirm this." The only male advantage, which shows up in late high school, is a meager 1.5 percent. When professor Diane Halpern did a major review of specific math and cognitive tests that purportedly show substantial sex differences, she also found such differences to be relatively small.[23] Overall, she says, although there are some differences, boys and girls are far more alike than different in their cognitive skills.

The three studies described above clearly conclude that girls' and boys' math scores are roughly equivalent. If, as some argue, women don't have a "math gene" or their brains are hardwired in a way that does not allow them to do well in math, then these graphs would look completely different.

Neither is there much support in these graphs for those who argue that the male hormones, which kick in at puberty, give boys a big edge

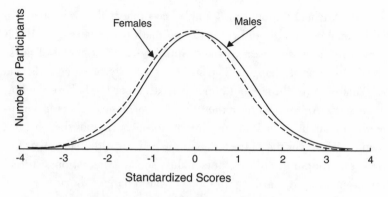

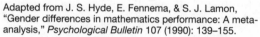

Adapted from J. S. Hyde, E. Fennema, & S. J. Lamon, "Gender differences in mathematics performance: A meta-analysis," *Psychological Bulletin* 107 (1990): 139–155.

FIGURE 7.1 Gender differences in mathematics performance

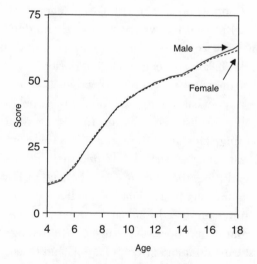

Adapted from E. Leahey & G. Guo, "Gender differences in mathematical trajectories," *Social Forces* 80 (2000): 713–732.

FIGURE 7.2 Math trajectories from ages 4 to 18

in math. Michael Gurian, for example, says that high levels of testosterone enable boys to perform better on math tests than girls.[24] If this
were true, boys' scores at this age would be soaring ahead of girls'.
Clearly this doesn't happen. The striking similarity between girls' and
boys' math scores throughout puberty makes it hard to believe the hormone story. Arguments over the effect of hormones on math performance remain lively in academia, but obviously hormones don't act in a
vacuum. Whatever their effect, they act in concert with many other factors—environment, culture, personality, social expectations, stereotypes—making it hard to pinpoint what changes hormones are
responsible for. But they don't play the major role in math ability—if
they did, the graphs would not look at all as they do.

Turn the math situation on its head, and you have the situation with
verbal abilities. As with math, there's a very small difference between
the sexes in this area. Because females outnumber males at the high
end of writing ability does not mean a man wouldn't have a good shot at
writing a screenplay, editing a newspaper, or winning the National
Book Award. CR notices no lack of writing skill among her male journalism students. But she does worry that boys who don't go to top
schools may shy away from careers that require writing skills. Because
they may read the headlines about boys' inferiority in this area, they
may believe that they aren't "naturally" good at it. Writing is key to
such good jobs as political reporter, editorial writer, political speechwriter, playwright, novelist, screenwriter. In fact, there are few jobs
where good writing skills aren't important. Boys who go to private
schools or affluent suburban schools will find their writing skills nur-
tured from an early age; the same may not be true of boys in urban
schools whose natural talents may fail to bloom if left untended. (Steering boys away from writing early on may have the same result as guiding girls away from math.) Boys who struggle with writing at first may
decide they just can't do it and give up. Parents and teachers who believe this is a natural male shortcoming may not push them to improve
their skills. But many successful authors and journalists were "late
bloomers" who didn't get wonderful grades early on. James "Scotty"

Reston, the legendary *New York Times* columnist, got Cs in his journalism courses.[25] Happily, he kept working on his writing.

Recently we've seen dozens of news stories about how boys are in trouble, about how their verbal abilities are falling far below girls'. Again, this is an exaggeration. What's the real picture? Gender differences are very small and have marginal importance for most boys and girls. Boys account for a disproportionate share of the extremely low ability end of the verbal abilities distribution.[26] They are more likely to stutter, have dyslexia, and suffer from mental retardation. But remember, the existence of great variation among males prevents drawing conclusions about individual abilities. Here's the overall picture:

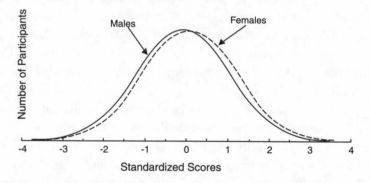

Adapted from J. S. Hyde, & M. C. Linn, "Gender differences in verbal ability: A meta-analysis," *Psychological Bulletin* 107 (1988): 53–69.

FIGURE 7.3 Gender differences in verbal ability

"I'm Just Not Smart"

As we've seen, there are few differences between the sexes in cognitive abilities across the board. Why, then, do so few girls choose careers in mathematics, when many are obviously equipped to do so? If not because of genes or hormones, perhaps they are discouraged by social attitudes and stereotypes. "Girls don't want to be computer geeks; it doesn't appeal," explained one woman, herself in a high-tech job, "but guys get hooked on playing games 24 hours a day."[27] The games draw boys but not girls into the world of high technology, and this difference takes hold early on. Boys get lots of encouragement and training, while girls get little. As boys take more math and science classes, the slight female advantage vanishes and a slight male advantage emerges. In the teen years, boys get increasingly comfortable with technology, as girls lose interest and become alienated from it. Fewer girls than boys enroll in computer science classes, feel confident with computers, or use computers outside of school.[28]

Under the intense peer pressure of adolescence, any activity that gets labeled "boy only" or "girl only" is off-limits to the other sex. These taboos apply even to girls who have shown interest in math and have been encouraged to pursue it. Eighth grader Karyn Greene, picked to attend a computer camp for talented kids sponsored by IBM, declared, "Science is boring; I want to argue with people, just like Reese Witherspoon."[29] (The actress played a Harvard Law School student in the film *Legally Blonde*.) Astronaut Sally Ride is so worried about the Karyns of the world that she started an organization to promote girls' interest in math and science. What drove her, she says, "was the sense that a lot of the stereotypes about girls and science and math that we all assumed would be gone by now have not gone away. Eleven-year-old girls still aren't encouraged as much as 11-year-old boys about science and math. A girl might still feel negative pressure from her peers if she's the best one in the math class."[30]

Rene is a good example of a girl with a flair for math who got the message that she didn't belong.[31] Rene remembers liking math in junior high, getting good grades, and having good teachers. She entered high school, she says, "with no feeling that I wasn't good at math." Then she ran into the football coach who also happened to teach geometry. Not only didn't he call on Rene or any of the other girls in class, but he peppered his lectures with sports analogies that Rene found mystifying. When she approached him for help and told him, "I'm just not getting it," the teacher brushed her off. "If you don't have any specific questions, I can't help you," he said. Rene took his rebuff to heart. "I guess I'm just not smart," she decided. The eager junior high girl who rushed to school every morning turned into a high school student who doubted her own ability. It was at this time, she remembers, that "I really did start to believe that girls were not as good as boys at math." The experience colored her idea of her future. "I didn't just say to myself *I'm not good at math*; I thought that bright people were good in math and science, so I began to think I just wasn't smart." No one said anything to her when her straight A's in junior high plunged in high school—except for one teacher who offered, "I guess you've got a boyfriend, that's why you're not doing as well." The school did nothing, and her parents were too distracted with issues in their own lives to pay attention to her grades.

Rene never applied to college because she was convinced she wouldn't achieve a high score on the math SAT. She trained instead to be an esthetician, performing facials and massages in beauty salons and spas. She spent ten years in this field, most of them "bored out of my mind" on the job. She married Evan, a college graduate who was studying for his MBA. When she told him that girls weren't good at math, he told her that was nonsense. His response shocked her; it was the first time she'd ever heard that point of view! He encouraged her to get her college degree. Indeed, Rene wanted to go to college—but that meant facing the math demon again. With great trepidation, she signed up for a low-level math course. To her surprise, she thoroughly enjoyed it and earned an A. Then she enrolled in a difficult statistics course with a wonderful math teacher. Rene says that in this class she actually experienced her mind learning to think in a new way. She remembers struggling with a hard problem one evening, then waking in the middle of the night with the answer. She jumped out of bed to write it down. In the next class, the teacher told her she was the only one to solve the problem. He also told her that she had excellent math skills and should apply to Harvard. "I could feel, in my mind, a light going on. That was a turning point. Everybody said that statistics was so hard, but I loved the class. I ended up getting 100 in my final. I cried the whole way home, I was so happy." The high school girl who thought she wasn't bright and couldn't do math is now, at 33, at the top of her class at Wellesley College, majoring in psychology and taking a large number of math courses. She will attend graduate school at Columbia University in 2004.

Rene was fortunate. She married a man who encouraged her and found a teacher who awakened her talents. Many other girls aren't so lucky. They have an awful high school math teacher, or a school that doesn't pay attention, or parents who don't encourage their math skills. Many girls will never feel the light going on inside their heads that Rene experienced and will end up in jobs far below their abilities.

There's no denying that a large percentage of top mathematicians are male. The reason for this is unknown—but most likely won't be found in studies of the early developmental years or girls' brains, say the Chapel Hill sociologists Leahey and Guo.[32] Rather, the ideas that young girls like Rene internalize make gifted women shy away from careers in math and science. Males are overrepresented among those scoring highest in math (and among those scoring lowest). But most men who hold good jobs in engineering, finance, design, and computer and information technology aren't Einsteins, and women don't have to be either.

In some parts of the world, particularly eastern Europe, there are more women working in technology than there are in the United States.[33] Nonetheless, some influential Americans adamantly oppose programs that encourage women to enter fields that involve math. Because it's hard to keep a straight face while arguing that women don't have the skills for high-level jobs in math, the argument has shifted. It used to be argued that women didn't "choose" to go into law, business, or journalism; now it's math-related careers. In *The Blank Slate*, Steven Pinker frowns on a plan, announced by the presidents of nine elite universities, to make a special effort to recruit women for fellowships and faculty positions in math and science.[34] Women, he says, don't *like* science, math, and engineering. They don't have the risk-taking impetus and tolerance for the "physical discomfort" required, he proclaims. He makes going into technical fields sound rather like going to Siberia—"working on oil rigs and jack-hammering sludge from the inside of oil rigs." (Of course, most male college graduates in science and engineering do not spend their lives on oil platforms in the North Atlantic. They lead comfortable lives in upscale suburbs, and the only vehicles from which they clean "sludge" are their SUVs.)

Pinker calls the idea of steering girls toward science and engineering at an early age "grotesque," equivalent to treating them "as if they were rats in a Skinner box." Oh, those poor girls, having to grow up to make six-figure salaries as engineers, automotive designers, architects, college math professors, and airline pilots. The "choice" argument is ludicrous on its face. Once upon a time, it was argued that women didn't "choose" to go into law, business, or journalism. Funny, isn't it, how women supposedly spurn certain well-paid occupations, but when they are given the least encouragement, they come flooding in.

The Power of Stereotypes

As we have seen, persistent stereotypes discourage girls from pursuing math starting at an early age. These stereotypes tend to take three main forms: (1) Math is not useful to women; (2) Women who pursue mathematical careers are masculine; (3) Women are more interested in social than theoretical fields.

Though these ideas may seem out of date in a world where women fly high-tech jets, they still have a lot of power, especially for kids in school—all the way from kindergarten to high school—precisely when career ideas start to bud. And stereotypes have the power to affect kids' achievement. Some studies find that boys behave negatively toward girls who are good at math, and male peers are the most responsible for the negative stereotypes about women and mathematics that women experience. K. C. Cole says that her stepdaughter, who earned the highest SAT grades ever recorded in her California high school, flunked calculus in her first year at Harvard. The young woman explained, "When I met a boy I liked and told him I was taking chemistry, he immediately said: 'Oh, you're one of those *science* types.'"[35]

The power of stereotypes is clear as kids progress through the grades—and it's not a pretty picture. Children learn at a young age that boys are supposed to be better at math than girls, and the downward spiral begins:[36]

- In the third and fourth grades, boys and girls like math equally. There's no change in fifth and sixth grade for boys, but girls' preference declines.[37]
- Between fourth and twelfth grades, the percentage of girls who say they like science decreases from 66 percent to 48 percent.[38]
- In those same years, the percentage of girls who say they would prefer not to study math any longer goes from 9 percent to a whopping 50 percent.[39]
- In the early grades, boys say that boys are better at math and girls say that girls are better; during the early pubescent years, girls and boys both say that boys are better.[40]
- Boys and girls in all grades believe that adult men are better than adult women at math, though boys hold that belief more strongly than girls.[41]
- For girls, but not boys, there is a relationship between their belief in stereotypes of adults in mathematics and their own math achievement. Boys are significantly more likely to see math as "male" than are girls, and over time girls rate math as less and less useful to them.[42]
- As grade levels increase, both girls and boys increase their perceptions of math as useful for men. By eighth grade, girls are less likely than boys to enjoy science or math and seem to have less confidence in these subjects.[43]

It's hard to believe that coincidence or choice causes the severe dip in girls' enjoyment of math and science. Rather, the culture has convinced them that girls don't belong in these fields. Media images of female scientists and engineers are rare; children's TV science shows feature three times as many male as female characters and twice as many adult male scientists as female scientists.[44] Of the female characters, most have secondary roles such as lab assistant or student.[45] Is it any wonder that many girls don't see themselves as "doers" of science and can't even imagine themselves in that role?[46]

Adults aren't much help either. A striking 34 percent of high school–age girls said a faculty member told them *not* to take senior math, and 16 percent fewer girls than boys reported ever talking to their parents about science and technology issues.[47] One fourteen-year-old Massachusetts girl, who transferred to a private school to get a better math education, said, "If a teacher always singles out the same person or picks the boys first, girls might feel discouraged or feel their answers are wrong. In my old school, if a boy and a girl had their hands up, the teacher picked him."[48]

The power of stereotypes isn't imaginary or hypothetical. It can actually be measured. In certain situations, people suffer an extra burden of anxiety because they are aware of the negative stereotype of the group to which they belong. African Americans perform significantly worse on a test when told that their intelligence is being measured.[49] (A fact that *The Bell Curve* didn't take into account.) Women perform worse on a math test when they are told that men usually do better than women on the test. Activate someone's awareness of a negative stereotype prior to a test, and that knowledge can cause a person to "clutch." Figure 7.4 offers a stark illustration of this phenomenon. When students are told that females generally don't do well on the difficult math test they are about to take, the women score much lower than the men. But without the comment, they score almost as well as men.[50]

Fortunately, many people, especially young people, make their life choices independent of stereotypes and conventional wisdom. What else accounts for the fact that 45 percent of the current freshman class at MIT is female? Or that the Rhode Island School of Design is 65 percent female? Or that more than half of all accountants in the United States are women?[51] Of course, MIT freshmen are a very select group—how many women set their sights that high? But if this group of women can do so well, think of how much better all women and girls would do if harmful stereotypes were swept aside. Some already are doing better; the trend is moving in the direction of equality.[52] One major meta-analysis of scores on seven academic subjects showed males scoring higher than females in math achievement, but the difference was the smallest of all the subjects assessed.[53] Trend analyses of vocabulary, reading, mathematics, science, social studies, nonverbal reasoning, and writing found that gender differences hadn't changed over time, with the exception of math and science.

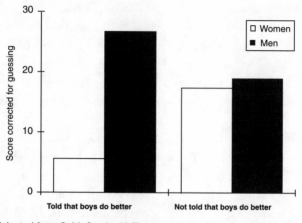

Adapted from C. M. Steele, "A Threat in the Air: How stereotypes shape the intellectual identities and performance of women and African Americans," *American Psychologist* 52 (1997): 613–629.

FIGURE 7.4 Mean performance on a difficult math test as a function of gender and test characterization

In these two cases, females are closing the gap—not surprisingly, since these are the two areas where major efforts have been made to improve girls' performance. When attention is paid, girls' scores get better and the gap narrows. This improvement came from a special push during the 1990s to get more girls interested in science, math, and technology. But there's a long way to go, and who knows whether such initiatives will be sustained, given recent and massive budget cuts.

Cutting such programs is tempting for those who believe, as many Ultra Darwinists do, that girls aren't equipped to do math. If math differences were genetically hardwired, all the training in the world wouldn't help women's performance—just as the average woman could bench-press weights for hours without developing the same upper body muscle mass as the average man. But a new climate for girls in math— new course offerings, increased parental and academic support, better employment opportunities, and more available role models—is changing the way girls perform. Training, not gender, is often what counts. Anyone who thinks it's not important for girls to feel the same natural affinity for math that boys do should read a recent report showing that girls who are not exposed to computers by age twelve effectively lock themselves out of 90 percent of all future jobs.[54]

Lost in Space

Did all that hunting and spear throwing (of which the Ultra Darwinists are so enamored) wire male brains more effectively for manipulating objects in space? Many think so. In their book *Brain Sex*, Anne Moir and David Jessel state that male superiority in spatial abilities is not in dispute: Men can "picture things, their shape, position, geography, and proportion."[55] Deborah Blum, a Pulitzer Prize–winning journalist, proclaims in her book, *Sex on the Brain*, the "well-documented superiority of boys in spatial analysis at handling maps and numbers," and she cites this superiority to bolster her conclusion that male and female brains evolved differently because of different roles in prehistory.[56] As one reviewer put it, "Basically, men had to keep maps in their heads because they were wandering all over the forest cruising for chicks. Women, meanwhile, were staying home tending the nest."[57]

The voices of some other researchers join in unequivocal unison: "Males have decidedly better spatial skill than females."[58] "Boys excel in visual-spatial ability. Male superiority on visual-spatial tasks is fairly consistently found in adolescence and adulthood, but not in childhood."[59] "Sex differences favoring males have been found consistently [in the area of spatial abilities] so perhaps there is a grain of truth to the old stereotype that women tend to have severe difficulties deciphering maps!"[60]

If these generalizations can be shown to hold water, what do they mean? Women who can't read maps have trouble with directions, can't visualize objects in space, and can't create computer models of objects that don't yet exist are unfit for a whole range of occupations. They can't be commercial pilots, they shouldn't drive trucks or taxis, they shouldn't be engineers, they can't design systems, they can't follow blueprints, they can't navigate at sea, and they can't command spaceships.

The assumption that women lack spatial skills is rooted in the evolutionary tale of Man the Hunter, which we have already shown to be highly suspect. Keep in mind that our hunter-gatherer ancestors, both male and female, mainly foraged for food. Success in foraging requires many of the same spatial abilities as hunting: reading animal signs, making mental maps, remembering directions. It makes evolutionary sense to imagine that successful females as well as males were those who had good spatial abilities. With 80,000 species of plants and vines, successful foragers had to be able to locate them and remember which were poisonous and which nutritious. Women had to walk many miles each day, often carrying babies, to find food and then find their way back to camp again. There is no reason to suppose that they were any less active and athletic in their pursuit of food than men were—as are females in today's hunter-gatherer tribes. As we've noted, women who hunted small birds with bows and arrows could certainly comprehend the movement of an object in space. As can the 42,000 female pilots who serve in the armed services as Apache helicopter pilots, military police commanders, tactical intelligence analysts, and combat engineers.

So why do women believe the myth that only men have superior spatial abilities? For one thing, only recently have women been permitted into jobs that require such skills. If you grow up seeing only male engineers, pilots, and truck drivers, then of course you accept the "fact" that only men have the ability to do such jobs. Also, many women grew up seeing only boys throwing baseballs, playing with erector sets, and building model airplanes. And even today college textbooks assert that "play patterns [of boys] reflect an evolved adaptation that prepares them for hunting and primitive warfare. Both the predisposition of this type of behavior and the play behavior itself may shape the male brain in ways that allow them to perform better than females on spatial tasks."[61]

These confident claims about men's superior spatial abilities are not surprising, but are they true? Once again, the answer is not simple. First, "spatial ability" does not exist as a stand-alone entity. Instead, there are many spatial abilities—the ability to determine how fast and in which direction something is moving, to picture an object rotating in space, to navigate through a maze, to remember where you've come from and how to find your way back. The field is so rife with disparities in definitions and measurements, and small sample sizes, that one major review questions whether "spatial ability" is even a legitimate concept.[62] Assuming for the moment that it is, are there any meaningful differences in people's abilities, and if so, do they have anything to do with gender?

One meta-analysis of cognitive differences found a consistent, although tiny, male superiority: Gender accounted for no more than 1–5 percent of the variance in cognitive abilities. With these numbers, knowing the sex of a child would tell you virtually nothing about his or her cognitive ability.[63] (Spatial ability is one form of cognitive ability.) Another meta-analysis of 100 studies found the magnitude of the sex-related cognitive differences to be "trivial";[64] others indicate a male advantage, especially in mentally rotating an object in three dimensions.[65] (Others claim that there are "pockets" of abilities where one sex or the other tends to excel. According to Diane Halpern, females are somewhat better at rapid access to and retrieval of information stored in memory, and males are somewhat better at the ability to maintain and manipulate mental representations.)[66] But the best available research shows us that with few exceptions the difference between males and females in spatial abilities is small indeed.

Round and Round

One area where boys consistently outperform girls is "mental rotation"—the ability to imagine how objects will appear when they are rotated in two- or three-dimensional space. But before we look to Stone Age male hunters for an explanation, consider a basic scientific principle: The most logical explanation for a phenomenon is probably the correct one. If a house is burning down, it might have been hit by a meteor from space—but if the neighbors saw a child playing with matches a few minutes before the fire, that's the more likely explanation. To account for boys' spatial abilities, we need look no farther than their tendency to play more games in childhood such as football, baseball, and blocks than do girls. One study found that boys threw better than girls did with their dominant arm—but when the kids were asked to throw with their other arm, there were no gender differences.[67] If biology alone determined throwing ability, then boys would throw better than girls with either arm. The researchers concluded that practice, not a hardwired ability, turned boys into better throwers. Parents are not off the hook here, either. A ten-year study of 4,000 children and 2,000 parents conducted by Jacqueline Eccles of the University of Michigan found that parents offer far more encouragement to boys than to girls to engage in problem-solving activities—playing with Legos, for instance—that may give them an early advantage in spatial skills.[68] And parents are more likely to attribute a boy's success in this realm to "natural talent," whereas a girl is seen as "hardworking."

Intriguing new research suggests that this gender difference vanishes in cyberspace, when subjects are tested using virtual reality technology. When psychologist Albert Rizzo of the University of Southern California gave men and women the standard paper-and-pen tests, the men scored much better than did the women.[69] High scores were obtained by those who could correctly and quickly identify which of two images of a three-dimensional figure was the same as another such figure portrayed in different rotations, as we see here:

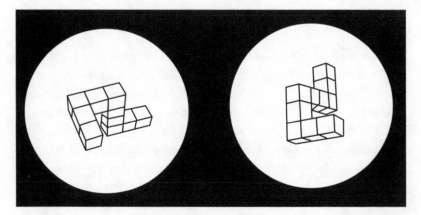

FIGURE 7.5   Three-dimensional mental rotation figure

This test, called the mental rotation task, when given in two dimensions, has consistently produced "one of the largest and most reliable gender differences favoring men," a skill that can clearly be useful in many instances. "The ability to manipulate objects mentally applies to many everyday life situations such as driving, sports or packing items into limited storage space," notes Rizzo. This skill has been linked to high-level mathematics performance. When you take this test in cyberspace, two large three-dimensional objects appear to be floating in space in front of you. You use a control device to manually manipulate the objects, as opposed to just mentally manipulating them. This is much closer to real-life situations than the widely used paper-and-pen version.

In 1999 Rizzo gave male and female college students the old test, then the cyber version, and then the old test again. Two startling results emerged. First, there were no gender differences on the cyberspace test with respect to either time or efficiency of completion. "Women can see and manipulate three-dimensional objects as efficiently and as quickly as men," notes Rizzo. Second, when women took the paper-and-pen test a second time, after spending as little as fifteen minutes with the cyberspace test, they scored as high as men.

This may be the strongest argument against Ultra Darwinism: A little training undoes a supposedly centuries-old difference. The adults whom Rizzo tested showed dramatic improvement, and studies with junior high students show that they too improve their spatial skills with brief training sessions. As Halpern states: "Virtually everyone can improve on cognitive tests, if they receive appropriate instruction."[70] If women's long established deficit on mental rotation tests is due to lack of practice, then girls need more chances to practice. In contrast to other areas of math and science, few interventions have been designed to improve girls' performance in spatial rotation. But things are changing. The supposedly "natural" male advantage will disappear as girls play high-level soccer, baseball, basketball, tennis, and golf at an early age. Does Annika Sorenstam's hand-eye coordination need buffing up? Is Mia Hamm unable to traverse the shortest route to where the ball is going to be? Hardly. Serena and Venus Williams certainly have no

trouble seeing objects in space. It can be argued that their father virtually manufactured his girls as tennis stars. After seeing how much
money women could make on the pro circuit, he gave his daughters
rackets almost as soon as they could walk and mapped their careers
from toddlerhood. They hit tens of thousands of tennis balls from a
very early age and were grandly rewarded for doing well.

But, if history is any guide, as girls improve their math and spatial
skills, someone is going find other reasons to discourage them. For example, Moir and Jessel write in *Brain Sex* that "it may be true that
women would make better neurosurgeons than men" because of their
superior fine motor coordination. But they caution, "To reach the
heights of a profession of this nature requires a single-minded desire to
be top, and for every woman who wants to be a top neurosurgeon there
will forever be ten men who want to be top neurosurgeons."[71] Women
simply don't have the drive and ambition for it, they claim. Just as one
stereotype falls to research, it appears, another pops up to replace it.

Women to the Rescue

The fields that require sophisticated math ability are among those that
offer the best salaries and the most opportunities for career advancement. If girls are discouraged from developing math ability, this will
spell disaster for women in particular and for the U.S. economy as a
whole. The studies we've cited above show girls drifting away from
math at an early age and getting little encouragement from either parents or schools. In an era in which scientific and technological talent
will determine a nation's standing in the world, consider the following
alarming statistics:

- A U.S. Department of Commerce report finds that only 9 percent
  of U.S. engineers and 27 percent of computer scientists/program-
  mers are women. Those numbers represent a decline over the past
  fifteen years.[72]

- In 1998, only 16 percent of computer science degrees were awarded to women, down from nearly 40 percent in 1984.[73]
- Women make up only 19 percent of the science, engineering, and technology workforce.[74]
- Women who earn terminal degrees in math and science often find their academic careers blocked. Women have earned a quarter of all science doctorates since the 1970s, and female associate professors of math and science have almost quadrupled in number. Yet women have made little progress in securing full professorships. In 1973 only 3 percent of female instructors had attained that level. By 1995 the figured had not reached 10 percent.[75]
- Of the ten fastest-growing occupations, eight are related to science, math, or technology.[76] Jobs requiring math and science skills will increase by 5.6 million by 2008. The highest median starting salary for college graduates is in computer science and engineering, which have the lowest percentage of women.[77]

With a little effort, the gap can be closed. Girls drop out of scientific pursuits at a higher rate than boys do. Carnegie Mellon Dean Barbara Lazarus traces the cause to a particularly American notion about "natural ability." Americans, she says, are less likely to encourage students to persevere at something they don't pick up immediately. In contrast, she notes, "in Japan, hard work is considered positive, not an indication that you're not really good at math or science."[78]

With sufficient training, women can excel in fields in which math abilities are critical. At Carnegie Mellon, aggressive outreach brought the incoming science class from 7 percent women in 1995 to 40 percent in 2000—an astonishing 500 percent increase. But this kind of progress won't be widespread until we stop believing that males are innately superior at math just as we have stopped believing that the earth is flat.

8

Leading Questions

F ORTY-FOUR-YEAR-OLD Charlotte was the CEO of a Boston-based biotechnology startup firm. In a predominantly male field heavily dominated by high-level scientists, she had parlayed a degree in business into an unusually prominent position in upper management. Charlotte had put together the seed money to bankroll the operation for the first year or so and was ready to take the next step. "This was a really tough job. I inherited all the internal battles between the factions in the company—the scientists who made the discoveries and the salespeople who promoted the products. Everyone had a huge ego and didn't appreciate a nonscientist—and a female to boot—coming in as the CEO."

She managed to overcome these obstacles and create a well-oiled team that met its objectives. When the fledgling company needed a big infusion of venture capital to keep going and build on its gains, Charlotte negotiated a deal to bring in the cash. She then bumped up against a hard reality. In her words, "when you swim with sharks, you run the risk of getting eaten." The moneymen she recruited wanted in—on the condition that *Charlotte* had to be out. They wanted a "marquee" CEO— code word for a prominent male. She was devastated when she was shown the door. "I'll never get a chance like this again," she moaned. She believed that because she was a woman, she'd never get to do the one thing she really wanted—build a company and take it public.

Despite flooding into the workplace in unprecedented numbers, women like Charlotte aren't moving up the career ladder as fast as they should. According to a 2003 study by Catalyst, women today cite the same barriers to senior leadership levels as women did way back in 1966: lack of general management experience, exclusion from informal networks, stereotyping, and preconceptions of women's roles and abilities.[1] Many influential voices argue that women will never rise in large numbers to the top of the ladder because of certain innate qualities they have or don't have, by virtue of having been born female.

Until relatively recently, the term "woman leader" would have been considered a paradox. Freud's claim that women who displayed assertive behavior were unfeminine and suffered from "penis envy" reigned through much of the 1960s.[2] It was buttressed by Erik Erikson's theory of "inner space," which decreed that because women produced babies, they had no desire to build skyscrapers, run for office, make art and music, or run businesses.[3] Such ambitions reflected a male drive to conquer "outer space," rooted in their inability to make babies. The accepted wisdom was that females were not biologically or psychologically fit for leadership. Some women—for the most part unmarried and childless—did reach the top of the heap, reinforcing the idea that only "unfeminine" women could succeed.

In the wake of 1970s feminism, women moved into managerial jobs in large numbers. But the dissenting voices have never quieted down. Susan Faludi documented the "backlash" against feminism in her book of the same name.[4] Postfeminism, the decline of feminism, the death of feminism—all have become media staples. *Time* ran a cover article about the decline of feminism picturing Gloria Steinem on one end of the line and at the other, Ally McBeal, the ditsy, desperate-to-get-a-man heroine of the TV show.[5] The backlash that Faludi documented never really went away but metastasized into new forms, including the "difference" argument. In its rumblings can be heard familiar echoes: Men are natural leaders while women are inherently unfit for leadership positions for the following reasons:

1. Women don't have the right hormones to be leaders. Political commentator and cultural critic Andrew Sullivan argued in a 2000

cover article in the *New York Times Magazine* that women's lower levels of testosterone make them timid and risk-avoidant in business.[6] This shortcoming, rather than discrimination, keeps women from climbing up the career ladder. UCLA psychologist Shelley Taylor argues that in times of stress, women's hormones lead them to avoid confrontation, preferring instead to "tend and befriend" others, which makes them unfit for aggressive leadership roles.[7]

2. Women's brain structures are poorly suited for leadership. In his book *The Essential Difference* (2003), psychologist Simon Baron-Cohen argues that male brains are created for systematizing—the drive to analyze, explore, and construct a system.[8] "The systemizer intuitively figures out how things work or extracts the underlying rules that govern the behavior of a system."[9] Such a brain is ideally suited for leadership and power. In contrast, women's brains are built for empathizing—the drive to identify another person's emotions and thoughts and respond to them with an appropriate emotion. The empathizer is motivated to "understand another person, to predict their behavior and to connect or resonate with them emotionally."[10] This type of brain is suited to making friends, mothering, and gossiping. Baron-Cohen's ideas have threaded their way through dozens of articles in the popular press.

3. Women lack the motivation for leadership. (Remember Steven Pinker's comment that men are the risk takers while women like low-level jobs in air-conditioned offices?) Syndicated columnist George Will declared in a 1999 essay that women are simply making "rational choices" when they opt for part-time jobs that offer flexibility but low pay, few benefits, and few chances for advancement.[11] He adds that such jobs are "cheerfully chosen" by women because of their preferences, motivations, and expectations. In *Brain Sex*, Anne Moir and David Jessel claim that men value high achievement, risk taking, and competition, while for women, "This all matters rather less."[12] The authorities claim that women do best in noncompetitive situations, and that women are paid less because money is not a high priority in their scheme of things.

Wayne State University law professor Kingsley Browne agrees.[13] In his 1999 book *Divided Labours*, he says that "women care less about money, status and power than do men." Robert Wright, in a *New Republic* article,[14] flatly declares women's lesser drive as a fact, not bothering to cite any evidence, while columnist Pat Buchanan argues, as already noted, that women are just not aggressive enough to succeed in modern American capitalism.[15] A recent *Fortune* cover story on the fifty most powerful women in America questioned their ambition, asking, "Power: Do Women Really Want It?"[16] And a cover piece in the influential *New York Times Magazine* asked, "Q: Why Don't More Women Get to the Top? A: They Choose Not To."[17] Women, the *Times* headline announces, are "Abandoning the Climb and Heading Home."

4. Women are violating their essential feminine natures when they try to lead. In *Women's Ways of Knowing*, Belenky and colleagues argue that men value excellence and mastery in intellectual matters and evaluate arguments in terms of logic and evidence.[18] Women, in contrast, are spiritual, relational, inclusive, and credulous—hardly the qualities desirable in any high-level position in society. F. Carolyn Graglia argues in *Domestic Tranquility: A Brief Against Feminism* that the assertiveness demanded by a career distorts women's maternal and sexual instincts.[19] Her fellow neo-traditionalists Wendy Shalit[20] and Danielle Crittenden[21] advise women that to be happy, they should marry young, postpone careers, and care for children in traditional marriages. (Of course, these authors couldn't have written their successful books if they'd followed their own advice.)

In short, these commentators believe that women will never achieve as much as men in the work world, an idea that resonates with the familiar Ultra Darwinist argument. When men lead, all's right with the world. When women lead, men are less manly and women are miserable. Andrew Hacker raises the same question when he speculates that women's achievements may diminish men's self-confidence and indeed their masculinity.[22] "We will soon see . . . how far the self-assurance associated with manliness can survive when each year sees more appointments and promotions going to the other sex."

Although women have indeed made strides in the executive suites of Fortune 500 companies, nearly doubling their numbers from less than 9 percent to about 16 percent between 1995 and the present, they are far from achieving parity with men.[23] Women hold a paltry 5 percent of top management positions; there is widespread sex segregation in the workplace; and the gender gap in wages persists. If women's inherent shortcomings are the real problem, if women are less well equipped than men to hold high-level jobs due to their hormones, brains, motivation, and innate femininity, then any attempt to advance women in the workplace is doomed. It's not the glass ceiling or lack of training or disrupted careers that holds them back, but their own nature. Women should gladly accept their "natural" inability to rise in the world of business and stop wasting their time on class action suits and antidiscrimination complaints. It's just the way things are, so why fight it? But this line of reasoning needs to be held up to the light. In the sections that follow, we will discuss each of the four main reasons given for why women are not natural leaders, sorting fact from fantasy, science from myth. We'll also show that both men and women lose out when these ideas remain in place.

The Test of Testosterone

Testosterone is a male sex hormone responsible for determining which embryos become baby boys and for making teenage boys' voices drop, their body hair develop, and their sexuality blossom. Testosterone increases muscle mass and can heighten sexual drive. Both men and women have this hormone. The amounts vary widely from person to person, but on average, men have ten times more testosterone than women. Much remains unknown about the hormone, including its relationship to aggression. Does testosterone cause aggression or does aggressive behavior trigger the release of testosterone? No one knows. In social groups, males with higher testosterone levels are not necessarily more aggressive. In a major review of the literature, John Archer of the University of Central Lancashire (United Kingdom) expresses doubt that there is any direct relationship between the level of testosterone in the bloodstream and aggressive behavior.[24]

The widely held idea that testosterone is linked to aggression—and by inference to the qualities needed for leadership—was given a big boost in 2000, when the *New York Times Magazine* ran a cover story titled "The He Hormone."[25] It was written by Andrew Sullivan, who is neither a scientist nor a science journalist. He is a gay conservative Catholic essayist who is HIV positive. A personal essay about the shots of testosterone Sullivan takes regularly to help manage his HIV would have made interesting reading. However, this was a full-fledged science article that purported to examine research on the hormone.

Sullivan cited the work of some scientists who were out of the mainstream and put forth several factual errors and incorrect assertions. Robert Sapolsky, an eminent Stanford University professor of biology and neurology and an expert on testosterone, told *Slate* that Sullivan "is entitled to his fairly nonscientific opinion, but I'm astonished at the *New York Times*."[26] Sapolsky notes that one of the studies cited by Sullivan is a scientific laughingstock that was discredited long ago. Three other respected researchers signed a letter to the *Times* about the article, stating, "In particular, there are scant results from well-controlled experiments showing that testosterone affects behavior of normal men in the ways asserted by Sullivan."

What was all the ruckus about? In his article Sullivan claimed testosterone was at the core of masculinity, responsible for "the ability to risk for good and bad; to act, to strut, to dare, to seize." It seems laughable to believe that one hormone could be responsible for this cartoonish version of masculine behavior, and that the lack of it would disqualify one from positions of leadership. And to many, this idea is ludicrous. Sullivan also admitted that too much testosterone is associated with depression and impatience, not a good recipe for the he-man manager. Even more ominously, Sullivan argued that because women have lower levels of testosterone than men, they will most likely be timid and risk-avoidant in business. "Low testosterone risk-aversion may lead to an inability to seize business opportunities," Sullivan writes. The article might well have been dismissed as the sloppy work of a journalist out of his league if it had not been put forth as an objective scientific report in perhaps the most influential newspaper in the country. Though Sullivan's science may be easily dismissed, the power of the *Times* to shape ideas is not.

It's clear how this argument hurts women. But what about men? Let's say you're a manager charged with picking the new director of a division. The leading candidates are Charlie and Joe. Charlie is domineering, always trying to take charge in any group; he's very competitive and talks constantly about his athletic prowess. Joe is quieter and more thoughtful, has good people skills, and is excellent at problem solving. Remembering the *Times* article, you might select Charlie, who certainly seems to have the high levels of testosterone needed to succeed in a leadership position. But would you be right? Probably not. Even if testosterone did influence leadership behavior, how would you know who really has high levels of it? Does Charlie have high testosterone? Or is his hypermale behavior a result of insecurity, making him a grown-up bully who will probably serve you very poorly. Maybe Joe in fact has higher levels of testosterone than Charlie. If you'd read the critics of the *Times* article, you'd understand that there is no way of predicting Charlie's and Joe's level of a single hormone from their behavior.

Fight or Flight

The complex link between hormones and behavior was illustrated particularly well in a classic study done by Marianne Frankenhauser in the 1970s.[27] Frankenhauser, an internationally renowned expert on stress hormones, found a consistent difference between women and men in response to the "fight or flight" challenge. She focused on situations involving competitive pressures—such as taking a demanding test—and found that men's hormone levels shot up but women's didn't. (Despite this, the women performed as well as or better than the men.) This research made perfect fodder for the Ultra Darwinists, who used it as further proof of innate biology at work. However, in stressful situations involving social relationships—such as taking a sick child to the hospital—women's stress hormones rose higher than the men's. The overall finding of her work was that people experience high stress in situations that involve a perceived demand on them to perform. For men, these were related to achievement, while for women, they had more to do with personal relationships.

In the 1990s, Frankenhauser began to study a new group: women in jobs traditionally held by men (lawyers, bus drivers, engineers, and managers). These women, she found, responded to competitive situations with almost as sharp an increase in endocrine secretions as men. Their levels of epinephrine, norepinephrine, and cortisol shot up. (And these were women whose stress reactions in regard to issues of typically female concern were higher than men's, as women's usually are. So they were not women with little interest in the traditional feminine activities, such as home and family.) As Frankenhauser says, "When men and women become more alike in their judgment of what is important in life and worth fighting for, their psychological stress reactions will become more similar."[28]

Another speculative theory that the media have embraced argues that women and men do indeed have sharply divergent reactions to stress. As we mentioned in Chapter 6, Shelley Taylor argues in her book *The Tending Instinct* that women bond with female friends in the face of stress and that this behavior may be innate.[29] She traces this "tending" instinct back to prehistory. Such a deeply rooted reaction would of course have an impact on women's leadership ability. A supervisor would understandably be reluctant to promote a woman to an important position if her reaction to stress was "tending and befriending," instead of tackling the problem at hand. Who could blame him for feeling uncomfortable if he thought she would run to her female colleagues whenever a crisis erupted or she couldn't provide the clear-headed authority her job demanded?

Taylor says that her interest in gender differences grew out of conversations with her female research assistant, who noticed that in times of stress, the women in her lab bonded, chatted over coffee, and seemed to benefit from their social connections—while the men withdrew into their own offices. Looking primarily at animal research, Taylor suggests that in human prehistory, "fight or flight" wasn't an option for our female ancestors, who had babies to protect. Instead, the mothers instinctively calmed their babies and banded with other females for protection. Underlying this pattern of behavior, Taylor suggested, was the hormone oxytocin and other hormones known to be produced by lactating mothers. (Oxytocin, also produced by massage, has a calming, soothing effect.)

The media went overboard with stories about the joys of friendship—experienced, it seems, only by women. "Female Bonding: Friendship's Therapeutic Value No Secret to Women," said *the Rocky Mountain News*.[30] "Fight Stress with Friends," advised the *San Francisco Chronicle*.[31] The *Boston Globe* chimed in, "Stressed Out? Try a Hug."[32]

To be taken seriously, a theory must be backed up by data. But Taylor did not actually measure levels of bodily hormones as Frankenhauser did, nor is she an endocrinologist. Dr. Sarah Knox, a stress researcher at the National Heart, Lung, and Blood Institute, says, "It's one thing to say that women behave differently than men—there's a whole body of literature on that, but to say that women don't have the same neuroendrocrine stress response as men is not supported by the literature."[33] She adds, "When a woman experiences chronic stress (i.e., she feels that she can't cope with the demands made on her or feels belittled) she has the same neuroendrocrine dysfunction as a man." Overall, Knox notes, "Taylor's theory appears to lack understanding of the neuroendrochrinic effects of chronic stress. The research argues that men and women's physiological reactions to stress are very much alike."

Here's another problem: Who says men don't bond in time of stress? There's a huge literature that says they do.[34] Men in wartime form strong bonds that are often credited with saving their lives. Research shows that men get an even higher return than women from bonding with others because women more often pay "the cost of care." In other words, they're the ones most often asked to put themselves out—to care for a sick child or relative, run errands, baby-sit for a friend's child, or cook a meal for an ailing friend. If you're a woman, having a large social network can *add* stress to your life and be detrimental to your health. Men tend to reap the benefits of such networks without the costs.[35]

As for the observation that sparked the research, might Taylor's lab assistant have been witnessing powerless behavior as opposed to innate female behavior? Were the women who were sipping coffee and chatting mainly lower-level assistants? Professor Rosabeth Moss Kanter of Harvard Business School, in her groundbreaking book *Men and Women of the Corporation*, notes that gossipy, bonding behavior in corporate offices is a trait of low-level employees of either sex.[36] One female manager remembers, "When our CEO was fired, the high-level managers, both men and women, gathered in the hallways and offices to strategize about what our next move was going to be. We could hear the secretaries talking among themselves, but we knew they had no power to change anything. Meanwhile, the rest of us were coping by making plans. We didn't separate out by sex; sex was irrelevant." Once again it's situation, not sex, that largely determines behavior. That's a message that people looking to identify leadership talent need to keep in mind.

Taylor does a service by highlighting the importance of tending and befriending as human characteristics. We are, after all, social animals, and the focus on caring is a refreshing counterpoint to all the babble about testosterone and aggression. Taylor herself points out that the most successful male is the cooperative male, the one with the best social skills—and that caring and friendship are essential to men as well as women. (Unlike Carol Gilligan, Taylor doesn't define "care" as a female-only prerogative.)

However, when Taylor ventures into evolutionary theory and proposes different physiological responses to stress for men and women, she is on shaky ground. And any social theorist on shaky ground can do damage. For example, building on Taylor's ideas, you could argue that women's supposedly superior "relational" skills would make them good managers. But the downside is that women may be asked to bear the weight of employees' emotional problems. Because you're a woman, will you be the one called on to pick up the pieces when an employee has a breakdown? And will you be called a bitch for insisting that your team pull together and get back to work?

Moreover, if you are an expert at tending and befriending, maybe you are less effective at making decisions, confronting people who disagree with you, and standing your ground. Like the male executive who reads Andrew Sullivan on women's lack of testosterone, a male supervisor who reads Taylor's work may be influenced to think that women belong in staff positions where their "people" talents will blossom, rather than in management.

Blaming hormones for women's "frailties" is an old story. During the 1970s it was seriously argued that women's behavior was so influenced by the menstrual cycle that they could not be relied on for important jobs. Neuroscientist Lesley Rogers, author of *Sexing the Brain,* remembers, "Even a woman with exceptional mathematical skills would be a liability for employment in a responsible position because there would be monthly periods during which she would be unable to exercise those skills. A similar argument was used to prevent women from becoming airline pilots."[37] (If that argument had prevailed, Killer Chick would not have piloted her Warthog, protecting troops in battle, and female pilots would not have roared off the decks of aircraft carriers, destroying important targets in Iraq.)

Rarely have such arguments advanced women. "When society wants to maintain inequality, biological explanations can be used to justify it," Rogers says.[38] Perhaps now that women are making so many gains, more and more is being said about women's "natural" deficiencies. Those who want to return to a more conservative, "traditional" world as far as the sexes are concerned rachet up the level of opposition to change. Relying on innate biology is a handy weapon. But, as Rogers points out, people often see differences and then speculate about causes. Speculations are, of course, shaped by ideology, cultural myths, and the power of the status quo. But speculations are not facts—even if they are made by scientists.

Human beings are always changing, Rogers points out, and "our biology does not bind us to remain the same, as implied by simplistic genetic and hormonal interpretations of our behavior."[39]

Sex on the Brain

If hormones don't explain why women can't be leaders, maybe brains do. The media seem to revel in the idea that the sexes have entirely different brains that propel them toward distinct behavior. Lately female brains have been portrayed as particularly unsuited for top leadership roles in society. This is sexy stuff, and those who make claims for great difference tend to get the sound bites and headlines, while those who offer more measured assessments are barely heard amid the excited din. Michael Gurian, speaking at a major conference of Canadian teachers, said that no more than 20 percent of girls have brains that work like boys' brains (he calls them "bridge brains," meaning they have equal characteristics of both the male and female brains).[40] He claims that the structure of girls' minds makes it hard for most of them to grasp subjects such as advanced math, calculus, and physics. This, of course, makes it nearly impossible for them to succeed in most MBA programs, to work as senior research scientists in high-tech firms, or to aspire to top management in aerospace companies, engineering firms, financial services, computer companies, and on and on. A number of experts find this notion ridiculous. One staffer at the Toronto school board called Gurian's ideas "voodoo science." Therezia Zoric told the *Toronto Star*, "It's bad research. He just hasn't met a reasonable standard of common-sense truth." Yet a news report on the conference said that teachers were "lining up" to buy his books, and he is widely quoted in the media.[41] (One shudders to think of those teachers taking notions of female inferiority back into their classrooms.)

In a more academic look at the subject, Simon Baron-Cohen of Cambridge University announces in *The Essential Difference* that there are two kinds of brains: As we noted earlier, he believes the male brain is the "systematizing brain," and the female brain is the "empathizing" brain.[42] The advantages of the male brain, he says, include a mastery of hunting and tracking, trading, achieving and maintaining power, gaining expertise, tolerating solitude, using aggression, and taking on leadership roles. The advantages of the female brain include making friends, mothering, gossip, and "reading" your partner.

Interesting how all the leadership roles in society require the male brain, while the female brain lends itself to the domestic arena. Baron-Cohen offers an evolutionary argument for these differences—based on the fanciful stories about active hunter males and passive homebody women we discredited in earlier chapters. He says male and female brains are perfectly suited for certain "specialist" niches—one adapted to predicting and controlling events and the other to survival and integration in the social world. Once again, we can say that he's describing power, not gender. The powerful control events; the powerless try to survive under the rules the powerful have created.

Not only are empathizing women expected to pick up on what others are *obviously* feeling, but according to Baron-Cohen, women are hardwired to respond to "any emotion or state of mind, not just the more obvious ones, such as pain."[43] The emotion of any other person— whether close or distant—triggers empathy in the "natural" woman. Describing this mechanism, he says, "Imagine that you not only see Jane's pain but you also automatically feel concern, wince, and feel a desire to run across and help alleviate her pain."[44] Would any woman so fully occupied with caring for everybody around her have the ability to lead others? Hardly. She'd barely have the time or energy to get dressed in the morning. She'd also be a prime candidate for depression and burnout.

And where are men in this picture? Stuck in the old male stereotype—detached, rational, unfeeling, unconcerned with others. In Baron-Cohen's worldview, the involved fathers we see around us would not exist—or would be very rare—and humane, caring male bosses would be in short supply. Men who read that they are not designed for empathy may simply give up. If their brain structure preordains them to detachment, why in the world would they try to develop the caring skills for which they are totally unsuited? The media, relying only, it seems, on his impressive credentials, reviewed the book as authoritative, and *Newsweek* gave it a cover story. However, Steven Rose, director of the Brain and Behavior Research Group of the Open University in Britain, took strong exception.[45] He says, "The author simply ignores credible research that does not agree with his essentialist position."

Baron-Cohen also ignores abundant examples of female "systematizing." Journalism, for example, is becoming a heavily female profession, and what does a journalist do but systematize: place events and ideas in space and time and link them up to make them comprehensible to readers. Other professional fields in which women are making strong gains—law, medicine, business—all require a strong ability to organize information and prioritize. Mere empathy and the ability to listen can't supply the skills to write a trenchant brief, organize a complex story on the city budget, plan a strategic marketing campaign, or make a sophisticated diagnosis from a cluster of difficult-to-sort-out symptoms. And how would theorists who claim that women's brains are not suited for systematizing explain the fact we noted earlier: the freshman class at MIT is 45 percent female.

Despite some outlandish statements, Baron-Cohen is widely cited on the issue of gender differences in the brain. In the *Building Design* article already mentioned, his ideas about female and male brains are quoted as established science.[46] He suggests (as does Gurian) that only a small percentage of women have the proper brain structure to be architects, but the magazine's readers have no way to identify this as pure speculation. What percentage of women would succeed in architecture if cultural ideas about girls' problems with math didn't exist, and if girls who showed early math ability got the same encouragement that research shows boys get?

In books that take an evolutionary stance on the brain, male activities are commonly described in serious, even reverential tones, while female activities are trivialized. Baron-Cohen,[47] the Peases,[48] and the *London Times*[49] specifically cite gossip as a female talent. If men engaged in the same activity, perhaps it would be called "extracting information from the environment." One news story says that females are good at "precision manual tasks, like sewing."[50] Why no mention of brain surgery, which also requires manual dexterity?

Now and then a plaintive voice makes a case for female superiority in the area of brains and hormones. In *The First Sex*, anthropologist Helen Fisher says that women have what she calls "web brains."[51] In her view, women engage in "synthesis thinking," seeing and integrating many sides of an argument, while men engage in more plodding "linear thinking." She says these special talents give women savvy, superior verbal abilities, and sharper senses—just what the global economy needs. The future, Fisher says, belongs to women. Her idea of what women are good at includes law, communications, medicine, education, government, and police work. Indeed, it's a relief to see the girls getting the good stuff for a change. But there's no more evidence for women having superior web brains than there is for men having superior systematizing brains—even when scientists suggest there is. Lesley Rogers says, "Scientists have always both reflected and reinforced the attitudes of society. In the past they have had an active role in 'sexing the brain,' and many of them continue to do so today."[52]

Sometimes Less Is Not Less

The past should have taught us that we get into trouble when we try to assess brains by race or sex. As Stephen Jay Gould pointed out in *The Mismeasure of Man*, scientists in the nineteenth century claimed that white men's brains were larger than those of women or blacks.[53] To "prove" their case, they packed cadaver brains of men and women, both black and white, with small lead pellets and then weighed them. The black skulls used were often those of Hottentots, who are very small in stature. (The lead was an easy way to fill the brain cavities and was thought to give reliable measurements.) Not surprisingly, the researchers reported that the brains of white males were the largest and heaviest, while the brains of women and blacks were smaller and lighter, akin to the brains of children or animals. In the 1970s, scientists recalculated the data from these old experiments and found that the measurements were very inaccurate.[54] Nonetheless, all sorts of discrimination against women and blacks was justified by this "evidence." We now know that women's brains are indeed smaller on average than men's, since their brains are in proportion to their body size. If absolute brain size really counted, a killer whale would be president of Harvard.

When it comes to brain studies, size does matter in one way: Small samples abound in the difficult area of brain research. The numbers are too small to tell us anything definitive, but they may suggest areas of promising research. In the mass media, however, these tiny—and preliminary—studies get blown out of proportion. In a classic example, researchers at Stanford used a brain scanner to see how twelve men and twelve women responded to photographs. Three weeks later, the women remembered events that had an emotional connotation better than the men did.[55] A study of twenty-four people can't tell us much— especially about such a complex subject as emotion. Nonetheless, a London newspaper soon reported that male brains "are just not built to recall things that women find easy to remember . . . such as a row with their boyfriend."[56] Shortly thereafter, Maureen Dowd of the *New York Times* used the study as the launching pad for a column in which she noted, "Women subjects who participated in the new study got more upset, for longer, than male subjects after being shown pictures of dead bodies, gravestones, crying people and dirty toilets."[57] The average reader was left with the "fact" that women's brains are hardwired to be better at emotions. But even if such findings hold up in studies with larger samples, there's a more reasonable explanation. In our culture, women are usually the ones in charge of managing the family's emotional life, and that could be why emotional issues trigger recall. Does a woman remember the birthday of her mother-in-law because her brain is wired for emotion? Or because it's her job to buy the present?

Brain research may be exploding, but many studies find differences that are hard to interpret. For example, when men and women perform certain tasks, different sections of their brains light up on PET scans.

That may or may not be significant. Steven Rose notes that the men and women who appear to be using different parts of their brains to solve problems come to the correct solutions in about the same amount of time.[58] And even Steven Pinker acknowledges that we do not know enough to assign importance to certain brain differences: "The brains of men differ from the brains of women in several ways. Men have larger brains with more neurons (even correcting for body size) though women have a larger percentage of gray matter. Since men and women are equally intelligent overall, the significance of these differences is unknown."[59]

Hocus Focus

It is easy to see how a researcher who takes "male" and "female" brains as a given will ignore a universe of other factors. If you wanted to, you could probably find evidence of "white brains" and "black brains" and "Asian brains." Some comparative studies find that Westerners focus more intently on a central object, while Asians see an object in a much broader field.[60] Is this evidence of an Asian brain? Or of attitudes and assumptions that could affect the way a person in an Asian culture thinks? Focusing only on male and female categories is equally limiting. Maybe fishermen have different brains than bankers. Maybe a lifetime of watching the sea, sailing the tides, and stalking fish sculpts the brains of the people who do it. But we will never know because nobody studies fishermen and bankers to compare their brains.

Similarly, when the media lock in on a male/female focus, they tend to ignore contradictory findings. As we pointed out, many news stories cited a study showing that boy babies, unlike girls, will look at a mechanical mobile more than at a human face.[61] This finding has been used to show that the female brain is wired to see people, while the male brain is wired to see things. William Pollack, professor of psychiatry at Harvard Medical School and author of *Real Boys*, however, points out that boy babies are actually *more* expressive and vocal with people than girl babies are.[62] "We now have executives paying $10,000 a week to learn emotional intelligence," he says. "These actually target skills boys are born with." But, he says, the strict "boy code" demands emotional rigidity and erodes those skills by the time boys are in the second grade.[63] One researcher followed boys from kindergarten through junior high and found that by junior high, boys in the classes that focused on both emotional development and academics were better adjusted than those whose classes focused only on academics.[64] Boys, like girls, are complex creatures with complex reactions, and emotions are no less important to them than they are to girls.

The Desire to Achieve

If differences in hormones or brains aren't responsible for keeping women out of top jobs, maybe motivation is the culprit. Perhaps women choose lesser jobs than men do because good wages, challenging jobs, and moving up the ladder are not as important to women. Maybe women simply lack the need for success. If that argument were true, working men and women would look very different from each other, and that difference could be empirically tested. Women would be considerably lower in motivation than men, so dead-end or boring jobs wouldn't be as stressful for them. And if men were more heavily invested in work, on-the-job problems would take a bigger toll on them than they would on women.

For the first time, we can test these ideas properly. Over many years, women were clustered in low-level jobs, and consequently there were not enough women in good jobs to draw a comparison to men. As we noted in the introduction, researchers compared men and women without regard to the jobs they did.[65] Top managers were compared with secretaries, each supposedly representing the "typical" male and female. Not surprisingly, males turned out to be ambitious and highly motivated whereas females were unambitious and more interested in relationships than advancement. When we look at men and women in comparable jobs, though, there is *no* evidence that women are less attached to the workplace than men are. Nor is there any evidence of gender differences in career motivation or job satisfaction. Here's forty-something Cynthia Cannady, a vice president at Apple: "I've been through all sorts of things and I've come to a point where I know what I'm talking about. Even when people and situations are difficult, you can learn from them. As you develop expertise, you gain confidence. If you know how to do something, people will respond positively to you because they need you. . . . in turn, as you feel respected and needed, you become more authoritative. As you gain authority, people begin to defer to you, and you gain even more confidence. As long as you keep learning and don't become arrogant, it's a positive cycle that builds and builds."[66] That's a description of a successful career path that fits both men and women.

Again and again, research finds women just as motivated as men. As already noted, *Business Week* in 2002 announced, "As Leaders, Women Rule," reporting on a number of comprehensive management studies from high-tech to manufacturing to consumer services companies.[67] "By and large, the studies show that women executives when rated by their peers, underlings and bosses, score higher than their male counterparts on a wide variety of measures, from producing high quality work to goal-setting to mentoring employees . . . women got higher ratings than men on almost every skill measured." Ironically, *BW* noted, "the researchers weren't looking to ferret out gender differences. They accidentally stumbled on the findings when they were compiling hundreds of routine performance evaluations and then analyzing the results." Clearly these women executives weren't lacking in motivation; in fact, motivation obviously drove them to produce high-quality work. *Business Week* concluded: "Management gurus now know how to boost the odds of getting a great executive. Hire a female."

Are women inherently better managers than men? Not according to most research, which shows few differences. Possibly women in management today get the subliminal message that they have to work harder than men to achieve, and so they do. Or it may be that skills like mentoring, which were formerly ignored, are now seen as key to good management, so women score better. Or it may simply be that, on average, women are *slightly* better, but plenty of men score as high or higher than women. There simply are not enough data to do sophisticated analyses.

A meta-analysis of studies of managers conducted by Gary Powell, a professor of management at the University of Connecticut, found female managers as motivated as male managers.[68] In one of the studies he examined—of nearly 2,000 managers—female managers actually reported "higher needs for self-actualization than male managers. Compared with males, female managers were more concerned with opportunities for growth, autonomy, and challenge." The women exhibited a "more mature and higher-achieving motivational profile" than their male counterparts.[69] This is almost the polar opposite of the argument that women are so tuned in to relationships, so "hardwired" for nurture, not achievement, that they are ill equipped for top jobs. It certainly casts doubt on Sullivan's theory that women will be timid managers because of low testosterone. Listen to Lucy Berroteran, a manager in the finance department of a major company: "I have a very aggressive attitude. I want to get things fixed. I don't have time to wait for everybody, so I get input and I act on it because I don't want to keep a particular job forever. I've had people challenge my aggressive style. But I keep moving forward until somebody tells me to stop. When you take risks and things work out, it gives you a level of confidence. You've got to be willing to take a risk. You've got to be willing to stand up for what you think is right."[70]

Vela McClam Mitchell, marketing director for a high-tech company, says, "I don't take things personally. Men curse each other out, but they don't get mad at each other. After they finish cursing, they talk to each other like it's no big deal . . . I've had men ream me, but I don't take it personally. If somebody starts yelling at me because I messed up, they're not yelling at me because they hate me, they're yelling at me because they are worried about the business. I can relate to that. I love the game as much as they do."[71] In the past, if women in business avoided risk, was it because of innate qualities? Or was it because, as tokens, they'd pay a higher price if they failed? Public relations expert Muriel Fox says, "Women cannot afford to make mistakes. If they did, they would hear, 'I told you so.' Since they had to be perfect, through the years they took fewer risks."[72]

The Opt-Out Myth

Even if women start out with the same motivation as men, some say, they give up faster and flee back home. The *New York Times* suggested this in a 2002 feature on female executives who had left their high-level jobs.[73] "They Conquered, They Left," announced the *Times*, and in a large black subhead added, "Some say women have less psychic investment in careers." The *New York Times* magazine reprised this theme in the 2003 cover article we noted earlier, "The Opt-Out Revolution."[74] The sweeping nature of the title and the placement of the article on the cover implies that the author, Lisa Belkin, is examining a pervasive national trend. "Many high-powered women today don't ever hit the glass ceiling, choosing to leave the workplace for motherhood. Is this the failure of one movement or the beginning of another?" asks the magazine.

Here is another example of overhyping a story to make it seem more important than it really is. This major article is not based on systematic research, but is a collection of anecdotes from a very nonrepresentative sample. Belkin based nearly her entire story on small groups of Princeton graduates who were members of book groups in several cities and had husbands affluent enough to finance a comfortable lifestyle on one income. And even though these women were presented as opting out "by choice," that's not quite an accurate picture. One television news reporter, for example, had asked her station for a part-time contract but was refused. They said it was all or nothing, so she left—and called it a wrenching decision. "It kills me that I'm not contributing to my 401(k) anymore," she said. Another woman, a lawyer, decided to leave her firm only after a judge made an arbitrary schedule change on a major case on which she had been working intensely for months—while nursing her daughter. The schedule change made her life nearly impossible.

Do these women in fact constitute a revolution? Are they even typical of their Princeton classes? That remains unknown because Belkin provides no data. Are these women really "opting out"? One woman Belkin quotes says, "It's not black or white, it's gray. You're working. Then you're not working. Then you're working part-time or consulting. Then you go back. This a chapter, not the whole book." Another says, "I'm doing what is right for me at the moment. Not necessarily what is right for me forever." The author herself writes that all the professional women she has spoken to who made the choice to stay home say they have made a temporary decision for just a few years, not a permanent decision for the rest of their lives. They have not lost their skills, just put them on hold.

One woman notes that "the exodus of professional women from the workplace isn't really about motherhood at all. It is really about work." She adds, "There a misconception that it's mostly a pull toward motherhood and her precious baby that drives a woman to quit her job . . . not that the precious baby doesn't magnetize many of us. Mine certainly did. As often as not, though, a woman would have loved to have maintained some version of a career, but that job wasn't cutting it anymore. Among women I know, quitting is driven as much from the job dissatisfaction side as from the pull to motherhood."

This would have been an interesting article about educated women making career decisions if it hadn't been oversold. Why did it need an overplayed title, a cover graphic that shows a woman holding a baby with the abandoned career ladder in the background, and the simplistic headline suggesting that this issue is only about women "choosing" to leave work? The article headline also suggests, hyperbolically, that this may be a "failure" of feminism (though later on the author herself contradicts that idea). In fact, wasn't feminism about giving women more choices? What the article really shows is the inflexibility of the workplace. Many of these women didn't opt out. They wanted to keep working but were presented with impossible choices—either working insanely long hours or not working at all.

The Belkin article suggests that professional and management-level women are focusing more on home and hearth and abandoning serious careers. Is this in fact true? Does such a major trend really exist? No. Over 78 percent of mothers with a graduate or professional degree are in the paid workforce, and they are three times as likely to work full-time as part-time, according to the 2002 U.S. Census.[75] Do women regularly opt out of demanding management jobs for home and hearth? In fact, they do not. There has been a small decline in the number of two-income families since 2000: 29 million then and 27 million in 2003.[76] This may be due to a temporary dip in the economy. In the early 1990s, with the same sort of dip, dozens of media stories announced that women were going home. Then the economy improved, and the long-standing upward trend in women's employment continued.[77] The head of the U.S. Bureau of Labor Statistics for the Northeast predicts that once again, women's employment will be on the uptick.[78] And since the Labor Department reports that about 45 percent of all managerial posts are held by females, the tide of women running home is more like a trickle.[79]

One major study of high-level women failed to uncover an "opt-out" trend. Linda Stroh and Anne Reilly of Loyola University and Jeanne Brett of Northwestern University compared 1,029 men and women managers who had the same level of jobs, education, and time in the workforce, and had relocated for their careers.[80] Not only did these women *not* opt out of demanding jobs, they were as devoted to their jobs as the men were to theirs. When they left, it wasn't to go home; it was for the same reason men left: better jobs and more advancement. Since women in corporations are more likely to stall out at lower levels than men, it's no surprise that more of them get frustrated and leave. Many form their own businesses, where they won't run into glass walls and ceilings. Stroh, Brett, and Reilly say that this defection is not due to qualities women managers lack or to anything they are doing wrong, but to persistent discrimination. One female investment professional told the *New York Times* that she believed she was denied a promotion because she was a woman, but decided not to waste time trying to prove it. Instead, she simply joined another firm.[81] And Janet Tiebout Hanson, who spent fourteen years at Goldman Sachs, asked, "Why spend ten or fifteen years hitting the glass ceiling? . . . Why not go directly to Go and collect $200?" She left Goldman and founded her own investment firm, Milestone Capital Management.[82] Stroh, Brett, and Reilly say, flatly, "Corporate America has run out of explanations that attribute women's career patterns to women's own behavior. It is time for corporations to take a closer look at their own behavior."

The Nature of Leadership

As one by one the straw men (so to speak) are knocked down, we come to the most fundamental and most difficult questions. Are men naturally better than women at making decisions and displaying authority? Do women, because of their feminine qualities, come in a distant second in their ability to lead others? Traditional notions would say that men are the "doers"—initiating subordinates' work, organizing it, and setting deadlines and standards. Women would be considered people oriented—watching out for subordinates' welfare, seeking to build their self-confidence, making them feel at ease, and soliciting their input about matters that affect them.[83] Much has been made of women's supposedly "democratic" leadership style, of their ability to make employees feel good about themselves and cooperate well together. And many of us probably remember such a female boss with fondness. But how many of us also remember the female boss who used attack as her weapon, put down subordinates in a public and painful way, and divided rather than pulled her team together? Similarly, while we can name some "kick butt" male bosses, we probably also know tactful ones who have the undying loyalty and affection of their employees.

Millions of dollars have gone into hundreds of studies of "task-oriented" versus "people-oriented" leadership behavior. And the research finds no significant difference between men and women on these parameters.

Moreover, in actual comparisons of men and women leaders in organizational settings, few differences in leadership style emerge.[84] Surprisingly, *Business Week* reports that a 2000 study of 41,000 executives (25 percent of them female) at 5,000 companies found that women are slightly *more* high-handed than men when making decisions. "In situations where an autocratic style was deemed appropriate, women chose 'my-way-or-the-highway' 35 percent of the time, guys only 31.5 percent." Women were also more likely than men to exclude key personnel needed to implement a decision, 37 percent to 32 percent. "If you're boss is a Ms., don't automatically expect her decisionmaking to be warm and fuzzy."

When differences *are* found, females have only a slight edge in being "democratic." This may be because women, on average, aren't as high in the pecking order, and so don't get to be as authoritative as men. Also, once again, behavior varies according to the situation. When women manage primarily male groups, they tend to be less democratic than when they manage groups with more women. Although many may think that men always command and women always nurture, the data don't agree.

Newer ideas about managers go deeper than just task-versus-people styles. The most effective manager, it's now believed, is the "transformational" leader, an innovative role model who gains the trust and confidence of followers, mentoring and empowering them to reach their full potential. Psychologist Alice Eagly of Northwestern University and her colleagues, in a meta-analysis, found that women managers were more "transformational" than men.[85] But the difference was small: 52.5 percent of females and 47.5 percent of males. Both sexes, it seems, are capable of leadership that enables employees to reach their full potential. One good example of the transformational leader is Supreme Court Justice Sandra Day O'Connor, described by the *New York Times* as "the most powerful woman in America."[86] Regarded as a brilliant jurist, she is also known for mentoring her law clerks and soliciting their active participation in her decisions. The *Times* notes, "O'Connor was the first woman to be elected majority leader of any state senate in the nation, and her experience as an Arizona legislator continues to influence the way she approaches her job. Most Saturdays when the court is in session, she and her clerks meet in chambers to discuss the cases that she will consider during oral arguments in the week to follow."

The question of "female" styles of leadership is a double-edged sword. Women may have won some success in business because of the belief that they have a lock on the intuitive skills and communication ability needed to heighten and encourage group performance. A number of executives may have agreed, *Yes, we need more women for the "sensitive" side of our organization.* But this notion can backfire, ghettoizing women in the "human relations" area of the corporation, far from the top management jobs that are seen as requiring authority and decisiveness.

Women often face a catch–22: If they're viewed as efficient, caring, and good with people, they can be dismissed for being not strong enough. Rosabeth Moss Kanter says: "If women are seen as only glorified office facilitators but not as tough-minded risk-takers, they will be held back from the CEO jobs."[87] But if they are seen as too strong, they can also lose out. Princeton psychologist Susan Fiske studied how this dynamic works.[88] She finds that outgroups—like women and minorities—tend to be viewed as either likable or competent, but not both. For example, nontraditional women tend to be respected but disliked, whereas traditional women are liked but not respected—putting women who want to be *both* liked and respected in a difficult position.

Robert Kabacoff of the Management Research Group in Portland, Maine, found this dynamic alive and well in the way CEOs and corporate boards view upper management.[89] He found a clear double standard. Male CEOs and senior vice presidents got high marks from their bosses when they were forceful and assertive and lower scores when they were cooperative and empathic. The reverse was true for women. Take the case of Ann B. Hopkins, who in 1989 was denied a partnership at Price Waterhouse.[90] Despite being a leading rainmaker in the firm, she was criticized for being "macho" and needing "a course at charm school." Hopkins had to go all the way to the Supreme Court before she was finally made a partner. Unfortunately, according to Catalyst, most women quietly leave the company instead. Kabacoff concluded, "At the highest levels, bosses are still evaluating people in the most stereotypical ways." *Business Week* notes: "That means that even though women have proven their readiness to lead companies into the future, they're not likely to get a shot until their bosses are ready to stop living in the past." So it would seem that it is not women's natures, but stubborn stereotypes held by their superiors, that are keeping women from the high-level jobs they deserve.

Holding on to myths about women's inability to lead harms not only women but also the corporations they work for. Research shows that diversity pays off. A 1998 American Management Association report found that senior management teams that were more inclusive of women and minorities showed "superior corporate performance."[91] The communications industry, which has senior management teams that are particularly hospitable to women, has above average reports of increased sales, operating profits, and worker productivity. And new companies that had higher numbers of women managers also had higher stock prices and earnings per share after their IPOs.

Men themselves may pay a price when stereotypes are operating. They may have benefited from the old conventional wisdom, but now winds are starting to blow in another direction. Does it seem farfetched to imagine that a qualified man could lose out on a top management position just because he's a male? Could he be seen as not "democratic" enough, not having the right people skills? *Business Week* reports that some executives are beginning to develop a new hiring bias. "If forced to choose between equally qualified male and female candidates for a top-level job, they say they often pick the woman—not because of affirmative action or any particular desire to give the female a chance but because they believe she will do a better job."[92]

The ideas we've tried to debunk in this chapter—that men and women have different brains, hormones, drives, and basic natures—reflect a pervasive tendency to see complicated systems in simple black-and-white terms. Do you believe that women's "inability" to lead is inborn and unchangeable? In fact, our genes, brains, hormones, environment, and experiences act together to shape our behavior. Consider this startling experiment. A study of female rats found that the mothers are attracted to a substance in the male babies' urine, and so they lick the male babies more than the female babies in their genital area. When researchers stroked the genital regions of female baby rats every day with a paintbrush, the females behaved like the males when they matured, mounting other females and secreting proteins in a male manner. In this case the mother's behavior, an environmental factor, apparently created male or female behavior. The fetal "wiring" of the babies' brains could not have predetermined their behavior.[93] This shows an amazingly complex interaction of brains, hormones, and environment in creating behavior. And if the process is complicated in rats, imagine how much more so it is in humans.

Simple beliefs about gender differences polarize the sexes and unfairly stereotype both men and women. All too often, they exaggerate differences between the sexes while minimizing their overwhelming similarities. Not long ago men were the beneficiaries of this rigid thinking, but today the stereotypes can cut both ways. As women, we don't want our daughters to have to fight the same battles we fought, but neither do we want our sons to lose out on good jobs that they might deserve. Just as we don't want our daughters to be seen as timid, risk averse, and passive, neither do we want our sons to be thought of as rigid, unable to deal with people, and naturally lacking in communication skills. We who are parents—and others who deal with children—can be a powerful force in breaking open the stranglehold of stereotypes. In Part III, we'll consider the ways in which these stereotypes play out in our children's early years.

part three

Parenting

As the Twig Is Bent

ARE BOYS MADE OF "snips and snails and puppy dog tails" while girls are "sugar and spice and everything nice"? Are boys and girls profoundly different from each other? Just as people assume there are strong gender differences in adulthood, they also take for granted gender differences in childhood. Indeed, as we'll show in this chapter, at least two influential theorists have argued that supposed gender differences in adults have their roots in the formative years of childhood.

One theorist maintains that the very dissimilar treatment mothers give to daughters and sons leads to strong gender differences in adulthood. As a result of this differential treatment, she claims, daughters grow up to be nurturers and sons grow up to be "antinurturers," almost alienated from the family. Another theorist argues that children themselves, in effect, create strong gender asymmetry by voluntarily separating themselves into single-sex groups. In this chapter, we demonstrate that these theorists are wrong. We show that, just as with adults, situation, not gender, determines children's behavior. The supposedly fixed gender roles observed in childhood are most often *not* actually characteristics of the children themselves but rather the stereotypes that are projected onto them. These stereotypes affect what researchers see and how they interpret their data. Even more significantly, they affect what we buy for our children, what activities we encourage them to participate in, and what the media and the manufacturers produce. Left to their own devices, children often operate in a much more gender-neutral fashion than we assume. We (parents, schools, media, and marketers), however, rarely let children operate for long in a gender-free zone. We're too busy handing them the merchandise, media messages, and activities that shriek "gender difference."

In recent years, rigid ideas about gender differences in children have taken hold, with some critics insisting that "common sense" tells us boys and girls are very different and that "gender-free" ideas should be jettisoned as misguided artifacts of the women's movement or the 1960s. But is this "commonsense" view in fact correct? As already noted, some theorists argue strongly that pervasive boy–girl differences do indeed exist and have lifelong impact. Their theories rest on two assumptions that we believe are questionable—first, that mothers (or the culture of childhood itself) create enormous gender differences and, second, that these supposed differences put boys and girls on separate paths for the rest of their lives. There are certainly cultural influences on children, but we believe them to be less widespread and less powerful than these trendy theories assume; they don't necessarily create strong gender differences that determine the course of adult development.

It's important to examine these theories critically because they have had—and continue to have—a profound influence on the way men and women deal with their ambitions, handle their jobs, and arrange their family lives.

How Much Does Mom Matter?

One of the most important proponents of the "mom is all" theory is psychoanalyst Nancy Chodorow, who presented her ideas in *The Reproduction of Mothering* (1978), which was chosen as one of the most influential books of the past twenty-five years by *Contemporary Sociology*.[1] Her arguments still influence therapists, educators, and the general public. Chodorow wrote earlier than Carol Gilligan and had a major effect on Gilligan's work. Although Chodorow is less of a household name than Gilligan, her influence has been just as pervasive, especially in psychoanalytic circles. The prestigious Women's Therapy Institutes in Paris and New York were founded in great part on her work.[2]

Like Gilligan, Chodorow considers herself a feminist and believes that her focus on mothers is a corrective to Freud's earlier ideas about the overwhelming power of the father in the child's early years. Based on her experiences with her patients, she argues that *mothers* are key. They raise their boys and girls differently, and this fact is critical to the kinds of people their children grow up to be. Mothers, she says, raise daughters to express their nurturing side and sons to suppress it. The daughters, kept emotionally close, never really "separate" from their mothers. Mother and daughter remain connected, and that connection enables daughters to bond closely with their own children. Because of their special capacity to bond, daughters are well equipped to mother and they naturally gravitate to spending their adult years tending the family hearth.

Sons, on the other hand, are encouraged to "individuate." Mothers push their sons away so that they can develop a healthy masculine identity. With their early connection to their mothers severed, men naturally turn to the impersonal world of work and public life, often turning their backs on the nitty-gritty of family life. For Chodorow, it was a short jump to claim that mothering resides deeply in the psychological life of women but is forever beyond the reach of men. "The mothering role has gained psychological and ideological significance, and has come increasingly to define women's lives."[3] Women are programmed by their mothers to become mothers themselves; it is the core element in female identity—integral to the fabric of femininity. Women who don't completely embrace motherhood—who choose to engage their husbands, day care providers, or baby-sitters in child rearing—are betraying their natural instincts and, by implication, doing damage to their children. If no one can mother like mommy—and she's not there—kids are in trouble. Daughters, in particular, may never develop their own mothering capacities. "For girls, beginning in the earliest period," she says, "the relationship to the mother leads to the development of mothering in girls."[4]

Along with putting a huge and exclusive emphasis on the role of mothering, Chodorow relegates fathers to a minimal role in parenting, especially in teaching girls how to be girls and boys how to be boys. The father is a rather shadowy figure to his children. Adult males, in this view, are ill equipped to father, given the nature of the early and all-important mother–son relationship. Interestingly, Nancy Chodorow once believed that social forces shape men's parenting limitations, and that these could be overcome. But she's changed her mind, becoming more convinced that early influences are so strong that they can't be cast aside. Motherhood, she now says, is so integral to the psychological life of women that it is not something that men can choose to take on. "Mothering is not simply another creative role that can be challenged like glass ceilings and discriminatory practices."[5]

Where do Chodorow's ideas come from and how valid are they? Chodorow presents no systematic data; she bases her generalizations about *all* boys and *all* girls, *all* men and *all* women solely on her own practice and the work of other psychoanalysts whose observations are based on highly nonrepresentative individual patients. Some critics note that Chodorow's patients were very narcissistic women who might have been overinvested in their daughters—as reflections of themselves—in ways that ordinary women are not.[6] The idea of the all-important mother defined by Chodorow runs through many best-sellers about child rearing; some cite her directly, and others simply repeat her ideas about the centrality of women's exclusive mothering. These include Burton White, *The First Three Years of Life;*[7] Selma Fraiberg, *The Magic Years;*[8] and Penelope Leach's phenomenally successful baby books, including *Children First.*[9] Leach argues that to meet their children's needs, women should stay home until their children are at least *eight years old.*

There is a second part to Chodorow's argument. By claiming that males are ill equipped to nurture, Chodorow finds no real emotional role for fathers during their sons' and daughters' childhood years. Even men who want to be active fathers aren't up to the job, no matter how hard they try. Chodorow says that men's nurturing capacities have been permanently and "systematically curtailed and repressed."[10] But the actions of both adult men and women disprove this theory time and again. National survey data and our own major study of dual-earner couples show that young fathers are spending more time with their kids, taking them shopping, dropping them off at day care, cheering at their soccer games, giving them their cough medicine, helping with their homework.[11] And new mothers are returning to work after a brief maternity leave. Yet books in line with Chodorow's thinking continue to become best-sellers and articles making the same claim can be found all over the newsstands. For example, David Blankenhorn of the Institute for American Values writes in *Fatherless America* that men are not "natural" parents in the way that mothers are.[12] He says that the correct role for fathers is to be providers to the family and "pals" to their children, but not primary caregivers. He rails against what he calls the New Age, sensitive father:

> He is nurturing. He expresses his emotions. He is a healer, a companion, a colleague. He is a deeply involved parent. He changes diapers, gets up at 2:00 A.M. to feed the baby, goes beyond "helping out" in order to share equally in the work, joys, and responsibilities of domestic life.[13]

Such intense involvement in caring for young children demasculinizes men, says Blankenhorn. As the *Washington Post* notes, Blankenhorn believes that men who reject the traditional breadwinner role and assume a fully involved, coparenting relationship with their partners are to be decried. "To Blankenhorn, these men have denied their own masculinity and need to realize that their role in the family really should be as junior partner to their wives. 'The New Father model is a mirage,' he writes. 'It purports to be about fatherhood, but it is not. There is no father there.'"[14] The father's proper role is family breadwinner.

Pediatrician Burton White decrees that only mothers can care for their children with the type of "delight" that enables babies to thrive.[15] Dad can never hope to compete. Rutgers anthropologist Lionel Tiger says, "Men don't possess a commitment to the offspring remotely comparable to the mothers."[16] Robert Wright says men are naturally sneaky.[17] They may be programmed to deceive women about what wonderful, caring dads they will be—while fully intending to have many dalliances that will take time away from their children. In his book *The Wonder of Boys,* Michael Gurian out-Chodorows Chodorow, arguing that it is simply not in the nature of males to display the emotional, relational behaviors that make for good parenting.[18] "Men are fueled by aggression . . . and wired for compartmentalized thinking," he writes, so men's brains aren't built for relationships. "Fighting and hunting, it was better to hold emotions back, so now they can't process emotive data so well."[19] Rutgers sociologist David Poponoe says, "Men are not biologically as attuned to being committed fathers as women are to being committed mothers."[20] In the absence of social coercion, men's commitment to their family is weak, he argues. The popular media have picked up on these ideas. One widely e-mailed Internet communiqué reads, "A woman knows all about her children. She knows about dentist appointments and romances, best friends, favorite foods, secret fears and hopes and dreams. A man is vaguely aware of some short people living in the house."

These notions put today's young women and men in a bind. If women believe that men are simply not fit by nature to care for young children and men believe the same thing, they may strap themselves into straitjackets of their own making—with harmful effects for fathers, mothers, children, and family relationships.

For example, RB's patient Carla is a thirty-nine-year-old OB-GYN; she is married to Frank, a research scientist. They have a six-month-old child, Dana. They live in the Boston area and have been married for four years. Carla has been working hard for the past decade to complete medical school, finish her residency, and build her practice. Frank works long hours in a research lab, but his schedule is more flexible than hers. He can come home and work on his computer when he needs to. Carla has very little control over her schedule. "Hey, when a baby's ready to be born, I have to be there. I can't say, 'How about we reschedule for Tuesday?'" It makes sense for Frank to take on greater child care responsibility—and he's willing to do so. But Carla, believing that only she has the innate capacity to mother, doesn't see any other option but to do it herself. "I don't think I have any choice. I don't want to cut back, but I don't want my child to suffer because of my career."

Asked why she couldn't take Frank up on his offer, she shakes her head. "He'd have one eye on his laptop and the other on the baby. I'm afraid he wouldn't be totally there for Dana." So, Carla cuts way back on her practice, disappoints her patients, and leads her medical partners to doubt her commitment to medicine. While she adores Dana, she misses the challenge of full-time medicine—and is unhappy when Frank starts to work even longer hours to make up for her lost income and appears to enjoy it. She once thought she was part of an ideal couple; now Carla has begun to wonder about the health of her marriage. Frank sees that Carla is unhappy and finds himself becoming anxious and depressed. Carla created this problem because of her rigid beliefs about what the sexes can and can't do, and now she and Frank are suffering the consequences of her rigidity.

Megan, a thirty-three-year-old television producer, took a year's unpaid leave to care for her baby boy. When John was a year old, she was offered a job as executive producer of a show that she had been pushing to get on the air for years. This was a once-in-a-lifetime opportunity, and she knew it. Megan was torn because she had been reading Burton White about the paramount importance of the baby's "first three years of life." She was convinced that John's emotional and intellectual development would be damaged if she weren't omnipresent during this period. Her husband, Ed, didn't buy that idea, assuring her that she could be a fine parent while she was working, as his own mother had been. "Let's get a nanny, or let's check out some day care centers," he urged her. "I don't want you driving yourself crazy or blaming me because you lost this great opportunity." Megan thought seriously about his suggestion—but timing is everything in life. She had started talking to child care providers when the story broke of the "nanny murder," in which a young British nanny in their town was convicted of shaking to death a baby in her charge. That did it for Meagan. As much as she wanted it, Meagan turned down the new job. With great reluctance, she watched as another producer took the helm of her dream show. A year later, restless at home, she told the station manager she was ready to return as a senior producer. But the station had cut back, and another producer has been hired in her place. Unable to move to another market because of Ed's job, Meagan wonders if she's ever going to get her career back on track.

Brian, a thirty-five-year-old journalist, has just had his first child, Alice. From the instant he saw her, he felt a powerful flush of love and protectiveness. Brian wants to take a paternity leave to spend time with Alice. His newspaper has just announced a policy of offering a three-month unpaid parental leave to new fathers. His wife's career is at a critical juncture, and Brian can more easily afford time away from the job than she can. But, like Megan, he's read the popular parenting books. Can he really mother Alice? He worries. His editor's attitude doesn't help. "The elections are coming up. Who's going to be able to pick up your beat?" the editor asks. Clearly, for him, flexibility is the F-word. With mixed feelings, Brian decides not to take the leave.

We all know people just like these—they are our sisters, our brothers, our daughters—maybe they are *us*. They have bought into the idea that mothers are all-important. But, in fact, are men unable to nurture? And do the sexes nurture in different ways? Chodorow makes two basic claims: The first, as we've noted, is that mothers raise their girls to nurture and their boys to separate. The second is that mothers and fathers differ greatly in their parenting. Mothers are more nurturing, warm, expressive, and interactive than fathers—especially in their relationship with their daughters.

The Deficient Dad

A number of studies that have evaluated Chodorow's notions fail to support either of her claims. They conclude that there is little difference between fathers and mothers in how they socialize their very young children. Sociologist Barbara Risman of North Carolina State University found that men who had primary responsibility for child care parented their kids the same way mothers did.[21] In her 1986 study of 141 single fathers, she found that "most men felt comfortable and competent as single parents."[22] When men have to shoulder the primary responsibility for raising their kids, they do all the things that have traditionally been thought of as "mothering."[23] Risman's findings echo a main argument of this book: situation, not gender, is the major key to behavior. The sexes aren't stuck with inflexible "gender-typical" roles. As situations change, so does their behavior. Men "mother" because they want to—or because they have to. Sometimes they are single fathers, sometimes they are the major caregivers while their wives are at work, or sometimes they are just heavily invested in coparenting.

Risman says that "when males take full responsibility for child care, when they meet expectations usually confined to females, they develop intimate and affectionate relationships with their children. Despite male sex-role training, fathers respond to the nontraditional role of single parent with strategies stereotypically feminine."[24] Here's how some of the single parents in Risman's study talked about their experiences:

They get hurt and they need somebody to rock them. They wake up in the middle of the night to a scary dream and they need somebody to comfort them." As for his own needs, [he] says, "If you're a single man with two children, you don't go out picking up women. You're a single man, but you're a family man.

Hair-braiding was something I had to learn to do," one father recalled proudly. "Sandy had long hair, and I realized that if you didn't take care of it, it looked like nobody loved her. And it couldn't be just any braid, I had to learn to make a French braid.[25]

These men had to struggle against the cultural idea that only women are supposed to do the day-to-day caring for children such as braiding a daughter's hair. Many studies find a strong tendency in American society for men to interact with their children mainly by roughhousing or playing with them.[26] This observation led to the conclusion that mothers and fathers interact with their children in ways that are inherently different. If this is so, it should hold true across income groups, racial groups, and cultures. But does it?

It does not. Parenting behavior is neither inborn nor socially transferred to one sex, but is learned by caregiving in a specific situation. (Just ask any mother with a newborn who says to herself, *Oh my God, what do I do now!*) This conclusion is drawn from studies of cultures similar to ours such as Sweden, Britain, and Ireland, as well as from studies of very different cultures, most notably the Aka pygmies of East Central Africa.[27] Since most studies of parental behavior are conducted during daytime hours, when fathers are at work and only mothers are home, theorists assume that fathers play a peripheral role in the development of young children. But what if research is done when fathers are actually present and interacting with their children? Barry Hewlett, an anthropologist at Washington State University–Vancouver familiar with Aka pygmy fathers, did just that.[28] He studied fifteen fathers of infants around the clock and compared the frequency and nature of many kinds of parent–child interactions. He found that while mothers more frequently fed the infants (obviously the case for nursing mothers), fathers were more likely to play with or hug and kiss their infants while holding them. Furthermore, the fathers did not engage in the sort of vigorous rough-and-tumble play seen as typical by American developmental psychologists.[29] Hewlett noticed that nonfathers, and fathers who didn't spend much time with their kids, were far more apt to engage in this type of activity than were involved fathers. In the absence of intimate knowledge of their children, men could stimulate a response by roughhousing with them.

In contrast, "Aka fathers [like Western mothers] know their infants intimately. Fathers know the early signs of infant hunger, fatigue and illness as well as the limits in their ability to soothe the infant. They also know how to stimulate responses from the infant without being vigorous. Unlike too many American fathers, Aka wait for infants to initiate interactions."[30]

Hewlett concludes that "the Aka father–infant relationship appears to be markedly different from the American father–infant relationship."[31] Fathers who get to know their children better are able to respond to them in a myriad of ways. Playing or roughhousing are just some of the ways in which fathers connect with their children. The "pal" dad who plays catch with his kids or tosses them in the air is not the *proper* father. In fact, if he can't go beyond roughhousing, he may be the "deficient dad."

Scott Coltrane, a sociologist at the University of California–Riverside, did a major study of fathers and found that men who actually took care of their kids on more than a casual basis underwent a transformation.[32] "They developed 'maternal thinking,'" he says. They became "sensitive and nurturing caregivers." Coltrane quotes one father who had to learn to parent:

> It was real hard to learn to sit down and hold them when they were sick. I had to keep telling myself that this is important, you need to be here with them doing nothing. (laughs) Which is the feeling I had, I'm not doing anything, but I was. Eventually those things really paid off with the trust the kids developed in me.[33]

Other evidence also debunks the idea that fathers can't parent. A major meta-analysis of studies of nearly 30,000 parents by psychologists Hugh Lytton and David Romney of the University of Calgary found *no* significant differences between mothers and fathers in seven crucial parenting areas: warmth, nurturance, responsiveness, encouragement of dependence, restrictiveness, low encouragement of independence, and disciplinary strictness.[34] In other words, mothers and fathers behaved similarly in these areas when interacting with their children. They did, however, differ in one respect. Fathers were more likely than mothers to offer sex-typed toys to their boys and girls. When father was in charge, sons were given trucks to play with, while girls were offered dolls. Hardly evidence that fathers can't "mother."

If Chodorow were right and full-time mothering was critical to children, then children in nonmaternal care should be less securely attached to their mothers. But major new research refutes this idea. Children are able to bond well with their mothers even when they spend a great deal of time with their fathers or other caregivers. In the "gold standard" study of early childhood research, 1,300 babies and their parents were recruited into an ongoing study of the effects of early maternal or non-maternal care on children's emotional, social, and cognitive development.[35] When the children were fifteen months of age, the researchers assessed the degree to which they were securely attached to their mothers. Those who had been in regular nonmaternal care (e.g., father care, other relative care, day care center, etc.) were just as likely to be securely attached to their mothers as those who were in regular maternal care.

What about Chodorow's argument that mothers' relationship with their girls differs from that with their boys? She claims that mothers establish a more intimate, or "enmeshed," emotional relationship with daughters than with sons. So there must surely be a different quality to those relationships. Mothers *must* have very special, exclusive relationships with their daughters that they can't have with sons. If Chodorow were right, you'd find more intense emotional reciprocity between mothers and daughters than between mothers and sons.[36] But this isn't the case. Emotional expression has *not* been shown to be greater between mothers and daughters than between mothers and sons.[37] There's no scientific evidence that mothers shape their daughters to be nurturers and their sons to be remote and unemotional. The caring potential in boys is not forever lost because of "natural" female mothering.

If the Chodorow thesis were true, it should hold across cultures. But cross-cultural studies don't point to greater mother–daughter "enmeshment."[38] In fact, in Chinese society, the mother–son relationship is more intense than the relationship between mothers and daughters.[39] So far, research does not support the popular notion that mothers construct a more enmeshed relationship with daughters than with sons in the early years.

Why are ideas about men's inability to parent so hardy? Why are men and women who happily share parenting in their own lives so vulnerable to theorists who say they are psychologically unsuited to be doing it at all? The following case from RB's practice may give us some hint as to why women, in particular, may be vulnerable to these mothering myths. Chad and Melissa, in their early forties, are devoted coparents, sharing both work and child care. Melissa says she believes deeply in the idea that fathers should be involved parents. "I love the idea that our son Joe (age 5) spends so much time with his father." At the same time, Melissa confesses to another feeling—jealousy. Joe and Chad have bonded intensely.

Two situations are particularly hard for Melissa. When she and Chad come home from work, Joe runs to his father and wants his dad to hold him. And Joe turns first to his father for comforting after he falls or has a nightmare. In her heart of hearts, Melissa thinks that Joe should be turning to *her* first for comfort. After all, she's the one who is supposed to have a special bond with her children. Instead of delighting in the closeness between Chad and Joe, she tries to get Chad to hold back on rushing to Joe, and make sure that *she's* included. Melissa feels that her femininity is on the line. (Indeed, this could be a real problem for women. When their husbands parent, women have to give up what had once been their exclusive turf.)

Perhaps for mothers, the idea of being the primary nurturer is akin to a security blanket, something to hang onto in a time of great change. If mothers believe that their nurturing is unique and can't be duplicated by fathers, then they don't have to worry about losing their status as "mommy" when they go to work. As others, including fathers, begin to take on more of the parental role, mothers can breathe easily, comfortable in the knowledge that they are still the supreme nurturer and hence the most important figure in their child's life. The idea that their care is unique and irreplaceable has to comfort women as they begin to turn over child care responsibilities to others and—naturally enough—begin to wonder if somebody else is going to be viewed as "mommy."

But there is a big drawback to this false theory of woman as preeminent nurturer. Although it may comfort women as they leave their homes, it may also make them feel enormous guilt when they aren't at home mothering. As we've seen in some of the cases described in this chapter, this idea may lead women to make poor career choices. With the massive movement of women into the workforce, something is gained and something is lost. Perhaps gender-difference theories helped women as they went out to work. Maybe these theories sent the message "you're still number one, and the fact that you're not there as much doesn't change that." But the comfort these ideas provide is outweighed by the guilt and inflexibility they foster. Maybe "mommy" should face the fact that she won't always be number one in her child's eyes. Perhaps that isn't a bad thing. In other cultures children who have many caregivers are happy and healthy. Maybe it's good for mothers, children, and fathers if dad gets to be number one sometimes. Perhaps women's conflicting emotions partly accounted for the success of Chodorow's work.

Ironically, Chodorow's ideas were being contradicted by the actions that adult women were taking at the time she was presenting her ideas. In 1978, when *The Reproduction of Mothering* was published, she took no cognizance of the fact that women, in record numbers, seemed to be outsmarting their nurturing socialization. First, women were putting their maternal imperative on hold, working outside the home and having their children later and later in life. (So late that Sylvia Ann Hewlett would argue in 2002 that these women somehow forgot or denied that they had a biological clock.)[40] Finally, there was a less obvious but equally important trend that began in this period. As workplace opportunities opened up for women, some men became stay-at-home dads while their working wives went out and brought in bigger and bigger paychecks.

Once freed from the guilt engendered by Chodorow's dire predictions, mothers (like Carla and Megan) and fathers (like Brian) can pursue their desires knowing that their children will not suffer. Parents can make reasoned decisions based on the realities of their lives rather than on nonscientific ideas that smack of gender stereotypes more than careful research. Embracing Gilligan's and Chodorow's idea that women are the natural, relational parents and that men can't measure up leads to unhappiness for many contemporary couples. Their message will return us to the unhappy days of "the second shift," when women did it all. Is that what we really want—high stress for women, just as their families are more dependent on their earnings?

If essentialist ideas prevail, kids will also suffer. Children will be deprived of the considerable benefits of involved fathering. Boston University's Leslie Brody found that for nine- to twelve-year-olds, the more time they spent with their fathers, the less they expressed "gender-stereotypic" emotions.[41] Compared to children who spent less time with their fathers, girls who were close to their dads expressed more competitiveness, less sadness, and more assertiveness. Boys who spent more time with their dads expressed more interpersonal affiliation, less competitiveness, more fear, more warmth, less anger, and less aggression than kids who had less father time. Of course, both boys and girls experience a wide range of emotions but are not always free to express them. Cultural taboos let boys get angry and let girls cry, but not the other way around. Just because boys or girls don't visibly express emotions that are supposed to belong to the other sex doesn't mean that they aren't *feeling* those emotions. Fathers, it seems, can give their children a valuable gift: freedom to express a full range of emotions without fear of being stigmatized.

On the other hand, if they believe they can't be good fathers, dads will hurt themselves as well as their kids, since research shows that fathers gain from close relations with their children.[42] Married men who have good relationships with their kids report fewer stress-related physical symptoms such as fatigue, insomnia, and back pain than those with poor relationships with their children. Close relationships with children spill over into men's work life. Involved dads suffer less from anxiety and depression when they have problems on the job.

The Culture of Childhood

Is there a culture of childhood that, rather than parents, powerfully shapes the nature of children? Do girls and boys inhabit very different and separate worlds and does this separateness create life-long sex differences?

Stanford psychologist Eleanor Maccoby,[43] a pioneer in sex role research, believes this to be the case.[44] "Boys and girls are indeed exposed to two somewhat different cultures," Maccoby says, and she believes that children's identities are often shaped by what she calls "membership in a same-sex collective."[45]

Maccoby claims that gender differences are created not by parental socialization but by pervasive sex segregation that emerges when children are about three years old. (Judith Rich Harris has an even more extreme view of the power of peers.[46] She argues in *The Nurturing Assumption* that besides contributing their genetic material, parents exert almost no influence on their children. Peers are everything.) As boys and girls increasingly segregate themselves, they begin to develop styles of playing, making friends, talking, learning, and relating to adults that heighten their differences and further separate their worlds. Maccoby believes in a universal tendency for this polarization that has its origins in our evolutionary past. She says that each sex develops its own unique style. Boys organize themselves into groups that are large and hierarchical, whereas girls form groups that are smaller, less organized, and characterized by turn taking.

There is a strong bias, Maccoby argues, "in every society" for children to be drawn toward playmates of their own sex. But, as we all know, cultures differ greatly. Some support rigid sex differences; in the *madrassas* (religious schools) of some Muslim countries, boys have no contact from a very young age with females other than aunts and mothers, and that only occasionally. In other cultures—like our own—boys and girls mix freely. Maccoby is careful; she cautions that "it is easy to overemphasize the differences. By no means all of what children say to each other in their segregated playgroups conforms to . . . gendered patterns . . . In fact, most utterances fall into neutral territory."[47] She also notes that "boys are more likely to act like boys when in public and when engaged in dominance encounters."

Still, the thrust of Maccoby's work argues forcefully that childhood play steers boys and girls onto disparate paths. If this sex segregation in early childhood is as pervasive as Maccoby suggests, if inevitable and tenacious gender differences emerge in early childhood and exert their influence throughout life, then there will be grave consequences for us all. Early on, each sex will stereotype the other in ways that make them seem unattractive, strange, and alien to the other. Maccoby believes that the ways kids learn to talk, act, and play in these sex-segregated groups follow them throughout life. What they learn colors their adult hetero-sexual relationships at home and at work. Maccoby cites solid research for the occurrence of same-sex segregation in childhood, especially in schools. The problem arises when she attempts to link children's behav-ior to the ways adults act, think, and feel. Do we really spend a great deal of time in segregated groups as children? Yes, we do. But as adults, do we behave the way we do *because* of the playing fields of childhood?

Can we really draw a direct line between kids' experiences in school and their whole range of adult relationships? This line of thinking ig-nores the influence of the experiences people have beyond childhood. Maccoby cites only three sources for the idea of the all-determining power of childhood: the very popular but seriously flawed works of Carol Gilligan,[48] Deborah Tannen,[49] and Mary Pipher.[50] (We'll discuss Pipher in detail in the next chapter.) Their work is a slim reed on which to hang so crucial an argument. A much stronger argument for the op-posite idea comes from New York University sociologist Kathleen Ger-son.[51] She conducted a detailed study of the life histories of young adults and found that the influence of childhood was "underdetermin-ing" when it came to the way their lives evolved. Many other events— their education, the line of work they chose, the bosses they had, the mentors who helped them, the spouses they married—all shaped their lives more powerfully than their early childhood experiences.

Another important question about the culture of childhood is whether sex-segregated play is rooted in our deep species history, as Maccoby claims. Do the boy–girl patterns of play on the school yard re-flect styles that date back to prehistory? Probably not, anthropologists say.[52] Our hunter-gatherer ancestors lived for eons in small nomadic groups. In all likelihood there were not many children in any one group, and the children were apt to be of different ages. (The sexes are more likely to separate from each other in same-age groups than in mixed-age groups.)[53] Both sexes most likely mingled freely with each other and the dominant "segregation" was between adults and children, not between boys and girls. We say that with some confidence because we see today that when children are in small groups, they play together without regard for sex. Moreover, in large extended families children tend to segregate by age, not sex: the older kids (or big kids) versus the younger kids (or little kids).

The child's play of our genetic ancestors was likely not "gendered." Toys were probably scarce and created from sticks, stones, or any available material. Children played most often with whatever was around, with no thought about whether it was a "girl thing" or a "boy thing." Our ancestors had no modern advertising to create pink and blue versions of the same toys to promote products for boys and girls.

So is sex-segregated play natural or created? Eleanor Maccoby seems to opt for the former. But other child developmentalists challenge her view. First, is what we see in school really typical of children's natural behavior, or does it come from a highly structured, rule-bound environment? Barrie Thorne, a highly respected sociologist at the University of California–Berkeley, points out that what science knows about kids comes mainly from only one place—the school yard—where most segregation among children occurs and most developmental research on children takes place—90 percent, according to Thorne.

She approaches the study of childhood differently. She doesn't hone in on school yard behavior but follows kids all day, in many settings. "Start with a sense of the whole rather than with an assumption of . . . separation and difference," argues Thorne.[54] Her work is extremely important because she collected her data by observing kids over long periods of time and she is very sensitive to context. Thorne understands that kids' behavior depends on what kind of school they are in, what kinds of teachers they have, and what activities they engage in; importantly, their behavior varies over time. She doesn't fall into the trap of making generalizations about *all* kids at *all* times.

Thorne reports in her 1994 book, *Gender Play*, that sex segregation only occurs when there are large groups of same-age children supervised publicly by a few adults. In more private and intimate settings, cross-sex play occurs often and easily. And these are the settings in which people spend most of their time—now and in the past. Not until the rise of industrialization were children sent out of the home to school, where there were enough of them to permit sex segregation and where there were few adults charged with their supervision. When you have forty kids playing in a school yard, watched over by one or two teachers, you have to find ways to organize them. Sex is the most obvious category. But it's unlikely that gender was important in determining how kids played back in hunter-gatherer times (roughly 2,000,000–8,000 B.C.), when children played in small groups of kin.

So the segregation we see among schoolchildren may itself be an adaptation to an "unnatural" set of circumstances for which humans are genetically ill prepared. That idea goes against the grain, since the tendency is to believe that what happens in school yards is natural. But sex-segregated play may have been created by the institution that was devised to educate children in the most convenient way, *not* by the nature of children themselves. "At school, no one escapes being declared male or female whether that difference is relevant or not," Thorne says.[55] What matters most in the school yard is the way in which children can be easily grouped (boys on the right, girls on the left). In families, on the other hand, parents are most concerned with the individual qualities of their children. In our culture, the model of sisters and brothers offers one of the few powerful images of relatively equal relationships between girls and boys and between adult men and women. The relationships between brothers and sisters begin in childhood, when gender relations in the family are relatively egalitarian.

When young kids aren't in school, they don't display much sex segregation. In neighborhoods, you find a lot more mixing of the sexes than in school.[56] In one neighborhood we know, girls and boys are in and out of each other's houses, they ride bikes together, roller-blade, and shoot hoops together. If there *are* two cultures, they are so fluid that many kids move in and out of them with ease. Even in schools, boys and girls often interact in classrooms, school plays, orchestras, and interest clubs. And a study of how kids behave in a children's museum finds very little segregation between boys and girls.[57]

But the focus on difference between the sexes is so overdone that little attention is paid to "within-sex" difference. Boys often differ more from one another in their temperaments and styles of play, than they do from girls. And vice versa. But too many experts ignore this reality and focus only on boy–girl differences. (Also, the situation makes a huge difference. When kids are roller-blading together, for example, their sex doesn't much matter. But when they are trying out for the gymnastics team or the football team, sex makes a big difference.)

When kids are being watched by adults, Thorne notes, boys and girls are more likely to avoid each other. When adults aren't around, kids are more flexible. Their behavior changes when the situation changes—when they're lining up on their own for the cafeteria, trying out for band, or playing spontaneously, boys and girls don't separate. At one elementary school Thorne studied, fifth grader Kevin arrived on the school yard with a ball. Seeing potential action, another boy, Tony, walked over "with interest on his face." Rita and Neera were already standing on the playground nearby. Neera called out, "Okay, me and Rita against you two," as Kevin and Tony moved into position. The handball game began in earnest with serves and returns punctuated by game-related talk—challenges between the opposing teams ("You're out!" "No, exactly on the line.") and supportive comments between team members ("Sorry, Kevin," Tony said when he missed his shot; "That's okay," Kevin replied). The game went on for about five minutes—no evidence of sex segregation here. Then other children began to arrive. One more girl joined Rita and Neera, and three more boys joined Kevin and Tony. One was John, a dominant leader among the boys. Suddenly the game changed from a casual one in which boys and girls happened to be on different sides to a "highly charged sense of girls-against-the boys/boys-against the girls." Each sex started jeering and teasing the other. Finally boys and girls started chasing each other, and that broke up the game.

Why did John's arrival have such a big effect? The other boys didn't want him to see them as sissies, and he encouraged the jeering at the girls. If you happened on the field at that moment, you would see a "snapshot" of highly segregated play. If you'd arrived a few minutes earlier, you'd have seen casual, relaxed mixed-sex play. John is a leader. He's dominant, assertive, and draws attention to himself. He's exactly the kind of boy researchers notice, and therein lies a major problem with the two-cultures model—*who* gets studied. The focus is usually on kids (like John) who behave the way they're expected to—the dominant boys and the passive girls. Kids who don't fit the pattern get ignored. Most boys, for example, aren't "dominant" most of the time. A hierarchy needs a lot of subordinates. Thorne sees "a skew toward the most visible and dominant" that leads to a silencing and marginalization of the majority.[58] She sees a "big man bias" in research on children, which equates the behavior of male elites with "typical" boy behavior. "Other kinds of boys may be mentioned, but not as the core of the gender story." However, more than half of the boys in a classroom she examined intensively did *not* fit into the rigid stereotype of the way boys are supposed to behave.

This bias is not limited to research. Many of the popular new books written for parents about how boys get shortchanged in school (e.g., *The War Against Boys* by Christina Hoff Sommers[59] and *The Wonder of Boys* by Michael Gurian[60]) portray only one kind of boy. He's dominant, rough-and-tumble, assertive, fidgety, and rather inarticulate. But many boys are not like that at all. They're not physically aggressive and not sports-minded; they are highly verbal, love to read, and are able to converse on a high level with adults.

In one of the classrooms Thorne observed, she found four boys— Jeremy, Scott, Bill, and Don—whose relationships were exactly like the intimate, sharing modes of connecting that are usually ascribed to girls.[61] "Jeremy, who had a creative imagination, spun fantasy worlds with one boy at a time . . . acting as detectives tracking footprints on the playground. Jeremy and his partner would share treasured objects." The identity of Jeremy's adventuring partner of the moment shifted between the boys via a "breakup" process often claimed to be typical of girls. "The boy on the outs would sometimes sulk and talk about the other two behind their backs." When Scott was excluded, he would activate a long-standing affiliation with Don. When Bill was on the outs, he went solo. "Over the course of the school year I saw each of the shifting pairs, Jeremy and Bill, Jeremy and Scott, Scott and Don—celebrate themselves as 'best buddies.'" The pattern of their relationships, Thorne says, "fit the shifting alliances claimed to typify girls' social relationships, but *boys* were the protagonists."

Toy Story

If childhood relationships between the sexes are more alike than different, what about the toys and games kids play with? Many children tend to prefer toys designed for their sex. Are such preferences due to deep-seated, inborn differences, as many experts and laypeople have assumed? Or can they be traced to early stereotyping, so that by the time kids are old enough to choose their own toys, they know what's for boys and what's for girls?

Experiences logged in the Fisher-Price experimental laboratory are revealing on this point.[62] The manager of the lab, Kathleen Alfano, noted that girls and boys will play with anything—from toy trains to vacuum cleaners—until age three. Then they go straight for the stereotypes. Girls gravitate toward art items, dolls, telephones, small manipulative toys like play dough, and pretend play accessories, like jewelry and hairpins. In contrast, boys prefer such toys as small blocks, vehicles, riding toys, tools, and balls. Why?

Their parents may have a role in this pattern. In the Fisher-Price lab, which encourages cross-gender play, boys lingered over a toy stove even longer than girls did. However, mothers bought it for their daughters, not their sons. Girls loved a fire truck that squirted real water, but parents usually bought it for boys. Once, when seven-year-old girls had finished painting their nails with polish and left the area, the seven-year-old boys descended and "spent the longest time painting their nails and drying them." Could boys get away with this at home or in school? Probably not. As Alfano said, "This is a safe environment. It's not the real world."

We've all seen kids heading for "gendered" toys starting at about age three or four and there may be a good reason for that. By age three or four, children go through a developmental phase in which they become less secure about what sex they really are. Sex-stereotyped toys help reassure them. It's a time when many girls who had shown no interest in dresses start asking for princess outfits, and boys gravitate to more "boyish" things. But children tend to outgrow this rigidity even if their parents don't.

Nor do the toy companies. Although their own research suggests that boys and girls will play with a wide range of toys, companies often heighten stereotypes. After years spent promoting a unisex approach to toys, many companies are now pushing aisles for boys and aisles for girls harder than ever—because this approach is more profitable. As sociologist Michael Kimmel says, in big toy stores "the gulf between His and Her sides looms like the parted Red Sea, and woe to him who strolls inadvertently into Barbie-land from Land of the Action Figures. It's not simply those cute blue-and-pink blankets anymore; everything is coded."[63]

Girls may be just as eager as boys to pick out a soccer ball, especially if it is displayed in a general sports aisle and not in a boy's aisle. If girls' participation in youth soccer, Little League, track and field, basketball, and swimming is any indication, sports may appeal equally to girls and boys. Fifteen years ago, no one would have predicted the explosion in girls' sports; but it happened.

Imagining the Future

The bottom line is that that when we all buy into boy–girl innate differences, we're limiting both sexes and, oddly enough, not preparing either sex adequately for the world as it currently exists. When we assume boys won't play with the nurturing and house-care toys—even though research shows they will—we're telling them that nurturing and domestic chores are not part of their future. But if we don't encourage boys to play with the toy vacuum cleaners now, they're going to need five "queer" guys showing them how to play with it when they grow up or risk losing the girl. If we don't encourage girls to play competitive sports and learn to "gut it out," they're going to be less prepared to enter a highly competitive workforce that demands that we do indeed "gut it out."

The message being sent by many scientists who study child development is that children are more flexible than some theorists—and much of the popular media—acknowledge or allow.[64] Children are not doomed to one-dimensional lives by the power of mothering, nor by behaviors cemented into their psyches by prehistory, nor by the sex-segregated playgrounds of childhood. Overall, science tells us, much of what we understand as "gender" is a social construct that we ourselves build, rather than something we inherit. Small differences between the sexes are blown out of proportion and take on nearly mythic dimensions. From minutiae like separate toy aisles to color-coded clothing to grand theories of how boys and girls learn and think differently, we have spun an elaborate fantasy about the sexes that is not moored to the solid dock of fact. We are only starting to realize the extent to which this is true. Our own actions and attitudes can indeed change the shape of the world that will be our children's legacy.

The Self-Esteem Swan Dive

ACCORDING TO HARVARD'S Carol Gilligan, adolescence is "a watershed in female development, a time when girls are in danger of drowning or disappearing."[1] This is the picture she drew from her widely publicized 1990 Dodge Study at the Emma Willard School, a private girls school in Troy, New York. In spite of the problems with this study (which we explore below), Gilligan's ideas have had amazing staying power. Her theme of decline for girls was echoed in 1994 by clinical psychologist Mary Pipher's surprise best-seller, *Reviving Ophelia*, which spent 135 weeks on the *New York Times* paperback best-seller list.[2] Drawing on case studies rather than systematic research, Pipher observed how naturally outgoing, confident girls get worn down by sexist cultural expectations. She argued that even though the girls she profiled were in therapy, they were typical, "normal" girls. The ideas espoused by Gilligan and Pipher were supported by a widely cited study by the American Association of University Women.[3] The 1990 AAUW study claimed that teenage girls experience a "free-fall in self-esteem from which some will never recover."

The barrage of dire predictions of a self-esteem swan dive—which received major play in the press—threw parents of young girls into a panic. A whole industry sprang up to help girls and their families cope with the inevitable crisis. The National Ophelia Project was founded in 1997 and continues to run workshops around the country; its most recent national conference was held in Pittsburgh in 2003.[4] Under its auspices, the Tampa YWCA staged a forum for middle schoolers in 2003 and four county public schools are running ongoing programs.[5] Mother–daughter book clubs, like one in Denver, were inspired by Pipher's book, along with countless summer camp and school programs.[6] A major Canadian corporation, Lever Pond, funded an ongoing project for 125,000 members of Boys and Girls Clubs in 2000.[7] Pipher's book has become a reference tool for educators, therapists, parents, teachers, and counselors. *Time* noted, "For troubled adolescent girls, and the people who love them, the best-selling *Reviving Ophelia* is a sacred text."[8]

The self-esteem swan dive story was trumpeted by the media. Early in the 1990s, news stories asked, "Teenage Turning Point: Does Adolescence Herald the Twilight of Girls' Self-Esteem?"[9] and promoted "the great teen girls self-esteem robbery."[10] The tide has not abated; recent media stories are as enchanted with girls' loss of self-esteem as ever. The *Hartford Courant* reported, "These days the female adolescent crisis is a known black hole in a parent's universe."[11] Note that the self-esteem crisis is no longer presented as a theory posited by a few researchers but now appears as unquestioned fact. Readers are not told that this information is in question.

Why did mothers whose daughters were playing a mean game of soccer—and were much more daring than the moms had ever been—suddenly become so worried about their girls? Perhaps they became concerned because they realized how challenging the future would be for their daughters. In a world in which demands were increasingly placed on girls to be independent and self-sufficient, Gilligan's well-publicized message was especially scary. If our daughters were going to face a world in which they had to earn their own way, achieve, and be independent, then losing their voices at an early age would be a disaster. Another likely reason for mothers' uneasiness was that they may have been remembering their own teenage years, when girls were told to never let a man see that you were smart, never beat a man at anything, and concentrate on your looks. In those days no one worried about teenage girls losing their voice—they weren't supposed to have one in the first place. Mothers who bought the Pipher book probably remembered how hard it had been for them to break free. The last thing they wanted for their daughters was to fall prey to the same messages they themselves had battled through. So widely did Pipher's idea spread that it became what social scientists call a "bandwagon"—a notion that takes off like a runaway train, moving far beyond its mooring in research or reality.

No wonder caring mothers became hypervigilant. Even mothers who weren't inclined to worry were affected. One woman, whose daughters are now college age, vividly remembers the angst she experienced after reading *Reviving Ophelia.* At the time, her girls were 10 and 12, and seemed to be fine, playing "heavy-duty sports" and getting good grades in math and science. After she read *Reviving Ophelia*, she started to worry about "things I'd never even considered." The only messages around, she recalled, were about how girls were losing their voice and facing inevitable crises. "There wasn't any other view—nothing to compare it to." As it turned out, both girls did fine and had no overwhelming adolescent crisis. Looking back, this mother now thinks she put herself through the wringer needlessly.

In her therapy practice, RB sees a number of hypervigilant mothers. For example, one mother wanted to go back to work but worried that her daughter would face a self-esteem crisis if she weren't at home seeing to her every emotional need. After all, Pipher suggests that women encourage their daughters to open up, to examine their lives in the company of an empathic, accepting mother. Mothers, she says, are "their daughters' shelter from the storm." Some mothers took this advice too literally—as this one did, asking, "What would my daughter do if she couldn't get hold of me? How would she manage? How will she handle problems with her friends?" Finally the mother went to work and the daughter—much to her mother's astonishment—was delighted that mom was no longer hovering all the time. Overprotective moms can unintentionally sabotage their daughters' self-confidence and independence.

Should parents watch their daughters like a hawk—even if they seem hardy and independent? Yes, if Carol Gilligan is right in saying that adolescent girls are headed for disaster. But scientists show that this vigilance may be misdirected.

The Vanishing Voice

Gilligan's Dodge Study was based on a small, highly nonrepresentative sample of girls attending an elite private all-girls school in the Northeast.[12] As Gilligan herself notes, "The isolated setting of the residential school and the walled enclosure made it something of a strange island in the stream of contemporary living; an odd mixture of old world and new."[13] Although she and her team interviewed 144 girls, no data were presented on the whole sample. Only eight girls were quoted in the book, leaving researchers to wonder how typical they were of the group. What were the other 136 girls experiencing? How would boys have responded to the interviewers' questions? Because the study is so limited and has no control group, it presents nothing more than interesting stories about an elite group of girls. There is no way of knowing whether these girls are even representative of the girls in their school—much less of girls in general. Further, there is no way of knowing whether these girls' problems are tied to any real-world outcomes. Do they do less well in school? Do they have different career choices? Do they finish college? All we have is a snapshot of one point in time. In this study, the questions were open-ended, and the answers subject to any interpretation. This sort of study, according to social critic Wendy Kaminer, is "useless, because interpretations of the answer[s] are hopelessly subjective."[14]

Because of their caring nature, Gilligan believes, female adolescents' experience of the world is difficult and differs from the world of young boys. "I heard girls speak about storms in relationships and pleasure in relationships revealing a knowledge of relationships that often was grounded in detailed descriptions of inner psychic words—

relational worlds through which girls sometimes moved freely and which at other times seemed blocked or walled. Listening for this knowledge, I felt myself entering, to some extent, the underground city of female adolescence."[15]

In Gilligan's worldview, boys have no comprehension of this "underground city," so detached are they from feelings and connections. But Barrie Thorne and others present clear evidence that boys too experience "relational storms," breakups, and disconnections. Even more disturbing is Gilligan's idea of the world awaiting these adolescent girls—a place filled with terror, violence, and threats. For Gilligan, girls are like tuning forks, vibrating to all the evils of the world. Are girls, she wonders, uniquely vulnerable to "the problems of violence in the world that they are entering as young women?"[16] Adolescence, she says, is a time when "girls are in danger of knowing the unseen and speaking the unspoken." She sees adolescent girls struggling with two choices: "being a good [i.e., caring and selfless] woman or . . . being selfish." Gilligan clearly links girls' self-esteem problems to the conflict between their relational natures and the demands of independence and achievement they encounter as they grow.[17] She adds, "They may be especially prone to notice the compliance of women to male authority."

Does Ophelia Need Reviving?

Echoing Gilligan, one after another pop psychology book proclaims that girls, especially adolescent girls, are headed for the therapist's couch because of the difficulties they will inevitably encounter as they progress through their teen years. They lose their voice, their self-regard takes a dive, they are prone to depression, eating disorders, and self-destructive behavior. Many of these books proclaim that the root cause of girls' universal malady lies in the conflict between their inherent nature and the demands of the adult world. Gilligan believes that because of their innate caring and selflessness, girls are ill prepared for the dog-eat-dog world beyond school. Mary Pipher, who cites Gilligan in her book, uses similar language but puts more emphasis on what she calls the "media saturated, girl-poisoning culture."[18] She says that cultural pressures on girls to be selfless and concerned about others weigh heavily on them. "Girls stop thinking, 'Who am I? What do I want?' and start thinking 'What must I do to please others?'"[19]

Pipher's *Reviving Ophelia*, the best-selling of these books, is based on the observations of a therapist who reported on her experiences with a small number of adolescent girls in psychotherapy.[20] Pipher does not say how many girls she saw in therapy, noting only that "I was mostly seeing white girls in therapy and I wrote about what I knew."[21] She also claims, "My clients are not different from girls who are not seen in therapy."[22] But since she has no control group, there's no way to know that this is true. It is highly unlikely that young adolescent girls who seek therapy are just like those who do not. In her examples, again and again Pipher writes of girls who were sexually abused, who witnessed parental suicides and violence, who abused drugs.

Popular worry about girls' self-esteem was also sparked by findings from the 1990 AAUW study[23] popularized in the book *Shortchanging Girls, Shortchanging America: A Call to Action* (1991).[24] The AAUW surveyed approximately 3,000 nine- to fifteen-year-olds, focusing on attitudes toward the self, family, friends, and school. This study was never submitted for scientific review, the accepted route to publication. Nevertheless, its main finding—the shocking suggestion that "little girls lose their self-esteem on the way to adolescence," appeared on the first page of the *New York Times*.[25] The book received worldwide attention and reignited concern about self-esteem issues in women and girls. The study breathed new life into scores of popular books assuming that females have substantially lower self-esteem than males and prescribing cures ranging from enrollment in single-sex schools to intensive programs in self-esteem training, for example, *Girl Stuff: A Survival Guide to Growing Up; Soul Searching: A Girl's Guide to Finding Herself; Brave New Girls: Creative Ideas to Help Girls Be Confident, Healthy, and Happy;* and *Girlwise: How to Be Confident, Capable, Cool, and in Control.*

Are Girls Unhappy?

The urgency about improving the self-esteem of teenage girls rests on the implicit assumption that high self-esteem is important because it is associated with a variety of constructive life choices or at least damps down destructive behaviors. On the positive end of the social spectrum, individuals with high self-esteem tend to be socially active, do volunteer work, and get involved in politics.[26] At the other end, researchers and educators have tried to link self-esteem scores to such negative outcomes as teenage pregnancy, use of alcohol, drug abuse, and deviant behavior (e.g., stealing, destroying property). Does this issue affect only girls? There has been no national outcry over boys' self-esteem. Should there be? These are critical questions. Before we get to the answers, we need to be clear about what exactly we mean by self-esteem: a generalized feeling of self-acceptance, goodness, worthiness, and self-respect. Those who believe that there is a national self-esteem crisis among young girls assume that the picture is much different for boys. But is it?

So much has been made of this issue that we expect boys and girls to be very different. Historically many scholars and serious writers have concluded that women and men differ in self-esteem, with men having the edge. Freud, for example, postulated that the female child experiences unconscious feelings of inferiority on realizing that she lacks a penis and "develops, like a scar, a sense of inferiority."[27] Psychoanalyst Karen Horney agreed that the little girl sees herself as comparatively disadvantaged in that she lacks a penis.[28] But according to Horney, the little girl's envy is based on the realistic assessment that she has fewer possibilities for gratification of her goals than does the little boy.[29] Horney's theme of disadvantage has been echoed by many others. Social psychologists point to a variety of social and cultural factors that collectively disadvantage, devalue, and disempower women.[30] These factors include an ongoing societal preference for males, a higher valuation of male over female attributes, negative stereotypes of women, minority group status, and institutional barriers that limit women's aspirations, potential for achievement, and economic advancement. Second-class status doesn't do a lot for self-esteem.

For Gilligan and Pipher, early adolescence is a watershed time for females, but not males. "Perhaps adolescence is an especially critical time in woman's development because it poses a problem of connection that is not easily resolved," Gilligan writes; it is a time when girls are marginalized and silenced.[31] Mary Pipher says that "junior high is when girls begin to fade academically." Why? Partly from "a shift girls make at this time from a focus on achievement to a focus on affiliation."[32] One girl who nearly flunked seventh grade told Pipher: "All I care about is my friends. Grades don't matter to me."[33]

Adolescent boys, on the other hand, are thought to be just fine as far as their self-esteem is concerned. But two important meta-analyses of self-esteem illuminate this issue and throw this assumption into doubt. In one, Brenda Major of the University of California–Santa Barbara and her colleagues analyzed scores of 82,569 participants.[34] In the other, Janet Hyde of the University of Wisconsin reviewed tests of 44,162 males and 52,431 females, conducted between 1987 and 1995.[35] Hyde wanted to know whether the AAUW results fit with those from peer-reviewed studies, so she included the AAUW data. In an attempt to be very thorough, Hyde and her colleagues also included data from three major national longitudinal studies that followed some 50,000 high school children across their young adult years.

The story these carefully conducted analyses tell us is very different from the headlines we have all read. Hyde's team found that the differences between boys and girls were very small,[36] and Major reported similar results.[37] Once again the within-gender difference is far greater than the between-gender difference. In fact, the overlap in self-esteem scores is well over 90 percent. Figure 10.1 starkly illustrates this similarity. Note how closely this figure matches the ones in Chapter 7 on math and verbal ability. There is simply no evidence here of girls' lagging self-esteem.

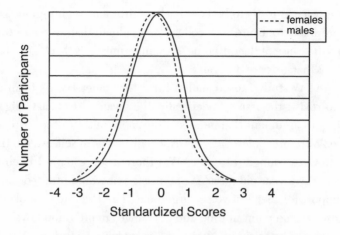

Adapted from K. C. Kling, J. S. Hyde, C. J. Showers, & B. N. Buswell, "Gender differences in self-esteem: A meta-analysis." *Psychological Bulletin* 125 (1999): 470–500.

FIGURE 10.1 Gender Differences in Self-Esteem

As for the influential AAUW study, critics found many faults.[38] When children were asked about their self-confidence and academic plans, 60 percent of girls and 69 percent of boys in elementary school said, "I am happy the way I am." But in high school, the percentage of girls happy with themselves fell to 29 percent. Could it be that 71 percent of the country's teenage girls were low in self-esteem? Not necessarily. Critics noted that the AAUW counted as happy *only* the girls who checked "always true" to the "happy" question. Girls who said they were "sometimes" happy with themselves or "sort of" happy with themselves were counted as *unhappy*. A more accurate count would show that only 12 percent of girls and 8 percent of boys were low in self-esteem.[39]

Another way of interpreting the AAUW results, suggests Wendy Kaminer, is that "girls are less complacent and more ambitious than boys, and more likely to hold themselves to high standards of performance."[40] In fact, eighth-grade girls are twice as likely to aspire to a business, professional, or managerial career than boys; eighth-grade boys are twice as likely to be held back as girls; and twelfth-grade girls are more likely to aspire to a college or graduate degree than boys.[41] Perhaps the cause of the difference, Kaminer muses, is that "boys are in a rut," not that girls are miserable.

The AAUW study caused such a furor that Janet Hyde's team decided to revisit the issue. Specifically, they wanted to test Gilligan's and Pipher's argument that gender differences in self-esteem are age specific. Were preadolescent girls especially lower in self-esteem than kids who were younger or older? Was there a self-esteem trench for nine- to twelve-year-old girls? If one existed, it would offer considerable support for the "lost voice" argument. The Hyde team looked at both sexes at one point in time and at changes in girls' and boys' self-esteem scores over time (National Longitudinal Study of Youth). What did they find? Whichever way they looked at the data, they found *no* evidence of a large gender difference in self-esteem emerging in early adolescence. In fact, the difference was tiny and in some cases favored girls.[42]

These findings were so different from those of the AAUW that the researchers were startled. They decided to take a much closer look at the AAUW data to see how that study could have reported such huge gender differences.[43] Hyde found that among fifteen- to eighteen-year-olds in the AAUW study, the male advantage was *twice* that of any other study. Furthermore, the AAUW claimed that gender differences in self-esteem increase with age during adolescence. Yet Hyde's analyses found self-esteem in both males and females between ages thirteen and thirty-two to be "relatively stable."[44]

How could this be? How could the AAUW findings be so different from what everybody else found? First, the AAUW constructed its own scale of self-esteem rather than use one of the several well-established scales. There is no way of knowing how their unusual results were affected by this previously untested measure of self-esteem. Second, the sample size for the preadolescent group was much smaller than in the other studies, so it's possible that the AAUW results were inflated by the relatively small numbers of subjects. Third, the AAUW data were collected at one point in time, whereas the national data were collected at several points over time. Notably, the AAUW can't legitimately claim that gender differences change over time because the children were not followed over time.[45]

Despite these findings, worries about girls' self-esteem continue to percolate through the media, perhaps because self-esteem has been called critical to academic achievement. Parents, corporations, and organizations rushed to remedy the gender difference in self-esteem in order to boost girls' school performance. The popular Take Your Daughter to Work Day grew out of this concern, and self-esteem seminars for women began to dot the landscape. But is self-esteem in fact linked to academic success? Social critic Alfie Kohn finds that the empirical evidence "offers meager support" for claims that self-esteem has a major impact on academic performance.[46] A review of 128 studies relating self-esteem to academic achievement found that differences in self-esteem can account for only about 4–7 percent of variation in academic performance. At the same time, academic achievement can account for only 4–7 percent of variation in self-esteem.[47] Morris Rosenberg of Cornell University, who developed the most widely used measure of self-esteem, concluded that self-esteem "appears to have little or no effect in enhancing academic performance."[48]

Importantly, little attention has been paid to intriguing contradictions in the scientific literature. Blacks in general score higher than whites in self-esteem. In the AAUW study, for example, black girls scored higher than both white girls and white boys, and black boys scored highest of all. Although much is made of improving girls' (i.e., white girls') self-esteem as a means of boosting their academic prospects, the group that is most at risk academically—black males—scored the highest in self-esteem. How is this possible? Because school performance is not the be-all-and-end-all for determining self-esteem. Research suggests that many young black men look to sports or music or to some area of life other than academics for their sense of self-esteem.[49] If black males have high self-esteem but are the group most at risk for low academic performance, there can't be a simple link between self-esteem and

achievement. It's a complex issue, one that needs thoughtful consideration and review, not boxcar headlines.

So, what are we to make of the "crisis" in girls' self-esteem? Why have
so many people uncritically accepted the unscientifically based thesis of
Ophelia and the skewed AAUW results? Perhaps one major reason for
the worry about girls was the changing nature of the media culture.
Pipher put her finger on this: "The script families have is about raising
wholesome, well-adjusted, productive individuals. The script the culture
has is primarily about selling people products and encouraging people to
be hedonistic consumers and to do what feels good at the moment."[50]
Parents, understandably concerned about noxious, hypersexual media
images, may have gazed in horror at those images while underestimating
the resilience of their daughters, who were able to thrive in spite of them.
In any event, a sophisticated look at the self-esteem data is far more reassuring than the headlines. Unfortunately, the "crisis" is a myth that has
created undue anxiety in parents and a rash of misguided social reactions.

Single-Sex Schools

Perhaps the most dramatic social reaction to the self-esteem scare was a
major effort to resurrect the single-sex classroom. Girls, it was said,
would flourish in a protected environment, safe from the demands of
male competition and aggression. Diane Pollard of the University of
Wisconsin specifically cites the AAUW study on self-esteem as a major
impetus to the single-sex school movement.[51]

The idea that women and men learn in different ways was the second
linchpin of the revived single-sex school movement. One private school
for girls in Toronto (grades 4–9) was set up specifically to implement
Carol Gilligan's theories. The headmistress said that the school carefully built its cooperative structure on the basis of ideas about how girls
learn best. She cites Gilligan's Dodge Study and says that girls in her
school would be able to benefit from the special "women's ways of
knowing" that would make education so much more effective for

them.[52] And the *New York Times* reports that a private Catholic school in Ohio, Ursuline College, offers a core curriculum based largely on the book *Women's Ways of Knowing*.[53] The authors of that book, psychologist Mary Belenky and her colleagues, argue that girls and women have more trouble than boys and men in asserting their authority or considering themselves authorities, in expressing themselves in public, and in gaining respect for their minds and their ideas. In the classroom, they say, women "often are unheard, even when they believe they have something important to say." Classrooms, they argue, "need to be more responsive to women's special ways of knowing."[54] One parent echoed this idea when she explained to the *New York Times* why she was sending her kindergarten-age daughter to an all-girls school. "I think girls' schools can teach to girls in a very concentrated way at the younger ages, teaching the way girls learn best."[55]

In the mid-1990s, proposals for new single-sex schools and classrooms began to pop up all over the country. In 1997, California Governor Pete Wilson set up six all-boys and six all-girls schools.[56] At the same time, other such schools opened their doors, including the Seattle Girls School and others in Minnesota, New York, and elsewhere. More numerous were single-sex classes within coed public schools, some designed to help kids learn, others designed to improve discipline and behavior. As this book is being written, President George W. Bush has called for more single-sex public schools, saying that he believes Title IX, which forbids gender discrimination in schools, should not stand in the way.[57]

Are single-sex schools the way to go? Not because of a difference in self-esteem between boys and girls, because, as we've seen, that doesn't exist. Maybe these separate schools are needed because of the special "women's ways of knowing" that makes girls learn differently from boys. But do the sexes, in fact, learn differently? Some theorists certainly think so. Belenky and her associates built on Carol Gilligan's observation that women have been left out of the theory-building studies in psychology and education.[58] To rectify this omission, they, like Gilligan, decided to listen only to women. Their intent was to learn about women's qualities as "learners and knowers." Based on open-ended interviews with 135 women from various backgrounds and educational institutions, they concluded that to learn, women need two basic conditions:

1. Confirmation that they could be "trusted to know and to learn"
2. Acceptance as a "person" as opposed to oppression and patronization

They further concluded that girls were drawn to the sort of knowledge that emerges from firsthand observation, not the abstract "out-of-context" learning typical of most schools. Specifically, women preferred to learn by moving from their own personal experiences to abstractions. Finally, all of the women wanted a system in which knowledge flowed in two directions, from teacher to student and from student to teacher.

Sounds wonderful; however, wouldn't male students also endorse these conditions? We'll never know, since no men were included in this study. But other evidence suggests that students—female and male alike—would benefit from the kinds of educational practices advocated by the women studied by the Belenky team. Indeed, the principles supposedly needed for women to flourish in school sound very much like the principles advocated by many charter and independent schools as well as by public schools that can afford these innovations. Who wouldn't want class sizes small enough to provide hands-on learning, group interaction, and one-on-one teacher–pupil exchanges? All children thrive in such educational environments, and the debate about whether teaching should progress from abstraction to specifics or vice versa goes on at all educational levels and at all types of schools. Moreover, hands-on experience is a requirement for entrance into perhaps the most male-dominated of all schools, graduate schools of business administration. Women's ways of knowing appear to be exactly like men's ways of knowing. In fact, sociologist Cynthia Epstein finds no evidence of psychological or cognitive differences between the sexes that would make them learn differently, and says that the "evidence" for the need for single-sex education is highly suspect.[59] "Many social science studies [of sex-based differences] do not support the idea that deep-rooted male and female natures require separate education or that segregated education can provide members of each sex with the same opportunities and development of skills."[60]

But if girls don't have different ways of learning, aren't they better off in all-female environments, free from the disrupting effects of boys? It has been argued that boys—whether scholars or troublemakers—suck up all the oxygen in the classroom; when boys are around, girls lose confidence and become passive and distracted and their self-esteem dips. Safety lies only in segregation. For example, picking up on Gilligan's language, the head of the Seattle Girls School says, "For me, having girls in an all-girl environment is an answer to making sure they don't lose their voices, that they stay strong, involved, all those good things."[61]

But even as some educators were talking about how caring, selfless, relational girls were losing their self-esteem and becoming quiet and passive, others were painting a totally different picture. "Mean Girls," as we've seen, became a banner headline around the country, even grabbing cover stories in the *New York Times Magazine*[62] and *Newsweek.*[63] "Relational aggression" became the topic du jour. Girls' lives were made miserable by petty jealousies, exclusive cliques, backbiting, and shifting alliances. In one school, kids told of leaving a message on a girl's answering machine, knowing the girl's parents would be the first ones to pick up the message: "Hello, it's me. Have you gotten your pregnancy test back yet?"[64] In another school, an outgoing, athletic, learning-disabled girl becomes the butt of cruel teasing from her "good friends." "I'm not that bright," says sixteen-year-old Heather. To escape the teasing, Heather goes into the backroom of her best friend Chelsea's basement. She lies on the floor and stares at the ceiling. She thinks how she wants to be a different person, how she is stuck because it is so hard to make new friends. Her dream is to transfer to a new school where she can stay quiet to avoid sounding stupid. "That's when I go home, yell at my mom, put on Eminem and go to sleep." She likes the singer because "he raps about how everything sucks and that's how I feel."[65]

How "safe" does this sound? How wonderful is this girl culture for building self-esteem? So much for the caring, cooperative, noncompetitive, nonaggressive world of teenage girls. Would being in a school without boys change this? Unlikely. As Emory University historian Elizabeth Fox-Genovese notes, "Those who have experienced dismissal by the junior-high-school girls' clique could hardly with a straight face claim generosity and nurture as a natural attribute of women."[66]

High Achievers

If single-sex schools aren't safe havens where self-esteem blossoms, and if girls don't have a special way of knowing, do these schools somehow provide a rigorous learning environment in which girls thrive academically? Some do—but some don't. The "Seven Sisters" colleges historically did well for women not because they produced safe, noncompetitive environments, but because they were highly selective and challenged the women they admitted to be as rigorous, competitive, and achievement oriented as men. Not surprisingly, many of the very bright women they recruited went on to successful careers: Madeline Albright (Wellesley), Gloria Steinem (Smith), Geraldine Ferraro (Marymount), and Katharine Hepburn (Bryn Mawr).

But many single-sex classrooms today are quite the opposite of the Seven Sisters. Instead of defying gender stereotypes, they reinforce them. Ironically, girls may be at risk in the single-sex classrooms that are designed to help them. A 2001 Ford Foundation report on Governor Pete Wilson's failed experiment noted that "traditional gender stereotypes were often reinforced in the single-gender academies. Boys tended to be taught in more regimented, traditional and individualistic fashion, and girls in more nurturing, co-operative and open environments."[67] Girls, the educators said, were told they had broader career options than in the past, but "they were also applauded for being feminine and being concerned about their appearance."[68]

Since successful women's schools often bucked the feminine stereotype, the findings of the California study are troubling. The California schools reinforced rather than challenged prevailing gender stereotypes. The Ford Report noted that "most educators did not adequately reflect upon the hidden or covert gender biases (to the disadvantage of both boys and girls) that often existed in the schools."[69] And, the Ford observers noted, the state of California did not provide guidance or special training in this area. This is probably typical of what would happen in most states, hard-strapped for the cash needed to support public schools. In the California schools, says the Ford Report, gender was portrayed in an "essentialist manner" as if girls and boys were very different.

This essentialism harms boys as much as girls. Valerie Lee, a professor of education at the University of Michigan, compared coed high schools with all-boys and all-girls independent high schools.[70] She found sexism in all the schools, but it was the most severe in the all-boys schools. This finding suggests that without daily interactions between genders to contradict the messages being sent by the media, boys have little chance to learn nonsexist behavior.

Moreover, the all-girls schools "perpetuated a pernicious form of sexism: academic dependence and non-rigorous instruction." For example, in all-girls chemistry classes, "undue attention was paid to neatness and cleanliness as well as to drawing parallels between domesticity and chemistry activities."[71] Wendy Kaminer (a Smith grad) calls the sexism in many new girls schools "insidious." She says that these schools have an approach to teaching that assumes a female penchant for cooperative or "connected" learning.[72] If girls are taught only in a cooperative, touchy-feely, "essentialist" manner, they may be missing out on the rigor that educational excellence demands. The idea that girls are fragile and "relational" has led some teachers to set up classrooms in which girls are never asked to defend their work or critique the work of others. Such classrooms may be safe but are hardly challenging—and they do not prepare girls for the world into which they will graduate.

There's another important downside to setting up segregated learning environments, notes Wendy Kaminer.[73] Many institutions for women and girls support female academic achievement but discourage competition with males. They encourage women to separate their social and intellectual lives, reinforcing the dissonance bred into many achievement-oriented females. Perhaps the best remedy, suggests Kaminer, lies not in legislation or in single-sex schools, but in the positive experience males gain from interacting with intelligent female classmates and colleagues. As a University of Virginia college athlete, Lindsay Walsh, puts it, "We [men and women] race against each other in practice, we cheer for each other at the regattas. When you are together with guys, striving under pressure for a common goal, a bond develops that helps you understand each other. We see our male teammates as close friends, not weekend dating material."[74]

Many young women today feel that the emphasis on "protecting" them is outdated and far from their concerns. An Alexandria, Virginia, senior, Lee Sparks, said that her friends don't fit the idea of girls as wilting flowers that advocates of single-sex education portray. At a three-week leadership conference sponsored by the American Legion, Sparks said, "The women in charge kept assuming that we felt we were limited in what we could achieve simply because we were females. They kept talking about female empowerment—telling us that we could make it, even though we were women. The girls were laughing about it because we never thought that being a female would keep us from succeeding." She thinks that older women don't realize how much her generation has profited from the feminist movement. "In most of my classes, the girls are the ones who excel above and beyond the boys. We expect to be able to excel and don't think twice about it."[75]

A Word of Warning

The studies we've reviewed conclude that the magnitude of gender difference in self-esteem is very small and unlikely to have important consequences, that girls don't learn in different ways from boys, and that single-sex schools may create as many problems as they solve. Overprotective parents obsessed with their daughters' self-esteem may unconsciously be communicating a message that they are too vulnerable to compete and achieve. As Janet Hyde and her colleagues warn, "If parents believe that their daughters have lower self-esteem than their sons, they may behave in ways that telegraph this message to their children . . . if girls believe they have lower self-esteem than boys and behave accordingly, it may be especially detrimental to their development."[76]

We saw exactly the same pattern with math ability. Girls are perfectly able to succeed in this arena, but the stereotypes say exactly the opposite—and parents believe them. As Professor Sylvia Rimm of Case Western Reserve Medical School notes, "It's really, really important not to overprotect our girls." She reports that in a study of 1,200 adult females, winning in competitive situations was identified most frequently as a positive event in childhood.[77]

Most young girls do not need special protection or self-esteem workshops to arm themselves against the "onslaught" of self-deprecation. But if parents heed the media story lines, they may wind up harming the daughters they are trying to protect.

The Road Ahead

IN CHAPTER 1, WE SAID that while the "difference" narrative is familiar, the *Same Difference* story, though firmly backed by reliable science, is much less so. The first narrative magnifies the differences between the sexes and slights the similarities. We have no illusions that this story line will be easy to change. What we've called the seduction of difference is palpable—even for women—and there's great irony in this.

Why would women living at a time of unprecedented professional success buy into the idea that men are from Mars and women from you know where? Or that men and women can't talk to each other? As they flood into college courses, why would they accept as immutable truth that women are less aggressive, less logical, emotionally weaker, and more naturally dependent than men? It may be that unlike older gender difference theories, which saw women as weak and unambitious, newer versions present women as *better* than men. According to this fresh perspective, it's okay for women to say that men are stubborn, that they refuse to admit when they don't know something, that they won't even ask for directions. And this demotion of men from rational perfection to flawed humanity makes a lot of women feel better about themselves. At last, women can believe that men themselves have a range of flaws that they themselves transcend.

According to the new gender-difference story, women are paragons of care, emotional intelligence, and warmth, and to any woman faced with an uncommunicative partner, this makes intuitive sense. But, as we have seen, there is a decidedly *un*reassuring side to this reassurance. The "care reasoning" and "empathizing" pacifiers that essentialist theorists hand out belittle women's ability to use logic, understand facts, argue their point, and stand their ground. These theories put women on a pedestal of motherly goodness while simultaneously promoting an almost unreachable standard of innate empathy. And it's important to note that the economic costs of these lovely "female" virtues are rarely discussed. As critic Katha Pollitt notes, "Money must come from somewhere. If women leave to men the job of earning the family income (an option fewer and fewer families can afford), they will be economically dependent on their husbands, a situation that, besides carrying obvious risks in an age of frequent divorce, weakens their bargaining position in the family." Also, the loss of the woman's income would plunge millions of families into financial chaos.[1] As for men, gender-difference theory suggests that they have little input in the emotional life of the family—and are betraying their masculinity if they ask their wives to carry part of the economic burden. Since more and more men are in dual-earner couples, this theory is a recipe for guilt and recrimination.

The gender-difference narrative is also appealing because it helps rationalize the sex segregation and discrimination that still pervade our society. It's easier to believe that men and women have different capacities and inclinations because of their genes, their hormones, their motivation, or their brain structures than it is to take the necessary steps to expand the opportunities of both sexes.

The renewed popularity of gender-difference ideas may be the inevitable fallout from women's success and men's changing roles. Today, 70 percent of women are in the workforce, many in professional fields, and new national surveys show that men are doing more child care than ever before. In fact, men with working wives are spending nearly as much time with their children as their wives spend and the trend is upward. With these changes have come questions that nobody had to ask before and which don't have easy answers. Have the baby now or go for the promotion? If you're married, how do you combine work and family? How do you decide who does the dishes, drives the kids to school, works the late shift? What trade-offs do you make between job success and personal satisfaction?

Consider, too, that with earning power comes responsibility—and often stress. Women now have to deal with office politics, layoffs, downsizing, pressure to do more in less time. While they get many benefits from being in the workforce—particularly a buffer against depression—they also have to give up some of the exclusive duties and privileges of the domestic area. It can be hard for a woman to watch her baby giving the rapt attention to her daddy that was once the sole province of "mommy."

For men, gender-difference theory may appeal because it recalls a golden past when men had all the power, got all the good jobs, and rarely had to make a meal or bathe a child. But the sons of those "distant" fathers grew up feeling unconnected to their dads and often vowed not to be like them.

Media "scare stories" also support a return to the gender-difference narrative. Many of the current books and articles that support the gender-difference argument focus on the extremes. Alarmist stories about innate differences—and the dire consequences of violating them—make better copy than the truth about the millions of ordinary men and women who are raising families while holding responsible jobs, who are neither in crisis nor free from worry, who are both taking care of others and taking care of themselves. Too often their voices are drowned out by dramatic stories of unhappy people: anguished teenagers who have lost their voices, "mean girls" who brutalize and taunt their peers, mothers who leave good jobs because they are too frazzled at work, career women who lament passing up the chance to have children. There are male versions of these scare stories as well: men now seen as the second sex, men losing their masculinity as women get good jobs, husbands becoming "henpecked" as they relinquish their authority at home, and boys becoming victims of teachers who conduct a so-called war against boys.[2]

What is real here? Are women miserable at work and happy at home, or vice versa? Are girls caring or mean? Are women dropping out or forging ahead? Are men enjoying their children or losing their manhood when they change a diaper? It all seems utterly confusing—especially the picture presented by the media. Maybe men and women buy into these stories because today we are making it up as we go along, with few role models to guide us. But these extreme, polarizing snapshots distort reality and obscure the complexities of real people's lives.

Lost Connections

Another possible reason for the staying power of the gender-difference message is the passing of the industrial era and the opening of the age of globalization and instant information. More than a century ago, as the new machines of the industrial age obliterated the old rhythms of the agricultural era, society faced the same sort of change. People on farms and in small villages once worked to the rhythm of nature—in tune with the seasons, daybreak, and sunset. They exchanged this for mammoth, in-human factories that cared nothing for sunset and sunrise—much less the wants and desires of human beings. At the same time, women were being idealized as the angels of hearth and home, the only ones who maintained the human virtues of connection and caring in a cold, impersonal time.

Today, in a world of the 24/7 work week, at a time when we can't es-cape our cell phones, pagers, e-mail, and faxes, when our jobs may dis-appear overnight to some place we've never heard of halfway around the world, we once again mourn the loss of caring and connection. In his book, *Bowling Alone*, Robert Putnam decries the demise of commu-nity, and he's not the only one.[3] The simplicity movement arose to reject mass consumerism and overprogrammed lives, while protesters rioted against the faceless minions of the global corporate state. And voices rise through this din saying that when each sex takes its place—men making money, women changing diapers—we can return to the human virtues we so cherish. But of course that is impossible. (As it was in the industrial age. The birth of trade unionism—not women's virtues—finally made life bearable for many people.)

Despite the seductive backward pull of traditional views, the real story of the sexes is the same-difference narrative. Most contemporary social and economic forces are moving men and women toward being more alike than different. With modern medicine, most children in the developed world survive into adulthood, meaning that couples do not have to produce large families to ensure that at least some of their children will grow to maturity. Most women will spend many years in the workforce, with childbearing and child rearing consuming a much smaller portion of their lives than in the past. In this emerging world, gender will be less important than it was. Today, research tells us, differences in income, class, and education are far more powerful in shaping behavior than gender differences. Middle-class men and women are much more like each other than they are like low-income people of the same sex. But as long as we are tied to the gender-difference story, we won't look at the real issues that divide people—the ones we can actually do something about.

Happily, we are already seeing evidence that gender stereotypes are no longer the engine of human destiny. In the past few years a woman was U.S. secretary of state and two female senators were elected to represent California; women serve as police chiefs and as CEOs of Fortune 500 companies; women now compete in Olympic sports like hockey, basketball, and pole-vaulting. And men are taking an increasingly active role in raising the children and running the household. The old "Ozzie and Harriet" couple with the breadwinner husband and homemaker wife now accounts for less than a quarter of all American families—and even that number is likely to dwindle.

The Change Virus

While the difference narrative exerts a powerful backward pull, we can't ignore forces moving us in the opposite direction. We have chosen the metaphor "change virus" to describe the process of rapid cultural transformation we see all around us. "Virus" is the word that biologist Richard Dawkins used in discussing the way ideas spread.[4] Drawing on Dawkins's work, Susan Blackmore of the University of the West of England offered some ideas that are relevant to the future of the sexes and the same-difference argument.[5] Asking which concepts tend to be imitated and spread, she notes that the more visible ones travel fastest. So, to the degree that nontraditional women are gaining more access to jobs, power, politics, and the media, their lifestyles are spreading faster. Journalists, actors, athletes, and businesswomen are visible in public roles. "Non-traditional women today are spreading [ideas] of equality and independence for women," notes Blackmore.[6] In contrast, traditional women, who are more apt to be at home, do not have media visibility and are less likely to trigger the change virus.

At the same time, powerful messages about men's caring qualities are reaching larger and larger audiences. Consider Disney's blockbuster 2003 film, *Finding Nemo*, in which the father fish openly expresses his love for his son and risks his life to find Nemo after he is swept up in a diver's net. Nemo's dad soothes and cuddles him and expresses feelings of tenderness for his son; he's not a distant, heroic figure but an "average" fish, who asks directions and displays his fears. Consider too the rash of single dads and sensitive guys on primetime TV—from *Friends* to *Six Feet Under* to *Arrested Development*. Many contemporary films also depict changing gender roles—from the girl who becomes a Maori leader and saves her tribe in *Whale Rider*, to the teenage girls in love with soccer in *Bend It Like Beckham*, to *About a Boy*, in which selfish cad Hugh Grant becomes a real human being when he bonds with a twelve-year-old who needs a father. But, as behavior is rapidly changing, there is a strong undertow of myth and misinterpretation that threatens to make coping with these changes very difficult. These retro forces include essentialist ideas, conservative Christian calls for women to be submissive toward men, government policy initiatives that reward traditional but declining family forms while punishing dynamic new ones, and chipping away at women's reproductive rights.

As a society we continue to grapple with change in a patchwork way. The gender-difference argument is still a big part of the problem. It frames many of today's social issues in a way that is out of synch with what's really happening. And as long as we're stuck in old ways of thinking about problems, we keep coming up with the same tired solutions. For example, do the 70 percent of women in the workforce need care for their children? Gender-difference theories merely offer the mantra that a woman's real role is to be at home taking care of her children. Each individual has to solve her (and his) own problems. On the other hand, the same-difference approach frees us to discover a wide variety of new understandings and solutions. When they recognize their similarities, men and women can actually do something about their work and family conflicts. They can push for expanded family leave, more flexibility, adequate paid parental leave, family-friendly workplace policies—all of which we know improve the health and welfare of families. When father–infant bonding was made a high priority, Sweden created the "daddy month"—entitling fathers to paid time off during a child's infancy. Under an earlier policy only 2.8 percent of parents who took leave were fathers. Was this because they weren't hardwired for nurturing? Hardly. When the new policies—specifically designed to encourage men to take parental leave—were put into place, the results were astonishing. In 1999, 36.2 percent of parents taking leave were fathers.[7]

The best solutions that individuals—men and women—can come up with under our slap-dash, difference-oriented system are often fragile, temporary, and improvised. Consider the story of Barbara, a manager at a manufacturing firm in Boston. She has what seems like an ideal situation. "I job-share the management role with a man. I work three days a week, and he works two." She had to devise this solution herself, though. When Barbara felt she needed more time with her children, she went to her boss and said, "I've got to reduce my hours." Her boss was amenable and encouraged her to find a way. Barbara says, "I ended up combining my job with this guy Jim who had to reduce his workload because of his wife's traveling schedule. She had the higher salary, so he was currently working two days a week."

Both Barbara and her male colleague are nervous because "all eyes are on us if it doesn't work." Earlier Barbara had inquired about working a flexible schedule at other companies. "I did that for six months, and I couldn't find anything. Nobody was willing to do it." Some of Barbara's coworkers are envious and would like to have an arrangement like hers. But Barbara knows how tenuous her situation is. "If I didn't have my boss, I don't think I would be in this position."

A lot of elements had to fall into place to make Barbara's situation work: a supportive boss with a lot of power, the right coworker, and a big chunk of luck. Few employees can count on that winning combination. With all this, Barbara's situation is still precarious. Her supervisor could leave the company, or her job-sharing partner could decide this arrangement wasn't working for him anymore. Even if Barbara wanted to change her job to find a new challenge, she couldn't, since there is little hope of finding such flexibility elsewhere. And this is a success story—one the women in the *Opt-Out Revolution* article would have been delighted to find, as would many men. But in a gender-difference world, few would even dare ask.

How much better it would be for everyone if a same-difference solution were in place, built on the knowledge that both sexes want to have a family life as well as pursue a career. This realization would lead companies to create more formal alternative career options that would both retain valuable employees and allow people to combine their work-family lives in a way that works for them.

Throughout this book, we have heard voices chanting that we must return women and men to a traditional past. This dated message belies the energy we see around us, as our society embraces new freedoms and discovers new tolerance, rejecting old stereotypes. No era is without its pressing social issues, but we are optimistic about the future of the sexes in a world of same difference. More freedom may indeed bring more anxiety; more choice may bring more confusion and less certainty. But it allows us to be more varied, complex, and unique than does a world shackled by the iron bars of a gender-difference culture.

The effort to understand women and men by one narrative—whether genes, drives, psychological mechanisms, biblical imperatives, or political ideology—is doomed to fail. Simple stories may be appealing, and the ones that catch on always contain grains of truth that make them seem plausible. But they can easily mislead us. Our complex same-difference tale may be harder to follow than a simple one, but it is the best path to discovering who we really are—and who we will become.

Notes

Chapter 1

1. R. C. Barnett and C. Rivers, *She works/he works: How two-income families are happier, healthier, and better-off* (San Francisco: Harper, 1996).

2. J. S. Bernard, *The future of marriage* (New Haven: Yale University Press, 1982).

3. F. Crosby, *Juggling: The unexpected advantages of balancing career and home for women and their families* (New York: Free Press, 1993); E. Galinsky and J. David, *Ask the children: The breakthrough study that reveals how to succeed at work and parenting* (New York: Morrow, 1999); S. Coltrane, *Family man: Fatherhood, housework, and gender equity* (New York: Oxford, 1996); and B. J. Risman, "Can men mother?" in B. J. Risman and P. Schwartz, eds., *Gender in intimate relationships* (Belmont, Calif.: Wadsworth, 1989).

4. E. Galinsky, J. David, and NICHD Early Child Care Network, "Relations between family predictors and child outcomes: Are they weaker for children in child care?" *Developmental Psychology* 34, no. 5 (1998): 1119–1128.

5. M. Gurian, *The wonder of girls: Understanding the hidden nature of our daughters* (New York: St. Martin's, 2003).

6. S. A. Hewlett, *Creating a life: Professional women and the quest for children* (New York: Talk Miramax, 2002).

7. S. Freud, *Psychopathology of everyday life* (New York: Macmillan, 1930).

8. J. DiStasio, "Primary campaign opens bag of tricks," *Manchester Union Leader*, February 17, 1996.

9. R. Maxa, "Long live men, the doctor says," *Washington Post*, November 19, 1978.

10. M. Kimmel, "About a boy," *Vassar*, Winter 2003, p. 72.

Chapter 2

1. *The new media Bible* (New York: Genesis Project, 1976).

2. *Homer, the Iliad, the Odyssey, and the lesser Homerica*, ed. A. Nicoll (New York: Pantheon, 1956).

3. C. G. Heilbrun, *Reinventing womanhood* (New York: Norton, 1979).

4. B. Ehrenreich and D. English, *For her own good* (New York: Anchor Doubleday, 1979), p. 190.

5. Ehrenreich and English, *For her own good*, p. 194.

6. C. Hymowitz and M. Weissman, *A history of women in America* (New York: Bantam, 1978).

7. S. Coontz, *The way we never were: American families and the nostalgia trap* (New York: Basic, 1992).

8. R. Rosen, *The world split open* (New York: Viking, 2000). and S. Coontz, 1992).

9. C. Gilligan, *In a different voice: Psychological theory and women's development* (Cambridge: Harvard, 1982). See also C. Gilligan, "In a different voice: Women's conception of self and morality," *Harvard Educational Review* 47 (1977): 481–517.

10. S. Freud, *Psychopathology of everyday life* (New York: Macmillan, 1930).

11. E. H. Erikson, *Identity and the life cycle* (New York: International Universities Press, 1959).

12. C. Gilligan, "In a different voice: Women's conceptions of self and of morality," in M. R. Walsh, ed., *The Psychology of women: Ongoing debates* (New Haven: Yale University Press, 1987), 278–320.

13. Gilligan, "In a different voice," p. 279.

14. B. Spock and S. Parker, *Dr. Spock's baby and child care* (New York: Pocket Books, 1998).

15. L. Kohlberg, "Stage and sequence: The cognitive–developmental approach to socialization," in D. A. Goslin, ed., *Handbook of socialization theory and research* (Chicago: Rand McNally, 1969).

16. Gilligan, "In a different voice," p. 288.

17. Gilligan, *In a different voice*.

18. Gilligan, "In a different voice," p. 299.

19. L. J. Walker, "Sex differences in the development of moral reasoning: A critical review," *Child Development* 55 (1984): 677–691.

20. Gilligan, "In a different voice," p. 318.

21. F. Crosby, *Juggling: The unexpected advantages of balancing career and home for women and their families* (New York: Free Press, 1993).

22. Crosby, *Juggling*, p. 129.

23. Crosby, *Juggling*.

24. A. Colby and W. Damon, "Listening to a different voice: A review of Gilligan's In a different voice," in M. R. Walsh, ed., *The psychology of women: Ongoing debates* (New Haven: Yale University Press, 1987), pp. 321–329.

25. D. Nails, "Gilligan's mismeasure of man," *Social Research* 50 (1983): 642–666.

26. J. Rosen, "A majority of one," *New York Times Magazine,* June 3, 2001.

27. J. Toobin, "Women in black," *New Yorker*, October 30, 2000.

28. J. Rosen, "Majority of one."

29. N. Banerjee, "The media business: Some "bullies" seek ways to soften up." *New York Times,* August 10, 2001.

30. L. A. Rydman and P. Glick, "Feminized management and backlash toward agentic women: The hidden costs to women of a kinder, gentler image of middle managers," *Journal of Personality and Social Psychology* 77 (1999): 1004–1010.

31. Rydman and Glick, "Feminized management."

32. C. Robb, "A theory of empathy over the last decade," *Boston Globe Magazine,* October 16, 1988.

33. K. Kisner, "Authors celebrate value of women's friendships," *Cleveland Plain Dealer,* June 25, 1996.

34. M. Rosenberg, "Teatime: Health care for women only," *New York Times*, January 26, 2003.

35. J. Gray, *Men, women, and relationships: Making peace with the opposite sex* (New York: Harper-Collins/Quill, 1993), pp. 11–12.

36. E. Eakin, "Fonda listening for the voices of women," *New York Times*, March 30, 2002.

37. Eakin, "Fonda listening."

38. A. Gates, "Rosa Parks, a not-so-timid woman who stayed in her seat," *New York Times*, February 22, 2002; J. Tierney, "The big city: GI stands tall again," *New York Times*, December 11, 2001; P. L. Brown, "Heavy lifting required: The return of manly men," *New York Times*, October 28, 2001.

39. Gilligan, "In a different voice."

40. R. Sharpe, "As leaders, women rule," *Business Week*, November 20, 2000.

41. N. Hentoff, "Justice O'Connor and the myth of the true woman," *Washington Post*, November 23, 1991.

42. J. Rosen, "Boys and girls," *New Yorker*, February 14, 1994.

43. M. F. Belenky, B. M. Clinchy, N. R. Goldberger, and J. M. Tarule, *Women's ways of knowing: The development of self, voice, and mind* (New York: Basic, 1986).

44. J. Gray, *Men are from Mars, women are from Venus: A practical guide for improving communication and getting what you want in your relationships* (New York: HarperCollins, 1992).

45. M. Gurian, *The wonder of girls: Understanding the hidden nature of our daughters* (New York: St. Martin's, 2003).

46. S. Baron-Cohen, *The essential difference: The truth about the male and female brain* (New York: Basic, 2003).

47. D. Brady, "Toronto feminists have customized a radical new curriculum for girls," *Maclean's*, April 25, 1994.

48. Anne Alonso, personal communication, October 3, 2003.

49. A. Kessler Harris, written testimony, *EEOC v. Sears Roebuck and Co.*, *Signs*, Summer, 1986.

50. K. R. Urbonya, "Supreme court report: Separate but equal revisited," *American Bar Association Journal*, February 1996.

51. Quoted in S. Reeves and A. Marriott, "A burst of popularity," *U.S. News & World Report*, September 26, 1994.

52. K. Kelly, "Pretty poison," *U.S. News & World Report*, May 20, 2002.

53. M. Biernat, "Toward a broader view of social stereotyping," *American Psychologist* 58 (12): 1019–1027.

54. A. Kuczynski, "They conquered, they left," *New York Times*, March 24, 2002.

55. L. K. Stroh, J. M. Brett, and A. H. Reilly, "All the right stuff: A comparison of female and male managers' career progression," *Journal of Applied Psychology* 77 (1992): 251–260.

56. J. M. Broughton, "Women's rationality and men's virtues: A critique of gender dualism in Gilligan's theory of moral development," *Journal of Social Research* 50 (1983): 597–642.

57. J. Gray, *Men, women, and relationships.*

58. Gilligan, "In a different voice."

59. J. K. Fletcher, *Disappearing acts: Gender, power, and relational practice at work* (Cambridge: MIT Press, 1999).

60. C. P. Cowan and P. A. Cowan, *When partners become parents: The big life change for couples* (Mahwah, N.J.: Erlbaum, 2000).

61. S. G. Boodman, "The last of the first-time mamas," *Washington Post*, April 29, 1990.

62. R. C. Barnett and K. G. Gareis, "Full-time and reduced-hours work schedules and marital quality: A study of female physicians with young children," *Work and Occupation* 29 (2002): 364–379.

63. P. Tyre and D. McGinn, "She works, he doesn't," *Newsweek*, May 12, 2003.

64. C. Hymowitz, "New exec learned to lead by shedding her old ways," *Wall Street Journal*, 1999, CareerJournalEurope.Com.

65. R. C. Barnett and C. Rivers, *She works/he works: How two-income families are happier, healthier, and better-off* (San Francisco: Harper, 1996).

66. Barnett and Rivers, *She works/he works*.

67. Radcliffe Public Policy Center, *Life's work: Generational attitudes towards work and life integration* (Cambridge: Radcliffe Institute for Advanced Study, 2000).

68. "Many caretakers relieved by loved one's death," *Milwaukee Journal Sentinel*, November 13, 2003.

Chapter 3

1. K. Glantz and J. Pearce, *Exiles from Eden* (New York: Norton, 1989), p. 5.

2. E. O. Wilson, *Sociobiology* (Cambridge: Harvard University Press, 1980).

3. R. Wright, *The moral animal: Evolutionary psychology and everyday life* (New York: Pantheon, 1994).

4. A. Ferguson, "Evolutionary psychology and its true believers," *Weekly Standard*, March 19, 2001, p. 31.

5. Quoted in H. Liebert, "The descent of men," *Weekly Standard*, October 25, 1999.

6. Quoted in S. Bordo, "Sexual harassment is about bullying, not sex," *Chronicle of Higher Education*, May 1, 1998, p. 86.

7. S. Pinker, *The blank slate: The modern denial of human nature* (New York: Viking Penguin, 2002), p. 356.

8. C. McEnroe, "Love between beauty, beast: Men value looks more than women," *Hartford Courant*, March 24, 1994.

9. Wright, *Moral animal*, p. 60.

10. D. M. Buss, *The evolution of desire: Strategies of human mating* (New York: Basic, 1994).

11. R. Trivers, *Social evolution* (Menlo Park, Calif.: Benjamin/Cummings, 1985).

12. J. Fischman, J. Rui Chong, and R. Hotinski, "It may be a many-splendored thing, but romance relies on Stone Age rules to get started," *U.S. News & World Report*, February 7, 2000.

13. S. J. Gould and R. Shearer, "Of two minds and one nature," *Science* 286 (1999): 1093–1094.

14. T. Morton, "The rise and rise of neo-Darwinism," *Australian Financial Review*, January 21, 2000.

15. A. H. Eagly and W. Wood, "The origins of sex differences in human behavior: Evolved dispositions versus social roles," *American Psychologist* 54 (1999): 408–423.

16. Eagly and Wood, "Origins," p. 413.

17. Eagly and Wood, "Origins," p. 413.

18. G. Lerner, *The creation of patriarchy* (New York: Oxford, 1986).

19. C. Darwin, *The origin of species* (London: Dent; Totowa, N.J.: Rowman & Littlefield, 1975).

20. C. Darwin, *The descent of man and selection in relation to sex* (1871; New York: Appelton, 1899, p. 273.

21. S. B. Hrdy, "Raising Darwin's consciousness: Female sexuality and the prehominid origins of patriarchy," *Human Nature* 8, no. 1 (1997): 1–49. See also Hrdy, *Mother nature: A history of mothers, infants, and natural selection* (New York: Pantheon, 1999), p. 9.

22. Hrdy, "Raising," p. 9.

23. Quoted in A. Fausto-Sterling, P. Gowaty, and M. Zuk, "Mr. Right—I mean Mr. Wright—meet Darwinian feminists" (unpublished paper, June 10, 1996).

24. Hrdy, "Raising."

25. Quoted in A. Ferguson, "Evolutionary psychology and its true believers," *Weekly Standard,* March 19, 2001.

26. Fausto-Sterling, Gowaty, and Zuk, "Mr. Right."

27. Hrdy, "Raising."

28. S. Beckerman et al., "The Bari partible paternity project: Preliminary results." *Current Anthropology* 39 (1998): 164–168. Also S. B. Hrdy, "New rules for an old game," *New Scientist* 46 (2003).

29. Hrdy, "Raising," p. 22.

30. S. Vedantam, "Desire and DNA: Is promiscuity innate?" *Washington Post,* August 1, 2003.

31. T. Spears, "You're wired for sex," *Ottawa Citizen,* August 9, 2003. See also D. P. Schmitt, "Universal sex differences in the desire for sexual variety," *Journal of Personality and Social Psychology* 85 (2003): 85–104.

32. M. Norman, "Getting serious about adultery," *New York Times,* July 4, 1998.

33. Vedantam, "Desire."

34. M. Wiederman, "Extramarital sex: The prevalence and correlates in a national survey," *Journal of Sex Research* 34 (1997): 167–174.

35. Wiederman, "Extramarital sex."

36. J. Gerstel, "If love is the disease, marriage is the cure," *Toronto Star,* August 8, 2003.

37. L. Kipnis, *Against love* (New York: Pantheon, 2003).

38. K. Hawkes, "Hardworking Hazda grandmothers," in V. Standen and R. A. Foley, eds., *Comparative sociology: The behavioral ecology of humans and other mammals* (London: Basil Blackwell), pp. 341–366.

39. R. Wright, "Feminists, meet Mr. Darwin," *New Republic,* November 28, 1994.

40. N. Angier, "Women, sex, and Darwin," *New York Times Magazine,* February 21, 1999, 48.

41. "Female baboons want mates that were friends first," *Orange County Register,* May 3, 1987. Also see B. B. Smuts and D. J. Gubernick, "Male-infant relationships in nonhuman primates: Paternal investment or mating effort?" in B. S. Hewlett, ed., *Father-child relations* (New York: Aldine De Gruyter, 1992), pp. 1–30.

42. E. Goodman, "A new model of masculinity?" *Boston Globe,* January 3, 2002.

43. Quoted in Goodman, "New model."

44. "The Bridget Jones economy—singles and the city," *Economist,* December 22, 2001.

45. W. Shalit, *A return to modesty: Discovering the lost virtue* (New York: Simon & Schuster, 1999).

46. Trivers, *Social evolution.*

47. C. T. Snowdon, "The nature of sex differences: Myths of male and female," in P. A. Gowaty, ed., *Feminism and evolutionary biology: Boundaries, intersections, and frontiers* (New York: Chapman & Hall, 1997).

48. Angier, "Women."

49. N. Blurton Jones, "The lives of hunter-gatherer children: Effects of parental behavior and parental reproductive strategy," in M. E. Pereira and L. A. Fairbanks, *Juvenile primates: Life history, development, and behavior* (Chicago: University of Chicago Press, 2002), pp. 309–326.

50. K. Bussey and A. Bandura, "Social cognitive theory of gender development and differentiation," *Psychological Review*, 1999, pp. 676–713.

51. K. Gerson, *No man's land: Men's changing commitments to family and work* (New York: Basic, 1993).

52. Snowdon, "Nature."

53. Snowdon, "Nature." Also W. K. Redican, "Adult male–infant interactions in nonhuman primates," in M. E. Lamb, ed., *The role of the father in child development* (New York: Wiley, 1976).

54. Snowdon, "Nature."

55. Hrdy, *Mother nature*, p. 226.

56. B. J. Risman and D. Johnson-Sumerford, "Doing it fairly: A study of postgender marriages," *Journal of Marriage and the Family* 60 (1998): 23–40.

57. Hrdy, *Mother nature*.

58. Bussey and Bandura, "Social."

59. Bussey and Bandura, "Social."

60. T. Bond, E. Galinsky, and J. Swanberg, *The national study of the changing workforce* (New York: Family and Work Institute, 1998). Between 1977 and 1997, the amount of time employed mothers spent caring for and doing things with their children on workdays decreased from 3.3 to 3.0 hours, according to the National Study of the Changing Workforce, whereas the time employed fathers spent with their children increased significantly by one-half hour per workday, from 1.8 to 2.3 hours per day. Over the same twenty-year period, mothers increased their time with children on non-workdays, nonsignificantly from 7.3 to 8.3 hours per day, whereas fathers increased their time significantly from 5.2 to 6.4 hours per day.

61. Gerson, *No man's land*.

62. S. Jones, *Y: The descent of men* (Boston: Houghton Mifflin, 2003).

63. C. McGinn, "Why sex matters," *New York Times Book Review*, January 9, 2000, 12.

Chapter 4

1. M. F. Stoeltje, "Evolution revolution: Why did the chicken cross the road? If it was male, probably for a tender young pullet; if it was female, probably for a powerful old rooster," *Texas Magazine*, June 20, 1999.

2. D. M. Buss, *The evolution of desire: Strategies of human mating* (New York: Basic, 1994).

3. D. M. Buss, "Sex differences in human mate preferences: Evolutionary hypotheses tested in 37 cultures," *Behavioral and Brain Sciences* 12 (1989): 1–49.

4. C. Suplee, "The evolution of desire: Strategies of human mating," *Washington Post*, March 27, 1994.

5. G. Cowley and K. Springen, "The biology of beauty," *Newsweek,* June 3, 1996.

6. W. F. Allman, "The mating game," *U.S. News & World Report,* July 19, 1993.

7. Buss, "Sex differences." The problems with Buss's sample include the following: (1) He computes group mean differences for men and women within each sample and then simply adds up the number of samples in which the data show significant male–female differences. (2) He recognizes that, in general, rural, less-educated, and lower-socioeconomic status groups are underrepresented as are less urbanized, noncash cultures. Thus his results might not generalize either within cultures (due to the nonrepresentativeness of the sample) or between cultures (due to the bias toward urbanized cash economies). (3) Although he concedes that there is considerable overlap in the

male and female preference distributions, he fails to note an important element, specifically the size of those overlaps.

8. Buss, "Sex differences."

9. Buss, "Sex differences."

10. Buss, "Sex differences."

11. C. Darwin, *The origin of species* (London: Dent; Totowa, N.J.: Rowman & Littlefield, 1975).

12. S. Vedantam, "Desire and DNA: Is promiscuity innate?" *Washington Post,* August 1, 2003.

13. D. McLellan, "In your face: Why do we like someone's looks?" *Washingtonian Magazine,* October 1992.

14. S. B. Hrdy, "Raising Darwin's consciousness: Female sexuality and the prehominid origins of patriarchy," *Human Nature* 8, no. 1 (1997): 1–49. See also S. B. Hrdy, *Mother Nature: A history of mothers, infants, and natural selection* (New York: Pantheon, 1999).

15. Hrdy, "Raising," p. 4.

16. Hrdy, "Raising," p. 5.

17. D. M. Buss and T. K. Shackelford, "From vigilance to violence: Mate retention tactics in married couples," *Journal of Personality and Social Psychology* 72 (1997): 346–361.

18. P. M. Buston and S. T. Emlen, "Cognitive processes underlying human mate choice: The relationship between self-perception and mate preference in Western society," *Proceedings of the National Academy of Science,* 2003, Early Edition, 1–6.

19. K. Bussey and A. Bandura, "Social cognitive theory of gender development and differentiation," *Psychological Review,* 1999, pp. 676–713.

20. P. C. Rosenblatt and P. C. Cozby, "Courtship patterns associated with freedom of choice of spouse," *Journal of Marriage and the Family* 34 (1972): 689–695.

21. Bussey and Bandura, "Social cognitive theory."

22. S. M. Kalick, L. A. Zebrowitz, J. H. Langlois, and R. M. Johnson, "Does human facial attractiveness honestly advertise health? Longitudinal data on an evolutionary question," *Psychological Science* 9 (1998): 8–13.

23. Bussey and Bandura, "Social cognitive theory."

24. B. Ehrenreich and D. English, *For her own good* (New York: Anchor Doubleday, 1979), p. 108.

25. H. Kirwan-Taylor, "The private life of the corporate wife," *Management Today,* February 15, 2000, p. 48.

26. V. K. Oppenheimer, "Women's employment and the gain to marriage: The specialization and trading model," *Annual Review of Sociology* 23 (1997): 431–535.

27. V. K. Oppenheimer, M. Kalmijn, and N. Lim, "Men's career development and marriage timing during a period of rising inequality," *Demography* 34 (1997): 311–330.

28. Quoted in A. P. Sanoff, "The economics of sex," *U.S. News & World Report,* May 4, 1992.

29. www.jdate.com

30. O. Craig and C. Milner, "First came the surrendered wife," *London Telegraph,* July 8, 2001.

31. H. Ono, "Husbands' and wives' resources and marital dissolution," *Journal of Marriage and the Family,* 1998, pp. 674–689; S. J. Rogers and D. D. DeBoer, "Changes in wives' income: Effects on marital happiness, psychological well-being, and the risk of divorce," *Journal of Marriage and Family* 63 (2001): 458–472. "Increases in married women's absolute and relative income significantly increase their

marital happiness and well being . . . the likelihood of divorce is not significantly affected by increases in married women's income" (p. 258).

32. Ono, "Husbands' and wives' resources."

33. Ono, "Husbands' and wives' resources."

34. Ono, "Husbands' and wives' resources."

35. R. C. Barnett and C. Rivers, *She works/he works: How two-income families are happier, healthier, and better-off* (San Francisco: Harper, 1996).

36. L. Goober, "Reversal of fortune: When you're more successful than he is," *Cosmopolitan*, September 2003.

37. J. S. Hyde, J. D. DeLamater, and E. E. Hewitt, "Sexuality and the dual-earner couple: Multiple roles and sexual functioning," *Journal of Family Psychology* 12 (1998): 354–368.

38. Oppenheimer, "Women's employment."

39. E. Wharton, *The house of mirth: Complete, authoritative text with biographical and historical contexts, critical history* (Boston: Bedford/St. Martin's, 1994).

40. Science update, *Independent*, June 29, 2001.

41. S. Schorow, "Love's rules on the rocks: Older woman–younger man couples more common as attitudes change," *Boston Herald*, March 4, 2002.

42. M. Norman, "Getting serious about adultery," *New York Times*, July 4, 1998.

43. B. D. Whitehead, "Forget sex in the city, women want romance in their lives," *Washington Post*, February 9, 2003.

44. R. Wright, "Feminists, meet Mr. Darwin," *New Republic*, November 28, 1994, p. 34.

45. Hrdy, *Mother nature.*

46. Hrdy, *Mother nature.*

47. Hrdy, *Mother nature.*

48. T. Egan, "The persistence of polygamy," *New York Times Magazine*, March 21, 1999.

49. Bussey and Bandura, "Social cognitive theory."

50. A. Eagly and W. Wood, "The origins of sex differences in human behavior: Evolved dispositions versus social rules," *American Psychologist* 54 (1999): 408–423.

51. N. D. Glenn, "Intersocial variation in the mate preferences of males and females," *Behavioral and Brain Sciences* 12 (1989): 21–23.

52. M. Ridley, *Nature via nurture: Genes, experience, and what makes us human* (New York: HarperCollins, 2003).

53. P. Gowaty, "Women, psychology, and evolution," in *Handbook of the psychology of women and gender* (New York: Wiley, 2001), p. 59.

54. K. Sexton, "Toyboy husbands: Australian women marry younger men," *Sydney Sunday Telegraph*, December 21, 2003.

55. Gallup survey of 1,003 Americans, age 20–29, Rutgers University, National Marriage Project, 2001.

56. E. Fein and S. Schneider, *The rules: Time-tested secrets for capturing the heart of Mr. Right* (New York: Warner, 1996).

57. D. McCullough, *John Adams* (New York: Touchstone/Simon & Schuster, 2002).

58. "Written on the body: An interview with feminist philosopher Susan Bordo," *Bitch*, Summer 2003.

59. J. Kagan, *Three seductive ideas* (Cambridge: Harvard University Press, 1999).

60. S. Freud, *Psychopathology of everyday life* (New York: Macmillan, 1930).

61. E. H. Erikson, *Identity and the life cycle* (New York: International Universities Press, 1959).

62. B. B. Smuts and D. J. Gubernick, "Male-infant relationships in nonhuman primates: Paternal investment or mating effort?" in B. S. Hewlett, ed., *Father–child relations* (New York: Aldine De Gruyter, 1992), pp. 1–30.

63. S. Taylor, *The tending instinct: How nurturing is essential for who we are and how we live* (New York: Times Books, 2002).

64. Taylor, *Tending instinct.*

65. R. Weiss, "Evolving view of chimp communities: Dominant females' reproductive success suggests new hierarchy model," *Washington Post,* August 8, 1997.

66. A. Zihlmann and N. Tanner, "Women in evolution, part 1: Innovation and selection in human origins," *Journal of Women in Culture and Society* 3 (1976).

67. R. Wright, "Feminists, meet Mr. Darwin," *New Republic,* November 28, 1994, p. 34.

68. Wright, "Feminists."

69. A. Fausto-Sterling, P. Gowaty, and M. Zuk, "Mr. Right—I mean Mr. Wright—meet Darwinian feminists" (unpublished paper, June 10, 1996).

70. S. J. Gould, "Evolution: The pleasures of pluralism," *New York Review of Books,* June 26, 1997, p. 47.

71. Ridley, *Nature via nurture.*

Chapter 5

1. D. Tannen, *You just don't understand: Women and men in conversation* (New York: Morrow, 1990).

2. T. Garbriel, "Call in the coach: How do you rehabilitate a personality-flawed exec?" *Ottawa Citizen,* May 11, 1996.

3. T. H. Ching, "Men, be the bullfighter, not the bull," *Singapore Straits Times,* January 23, 2001.

4. D. Tannen, *Talking from nine to five* (New York: Morrow, 1999).

5. D. Tannen *Talking,* p. 49.

6. Tannen *Talking,* p. 294.

7. Tannen *Talking.*

8. Tannen *Talking,* p. 81.

9. Tannen *You just don't understand.*

10. American Management Association Survey, *Senior management teams: Profiles and performance* (New York: American Management Association International, 1998), pp. 1–8; Catalyst, *The bottom line: Connecting corporate performance and gender diversity,* 2004.

11. Tannen *You just don't understand.*

12. Tannen *Talking,* p. 83.

13. Tannen, *You just don't understand.*

14. Tannen, *You just don't understand.*

15. E. Aries, *Men and women in interaction: Reconsidering the differences* (New York: Oxford, 1996).

16. Aries, *Men and women.*

17. S. E. Snodgrass, "Further effects of role versus gender on interpersonal sensitivity," *Journal of Personality and Social Psychology* 61 (1992): 154–158.

18. Aries, *Men and women.*

19. Aries, *Men and women.*

20. M. Wolf, "Lovelorn beware: Few books about relationships keep their promises," *Rocky Mountain News,* June 16, 2001.

21. "Novato 'diploma mill' shut down by state," *San Francisco Chronicle*, March 14, 2001.

22. J. Gray, *Men, women, and relationships: Making peace with the opposite sex* (New York: HarperCollins, 1993).

23. Gray, *Men, women*, p. 96.

24. Gray, *Men, women*, p. 96.

25. Gray, *Men, women*.

26. Gray, *Men, women*.

27. Gray, *Men, women*.

28. Wolf, "Lovelorn beware."

29. N. Banerjee, "The media business: Some 'bullies' seek ways to soften up," *New York Times*, August 10, 2001.

30. R. Sharpe, "As leaders, women rule," *Business Week*, November 20, 2000.

31. Sharpe, "As leaders, women rule."

32. P. Sellers, "The 50 most powerful women in America," *Fortune*, October 13, 2003.

33. M. Conlin, "From kindergarten to grad school, boys are becoming the second sex," *Business Week*, May 26, 2003.

34. L. Tiger, *The decline of males: The first look at an unexpected new world for men and women* (New York: St. Martin's Griffin, 1999).

35. A. Hacker, *Mismatch: The growing gulf between men and women* (New York: Scribner, 2003).

36. S. Jones, *Y: The descent of men* (Boston: Houghton Mifflin, 2003).

37. A. Ferguson, "Evolutionary psychology and its true believers," *Weekly Standard*, March 19, 2001, p. 31.

38. M. Conlin, "The new gender gap," *Business Week,* May 26, 2003.

39. R. Lim, "Women are taking over the workplace in the developed world and men are increasingly being marginalised," *Straits Times, Singapore,* September 29, 2002.

40. "Girls get extra school help while boys get Ritalin," editorial, *USA Today*, August 29, 2003.

41. D. Goldman, "The male ego takes a beating," *Adweek*, March 3, 2003, p. 9.

42. A. Argetsinger, "Women outnumber men at many colleges," *Washington Post*, November 17, 1999.

43. D. Abel, "Male call on campus enrollment trends widen gender gap, upset social scene," *Boston Globe*, November 5, 2000.

44. M. Kimmel, "Taking back the terms" (paper presented at the 2nd Annual Invitational Journalism-Work/Family Conference, Boston, May 2–3, 2003).

45. J. O. Robertson, *American myth, American reality* (New York: Hill & Wang, 1980).

46. G. Bederman, *Manliness and civilization: Cultural history of gender and race in the United States, 1880–1917* (Chicago: University of Chicago Press, 1995).

47. M. Kimmel, *Manhood in America: A cultural history* (New York: Free Press, 1996).

48. Quoted in Bederman, *Manliness*, p. 16.

49. Quoted in Bederman, *Manliness*, p. 99.

50. W. E. Leuchtenberg, *Franklin Roosevelt and the New Deal* (New York: Harper, 1963).

51. W. H. Whyte, *The organization man* (New York: Simon & Schuster, 1956).

52. Tiger, *Decline of males*.

53. Tiger, *Decline of males*, p. 243.

54. S. Coontz, *The way we never were: American families and the nostalgia trap* (New York: Basic, 1992).

55. Coontz, *The way we never were.*

56. Coontz, *The way we never were.*

57. Coontz, *The way we never were.*

58. T. Bond, E. Galinsky, and J. Swanberg, *The National Study of the Changing Workforce* (New York: Family and Work Institute, 1998).

59. E. Galinsky and J. David, *Ask the children: The breakthrough study that reveals how to succeed at work and parenting* (New York: Morrow 1999).

60. K. Gerson, *No man's land: Men's changing commitments to family and work* (New York: Basic, 1993), p. 162.

61. Gerson, *No man's land,* p. 168.

62. D. Sadker, "Gender games," *Washington Post,* July 31, 2000.

63. B. Fine, *1,000,000 delinquents* (Cleveland: World, 1955).

64. *Catalyst census of women corporate officers and top earners.* www.catalystwomen .org/research/research1.html.

65. J. E. Woods, "Don't blame girls, women," *USA Today,* August 29, 2003.

66. Sadker, "Gender games."

67. S. Faludi, *Stiffed: The betrayal of the American man* (New York: Morrow, 1999).

68. Tiger, *Decline of males,* p. 9.

69. Hacker, *Mismatch.*

70. G. F. Gilder, *Sexual suicide* (New York: Quadrangle, 1973).

71. J. S. Hyde, J. D. DeLamater, E. A. Plant, and J. M. Byrd, "Sexuality during pregnancy and the year postpartum," *Journal of Sex Research* 33 (1996): 143–151.

72. Barnett and Rivers, *She works/he works.*

73. Gerson, *No man's land,* p. 168.

74. Barnett and Rivers, *She works/he works.*

75. Barnett and Rivers, *She works/he works.*

76. Barnett and Rivers, *She works/he works.*

77. Barnett and Rivers, *She works/he works.*

78. V. K. Oppenheimer, "Women's employment and the gain to marriage: The specialization and trading model," *Annual Review of Sociology* 23 (1997): 431–535.

79. Oppenheimer, "Women's employment."

80. Oppenheimer, "Women's employment."

81. R. B. Freeman, "The feminization of work in the United States: A new era for (man)kind?" in S. Gustafsson and D. Meulders, eds., *Gender and the labor market: Econometric evidence on obstacles in achieving gender equality* (New York: Macmillan) pp. 3–21.

82. J. Waldfogel, "Understanding the 'family gap' in pay for women with children," *Journal of Economic Perspectives* 12 (1998): 137–156.

Chapter 6

1. M. Gurian, *The wonder of girls: Understanding the hidden nature of our daughters* (New York: Pocket Books, 2002).

2. B. Pease and A. Pease, *Why men don't listen and women can't read maps* (New York: Broadway, 2002).

3. P. Brennan, "Equal, but different: Desmond Morris surveys dating, mating, creating," *Washington Post,* February 1, 1998.

4. K. Wood, "Global layer added to glass ceiling," *Financial Times* (London), March 9, 1998.

5. M. Dowd, "Liberties: The abyss of desire," *New York Times*, January 13, 1999.

6. D. Harraway, *Primate visions: Gender, race, and nature in the world of modern science* (New York: Routledge, 1989) p. 201.

7. Harraway, *Primate visions,* p. 201.

8. Harraway, *Primate visions.*

9. R. Ardrey, *The hunting hypothesis* (New York: Athenaeum, 1976).

10. D. Morris, *The naked ape* (New York: McGraw-Hill, 1967).

11. L. Tiger, *Men in groups* (New York: Scribner, 1984).

12. E. O. Wilson, *Sociobiology* (Cambridge: Belknap Press of Harvard University Press, 1980).

13. L. Tiger and R. Fox, *The imperial animal* (New York: Holt Rinehart & Winston, 1971).

14. Harraway, *Primate visions*, p. 328.

15. Quoted in Harraway, *Primate visions,* p. 201.

16. R. Compton, *Old bones shatter new myths, biology as destiny* (Sociobiology Study Group, Science for the People, 1984).

17. Compton, *Old bones.*

18. Quoted in N. Weisstein, "Tired of arguing about biological inferiority?" *Ms.,* November 1982, p. 41.

19. Harraway, *Primate visions.*

20. H. Pringle, "New women of the Ice Age," *Discover,* April 1998, pp. 62–69.

21. Pringle, "New women."

22. Pringle, "New women."

23. M. Z. Stange, "Woman the hunter," in B. Ehrenreich, "The real truth about the female body," *Time,* March 8, 1999, 57.

24. J. S. Hyde, "How large are gender differences in aggression? A developmental meta-analysis," *Developmental Psychology* 20 (1984): 722–736.

25. B. A. Bettencourt and N. Miller, "Gender differences in aggression as a function of provocation: A meta-analysis," *Psychological Bulletin* 119, no. 3 (1996): 422–447.

26. M. A. Straus, "Physical assaults by women partners: A major social problem," in M. R. Walsh, ed., *Women, men, and gender: Ongoing debates* (New Haven: Yale University Press, 1997), pp. 210–221.

27. Straus, "Physical assaults."

28. J. R. Lightdale and D. A. Prentice, "Rethinking sex differences in aggression: Aggressive behavior in the absence of social roles," *Personality and Social Psychology Bulletin* 20 (1994): 34–44.

29. Lightdale and Prentice, "Rethinking sex differences," p. 35.

30. C. T. Snowdon, "The nature of sex differences: Myths of male and female," in P. A. Gowaty, ed., *Feminism and evolutionary biology: Boundaries, intersections, and frontiers* (New York: Chapman & Hall, 1997).

31. S. B. Hrdy, *The woman that never evolved* (Cambridge: Harvard University Press, 1981).

32. S. Taylor, *The tending instinct: How nurturing is essential for who we are and how we live* (New York: Times Books, 2002).

33. C. Martin, "Overlooked side of sexism: Women mistreating women," *Denver Post,* April 8, 2002.

34. N. R. Crick, M. A. Bigbee, and C. Howes, "Gender differences in children's normative beliefs about aggression: How do I hurt thee?" *Child Development* 67 (1996): 1003–1014.

35. Crick, Bigbee, and Howes, "Gender differences."

36. B. L. Foster, "The secret life of teenage girls," *Washingtonian*, November 2000.

37. Foster, "Secret life."

38. H. E. MacGregor, "Girl fight club," *Los Angeles Club*, September 30, 2003.

39. "Three teens get community service for hazing," *Milwaukee Journal Sentinel*, August 16, 2003.

40. H. Evans, "Young, female, and turning deadly: More and more teenage girls are getting busted in serious crimes," *New York Daily News*, December 19, 1999.

41. Evans, "Young, female."

42. Evans, "Young, female."

43. J. Ryan, "Girl gang stirs up false gender issue," *San Francisco Chronicle*, September 5, 2003.

44. K. Lazar, "Fighting like a girl—female adolescents catching up to boys in aggressive behavior," *Boston Herald*, March 11, 2001.

45. E. Moyle, "More girls looking for trouble," *Toronto Sun*, August 16, 1996.

46. K. Bjokqvist, K. M. J. Lagerstetz, and A. Kavkiainen, "Do girls manipulate and boys fight?" *Aggressive Behavior* 18 (1992): 117–127.

47. D. Ransom, private conversation with author, 1998.

48. J. Meek, "Russians claim to unearth steppes' ancient Amazons," *Guardian*, November 23, 1998.

49. Meek, "Russians."

50. D. H. Hackworth, "War and the second sex," *Newsweek*, August 4, 1991.

51. D. Dickerson, "Warrior's creed: I was trained to fight," *Ottowa Citizen*, February 8, 1999.

52. S. H. Greenberg et al., "Get out of my way," *Newsweek*, October 29, 2001.

53. R. Slattery, "Rebuilding Iraq: US fighter pilot recounts her harrowing flight over Iraq," *Boston Globe*, September 7, 2003.

54. M. W. Segal, "Women's military roles cross nationally," *Gender and Society*, December 1995, pp. 757–775.

55. Segal, "Women's military roles."

56. L. Tiger, *The decline of males: The first look at an unexpected new world for men and women* (New York: St. Martin's Griffin, 2000).

57. M. N. Coppola, K. G. LaFrance, and Henry J. Carretta, "The female infantryman: A possibility?" *Federal Information and News Dispatch Military Review*, December 2002.

58. Quoted in Coppola, LaFrance, and Carretta, "Female infantryman."

Chapter 7

1. "Boys and Girls Are Different," *ABC*, 1994.

2. S. Pinker, *The blank slate: The modern denial of human nature* (New York: Viking Penguin, 2002).

3. M. Gurian, *Boys and girls learn differently* (New York: Wiley, 2001).

4. K. Glaser, "Designer genes," *Building Design*, May 23, 2003.

5. K. C. Cole, Hers column, *New York Times*, December 3, 1981.

6. C. P. Benbow and J. Stanley, "Sex differences in mathematical ability: Fact or artifact?" *Science* 210 (1980): pp. 1262–1264.

7. Benbow and Stanley, "Math and sex."

8. "Are boys better at math?" *New York Times*, December 7, 1980.

9. "The gender factor in math," *Time,* December 15, 1980.

10. J. S. Eccles, B. Barber, and D. Jozefowicz, "Linking gender to educational, occupational, and recreational choice: Applying the Eccles et al. model of achievement-related choices," in W. B. Swann, J. H. Langlois, and L. A. Gilbert, eds., *Sexism and stereotypes in modern society: The gender science of Janet Taylor Spence* (Washington, D.C.: American Psychological Association, 1999), pp. 153–191.

11. L. Mundy, "The doll's house," *Washington Post,* December 6, 1998.

12. Quoted in A. Fausto-Sterling, *Myths of gender: Biological theories about men and women* (New York: Basic, 1985).

13. L. Fox, "Sex differences among the mathematically precocious," *Science* 224 (1984) p. 1292.

14. E. H. Luchins and R. Levin, "Women and the pursuit of a career in mathematics," *Christian Science Monitor,* May 27, 1981.

15. SAT scores. The effect size is 0.0 among Latinos (zero gender difference), -.02 among African Americans (tiny difference favoring females), and -.09 among Asian Americans (again, a very small difference favoring females).

16. R. J. Herrnstein and C. Murray, *The bell curve* (New York: Free Press, 1996).

17. B. Bridgeman and C. Wendler, "Gender differences in predictors of college mathematics performance and in college mathematics course grades," *Journal of Educational Psychology* 83, no. 2 (1991): 275–284.

18. D. F. Halpern, *Sex differences in cognitive abilities* (Mahwah N.J.: Erlbaum, 2000).

19. M. Carpenter, "Why girls score low on SATs baffling," *Pittsburgh Post-Gazette,* August 27, 2003.

20. Halpern, *Sex differences.*

21. In the scientific literature, this relationship is referred to as the "effect size" or "sensitivity index," and it is denoted by d'. Technically, this quantity is measured by dividing the group mean difference score by a parameter that reflects the widths of the two distributions. For example, if the two distributions are identical, except for a shift in the mean, the parameter is normally chosen to be the standard deviation of the distributions. In mathematical terms, the quantity d' is then given by $d' = (M_M - M_F)/s.d.$, when M_M and M_F are the means of the distributions for males and females and s.d. is the standard deviation of each distribution around its mean.

22. J. S. Hyde, E. Fennema, and S. J. Lamon, "Gender differences in mathematics performance: A meta analysis," *Psychological Bulletin* 107, no. 2 (1990): 139–155.

23. Halpern, *Sex differences.*

24. Gurian, *Boys and girls.*

25. J. Reston, *Deadline: A memoir* (New York: Random House, 1991).

26. L. V. Hedges and A. Nowell, "Sex differences in mental test scores, variability, and numbers of high scoring individuals," *Science* 269 (1996): 41–45.

27. A. Gifford, "Time for women to look past IT's geek image," *New Zealand Herald,* August 27, 2003.

28. *Report of the Congressional Commission on the Advancement of Women and Minorities in Science, Engineering, and Technology Development,* 2000.

29. E. Armstrong, "Where are the future scientists?" *Christian Science Monitor,* July 29, 2003.

30. C. Dreifus, "A conversation with Sally Ride: Painful questions from an ex-astronaut," *New York Times,* August 26, 2003.

31. Private patient, personal communication with RB, July 2003.

32. E. Leahey and G. Guo, "Gender differences in mathematical trajectories," *Social Forces* 80 (2001): 713–732.

33. Gifford, "Time for women."

34. Pinker, *Blank slate*.

35. K. C. Cole, Hers column, *New York Times*, December 3, 1981.

36. S. L. Boswell, "The influence of sex-role stereotyping on women's attitudes and achievement in mathematics," in S. F. Chipman, L. R. Brush, and D. M. Wilson, eds., *Women and mathematics: Balancing the equation* (Mahwah, N.J.: Erlbaum, 1985), p. 91.

37. Boswell, "Influence of sex-role stereotyping."

38. Boswell, "Influence of sex-role stereotyping."

39. Boswell, "Influence of sex-role stereotyping."

40. Boswell, "Influence of sex-role stereotyping."

41. Boswell, "Influence of sex-role stereotyping."

42. Boswell, "Influence of sex-role stereotyping."

43. Boswell, "Influence of sex-role stereotyping."

44. Congressional Commission on the Advancement of Women and Minorities in Science, Engineering, and Technology Development, *Land of plenty: Diversity as America's competitive edge in science, engineering, and technology*, www.nsf.gov/od/cawmset/report.htm.

45. *Land of plenty*.

46. *Land of plenty*.

47. *Land of plenty*.

48. C. Nissan, "Science programs experiment with instructing girls in science," *Boston Herald*, June 9, 2002.

49. C. M. Steele, "A threat in the air: How stereotypes shape the identities and performance of women and African Americans," *American Psychologist* 52 (1997): 613–629.

50. Steele, "Threat in the air."

51. Registrar's office, MIT and Rhode Island School of Design, personal communication with RB, October 2003.

52. Hedges and Nowell, "Sex differences."

53. Hedges and Nowell, "Sex differences."

54. *Land of plenty*.

55. A. Moir and D. Jessel, *Brain sex: The real difference between men and women* (New York: Dell, 1991).

56. D. Blum, *Sex on the brain: The biological differences between men and women* (New York: Viking, 1997).

57. K. Santich, "Men, women, and sex on the brain," *Orlando Sentinel*, July 5, 1998.

58. L. J. Harris, "Sex differences in spatial ability: Possible environmental, genetic, and neurological factors," in M. Kinsbourne, ed., *Asymmetrical function of the brain* (New York: Cambridge University Press, 1978), 405–533.

59. E. E. Maccoby and C. N. Jacklin, *Psychology of sex differences* (Stanford: Stanford University Press, 1974), p. 351.

60. H. Lips, A. Myers, and N. Colwill, "Sex differences in ability: Do men and women have different strengths and weaknesses?" in H. Lips and N. Colwill, eds., *Psychology of sex differences* (Englewood Cliffs, N.J.: Prentice-Hall, 1978), pp. 145–173.

61. L. Barker, *Psychology* (Upper Saddle River, N.J.: Prentice-Hall, 2002).

62. P. J. Caplan, G. M. MacPherson, and P. Tobin, "Do sex-related differences in spatial abilities exist: A multilevel critique with new data," *American Psychologist* 40, no. 7 (1985): 786–799.

63. M. Kinsbourne, ed., *Asymmetrical function of the brain* (New York: Cambridge University Press, 1978).

64. M. C. Linn and A. C. Petersen, "Emergence and characterization of sex differences in spatial ability: A meta-analysis," *Child Development* 56 (1985): 1479–1498.

65. J. S. Hyde, "How large are cognitive gender differences?" *American Psychologist 36*, no. 8 (1981): 892–901; D. Voyer, S. Voyer, and M. P. Bryden, "Magnitude of sex differences in spatial abilities: A meta-analysis and consideration of critical variables," *Psychological Bulletin* 117 (1995): 250–270.

66. Halpern, *Sex differences.*

67. C. Dowling, *The frailty myth: Redefining the physical potential of women and girls* (New York: Random House, 2000).

68. D. K. Yee and J. S. Eccles, "Parent perceptions and attributions for children's math achievement," *Sex Roles* 19 (1988): 5–6.

69. M. A. Larson et al., "Gender issues in the application of a virtual environment spatial rotation project," *CyberPsychology and Behavior* 2 (1999): 113–124.

70. D. F. Halpern, "Sex differences in intelligence: Implications for education," *American Psychologist* 52 (1997): 1091–1102.

71. Moir and Jessel, *Brain sex.*

72. M. Geewax, "If women ruled . . . Female techies imagine a world," *Atlanta Journal and Constitution,* August 27, 2000.

73. M. Thom, *Balancing the equation: Where are women and girls in science, engineering, and technology?* National Council for Research on Women (2001).

74. *Land of plenty.*

75. N. Hopkins, L. Bailyn, L. Gibson, and E. Hammonds, *The status of women faculty at MIT: An overview of reports from the schools of architecture and planning, engineering, humanities, arts, and social sciences and the Sloan school of management* (2002).

76. *Before it's too late: A report to the nation from the national commission on mathematics and science teaching for the 21st century* (2000).

77. *Educational Equity of Girls and Women* (National Center for Education Statistics, 2000).

78. Barbara Lazarus, personal communication to RB, March 2003.

Chapter 8

1. *Women in U.S. corporate leadership: 2003* (New York: Catalyst, 2003).

2. S. Freud, *Psychopathology of everyday life* (New York: Macmillan, 1930).

3. E. H. Erikson, *Identity and the life cycle* (New York: International Universities Press, 1959).

4. S. Faludi, *Backlash: The undeclared war against American women* (New York: Crown, 1991).

5. "Is Feminism Dead?" *Time,* July 29, 1998.

6. A. Sullivan, "Why men are different," *New York Times Magazine*, April 2, 2000.

7. S. Taylor, *The tending instinct: How nurturing is essential for who we are and how we live* (New York: Times Books, 2002).

8. S. Baron-Cohen, *The essential difference: The truth about the male and female brain* (New York: Basic, 2003).

9. S. Baron-Cohen, "The opposite sexes," *Sydney Morning Herald,* August 16, 2003.

10. Baron-Cohen, "Opposite sexes."

11. G. Will, "Damned Lies and . . . " *Newsweek*, March 29, 1999, p. 84.

12. A. Moir and D. Jessel, *Brain sex: The real difference between men and women* (New York: Dell, 1991).

13. K. Browne, *Divided labors* (New Haven: Yale University Press, 1999).

14. R. Wright, "Feminists, meet Mr. Darwin," *New Republic*, November 28, 1994.

15. J. Stasio, "Primary campaign opens bag of tricks," *Manchester Union Leader*, February 17, 1996.

16. P. Sellers, "Power: Do women really want it?" *Fortune*, October 13, 2003.

17. L. Belkin, "The opt-out revolution," *New York Times Magazine*, October 26, 2003.

18. M. F. Belenky et al., *Women's ways of knowing: The development of self, voice, and mind* (New York: Basic, 1986).

19. F. C. Graglia, *Domestic tranquillity: A brief against feminism* (Dallas: Spence, 1998).

20. W. Shalit, *A return to modesty: Discovering the lost virtue* (New York: Simon & Schuster, 1999).

21. D. Crittenden, *What our mothers didn't tell us: Why happiness eludes the modern woman* (New York: Simon & Schuster, 1999).

22. A. Hacker, *Mismatch: The growing gulf between men and women* (New York: Scribner, 2003).

23. S. Armour, "More women cruise to the top," *USA Today*, June 25, 2003.

24. J. Archer, "The influence of testosterone on human aggression," *British Journal of Psychology* 82 (1991): 1–28.

25. Sullivan, "Why men are different."

26. Quoted in J. Shulevitz, "Rethinking testosterone," *Slate*, April 7, 2000.

27. M. Frankenhauser, *Stress, health, job satisfaction* (Stockholm: Swedish Work Environment Fund, 1989), pp. 1–20.

28. M. Frankenhauser, "The psychophysiology of sex differences as related to occupational status," in M. Frankenhauser, U. Lundberg, and M. Chesney, eds., *Women, work, and health* (New York: Plenum, 1991).

29. S. Taylor, The tending instinct: How nurturing is essential for who we are and how we live (New York: Times Books, 2002).

30. D. Merlani, "Female bonding: Friendship's therapeutic value no secret to women," *Rocky Mountain News*, July 29, 2003.

31. R. Rosen, "Fight stress with friends," *San Francisco Chronicle*, April 1, 2002.

32. J. Foreman, "Stressed out? Try a hug," *Boston Globe*, August 13, 2002.

33. S. Knox, personal communication to RB, October 16, 2003.

34. L. Tiger, *Men in groups* (New York: Scribner, 1984).

35. D. Belle, *Lives in stress: Women and depression* (Beverly Hills: Sage, 1982).

36. R. M. Kanter, *Men and women of the corporation* (New York: Basic, 1977).

37. L. Rogers, *Sexing the brain* (New York: Columbia University Press, 2001).

38. Rogers, *Sexing the brain*, p. 12.

39. Rogers, *Sexing the brain*, p. 111.

40. G. Swainson, "Girls not wired for science, author claims," *Toronto Star*, January 10, 2002.

41. Swainson, "Girls not wired."

42. Baron-Cohen, "Opposite sexes."

43. Baron-Cohen, "Opposite sexes," p. 2.

44. Baron-Cohen, "Opposite sexes," p. 2.

45. S. Rose, "Gender surrender," *London Sunday Times,* April 27, 2003.

46. K. Glaser, "Designer Genes," *Building Design,* May 23, 2003.

47. Baron-Cohen, "Opposite sexes."

48. B. Pease and A. Pease, *Why men don't listen and women can't read maps* (New York: Broadway, 2000).

49. S. Connor, "Men and women: Minds apart," *London Times,* March 2, 1997.

50. Connor, "Men and women."

51. H. Fisher, *The first sex: The natural talents of women and how they are changing the world* (New York: Random House, 1999).

52. Rogers, *Sexing the brain,* p. 111.

53. S. J. Gould, *Mismeasure of man* (New York: Norton, 1981), pp. 228–229.

54. Gould, *Mismeasure.*

55. T. Canli et al., "An fMRI study of personality influences on brain reactivity to emotional stimuli," *Behavioral Neuroscience* 115 (2001).

56. Connor, "Men and women."

57. M. Dowd, "Men: Too emotional?" *New York Times,* July 24, 2002.

58. S. Rose, "Gender surrender," *London Sunday Times,* April 27, 2003.

59. S. Pinker, *The blank slate: The modern denial of human nature* (New York: Viking Penguin 2002), p. 347.

60. N. Angier, "A revolution at 50; not just genes: Moving beyond nature vs. nurture," *New York Times,* February 25, 2003.

61. Glaser, "Designer genes."

62. W. Pollack, *Real boys: Rescuing our sons from the myths of boyhood* (New York: Holt, 1998).

63. M. Conlin, "The new gender gap: From kindergarten to grad school, boys are becoming the second sex," *Business Week,* May 26, 2003.

64. R. A. Marcon, "Moving up the grades: Relationship between preschool model and later school success," *Early Childhood Research and Practice* 4 (2002).

65. P. D. Cleary and D. Mechanic, "Sex differences in psychological distress among married people," *Journal of Health and Social Behavior* 24 (1983): 111–121. Also L. Pearlin, "Sex roles and depression," in N. Datan and L. H. Ginsberg, eds., *Life-span developmental psychology: Normative life crises* (New York: Academic, 1975), pp. 191–207.

66. V. O'Brien, *Success on our own terms* (New York: Wiley, 1998), p. 229.

67. R. Sharpe, "As leaders, women rule," *Business Week,* November 20, 2000.

68. G. N. Powell, *Women and men in management,* 2d ed. (Newbury Park, Calif.: Sage, 1993).

69. Powell, *Women and men,* p. 164.

70. O'Brien, *Success,* p. 97.

71. O'Brien, *Success,* p. 137.

72. M. Loden, *Feminine leadership: How to succeed in business without being one of the boys* (New York: Times Books, 1985), p. 110.

73. A. Kuczynski, "They conquered, they left," *New York Times,* March 24, 2002.

74. Belkin, "Opt-out revolution."

75. U.S. Census Bureau, *Fertility of American Women,* (June 2002) Table 6, p. 9.

76. K. Blanton, "Two-income families decline, economists blame the drop on unemployment," *Boston Globe,* September 23, 2003.

77. R. C. Barnett and C. Rivers, *She works/he works: How two-income families are happier, healthier, and better off* (San Francisco: Harper, 1996).

78. Blanton, "Two-income families."

79. Sharpe, "As leaders," p. 45.

80. L. K. Stroh, J. M. Brett, and A. H. Reilly, "All the right stuff: A comparison of female and male managers' career progression," *Journal of Applied Psychology* 77, no. 3 (1992): 251–260.

81. R. Abelson, "If Wall Street is a dead end, do women stay to fight or go quietly?" *New York Times*, August 3, 1999.

82. Abelson, "Wall Street."

83. Powell, *Women and men*.

84. R. McNatt, "Don't mess with these ladies," *Business Week*, February 28, 2000, p. 8.

85. A. H. Eagly, M. C. Johannesen-Schmidt, and M. L. van Engen, "Transformational, transactional, and laissez-faire leadership styles: A meta-analysis comparing women and men," *Psychological Bulletin* 129 (2003): 569–591.

86. J. Rosen, "A majority of one," *New York Times,* June 3, 2001.

87. Kanter, *Men and women.*

88. S. T. Fiske et al., "A model of (often mixed) stereotype content: Competence and warmth respectively follow from perceived status and competition," *Journal of Personality and Social Psychology* 82 (2002): 878–902.

89. Sharpe, "As leaders."

90. Abelson, "Wall Street."

91. *1998 AMA Survey: Senior management teams: Profiles and performance* (New York: American Management Association International, 1998).

92. T. Gutner, "Do top women execs = stronger IPOs?" *Business Week*, February 5, 2001, p. 122.

93. C. L. Moore, "Maternal contributions to the development of masculine sexual behavior in laboratory rats," *Developmental Psychobiology* 17 (1984): 347–356.

Chapter 9

1. N. Chodorow, *The reproduction of mothering: Psychoanalysis and the sociology of gender* (Berkeley: University of California Press, 1974).

2. G. Bedell, "Emotion Without Tears," *Independent*, November 26, 1995.

3. Chodorow, *Reproduction of mothering*, p. 4.

4. Chodorow, *Reproduction of mothering*, p. 91.

5. N. Chodorow, "The reproduction of mothering" (paper presented at the Tillie K. Lubin Symposium, Brandeis University, April 1997).

6. E. E. Maccoby, *The two sexes: Growing up apart, coming together* (Cambridge: Harvard University Press, 1998). Also D. Dien, "The evolving nature of self-identity across four levels of history," *Human Development* 43 (2000): 1–18.

7. B. White, *The first three years of life* (New York: Prentice-Hall, 1975).

8. S. H. Fraiberg, *The magic years* (New York: Scribner, 1996).

9. P. Leach, *Children first* (New York: Knopf, 1994).

10. Chodorow, *Reproduction of mothering*, p. 7.

11. R. C. Barnett and C. Rivers, *She works/he works: How two-income families are happier, healthier, and better-off* (San Francisco: Harper, 1996); T. Bond, E. Galinsky, and J. E. Swanberg, *The 1997 national study of the changing workforce* (New York: Families and Work Institute) 1998.

12. D. Blankenhorn, *Fatherless America: Confronting our most urgent social problem* (New York: Basic, 1995).

13. E. Schoenfeld, "Our Foundering Fathers," *Journal of American Citizenship Policy Review,* January-February 1996.

14. Quoted in A. Brott, "The sins of the fathers," *Washington Post,* April 17, 1995.

15. White, *First three years.*

16. L. Tiger, *The decline of males: The first look at an unexpected new world for men and women* (New York: St. Martin's Griffin, 2000), p. 162.

17. R. Wright, *The moral animal* (New York: Pantheon, 1994).

18. M. Gurian, *The wonder of boys: What parents, mentors, and educators can do to shape boys into exceptional men* (New York: Tarcher 1997).

19. Quoted in P. Dimeo, "Men behaving badly? Yes, but it's only natural," *Scotsman,* July 24, 1997.

20. Quoted in Tiger, *Decline of males,* p. 69.

21. B. J. Risman and D. Johnson-Sumerford, "Doing it fairly: A study of postgender marriages," *Journal of Marriage and the Family* 60 (1998): 23–40.

22. Risman and Johnson-Sumerford, "Doing it fairly."

23. Risman and Johnson-Sumerford, "Doing it fairly."

24. Risman and Johnson-Sumerford, "Doing it fairly."

25. Risman and Johnson-Sumerford, "Doing it fairly."

26. M. E. Lamb, *The role of the father in child development* (New York: Wiley, 1976).

27. B. S. Hewlett, *Intimate fathers: The nature and context of AKA pygmy paternal infant care* (Ann Arbor: University of Michigan Press, 1991).

28. Hewlett, *Intimate fathers.*

29. Hewlett, *Intimate fathers.*

30. Hewlett, *Intimate fathers.*

31. Hewlett, *Intimate fathers.*

32. S. Coltrane, *Family man: Fatherhood, housework, and gender equity* (New York: Oxford, 1996), p. 12.

33. Coltrane, *Family man.*

34. H. Lytton and D. M. Romney, "Parents' differential socialization of boys and girls: A meta-analysis," *Psychological Bulletin* 109 (1991): 267–296.

35. NICHD Early Child Care Network, "Relations between family predictors and child outcomes: Are they weaker for children in child care?" *Developmental Psychology* 34, no. 5 (1998): 1119–1128.

36. N. Chodorow, *The Reproduction.*

37. M. Siegal, "Are sons and daughters treated more differently by fathers than by mothers?" *Developmental Review* 7 (1987): 183–209.

38. Siegal, "Sons and daughters."

39. Dien, "Evolving nature of self-identity," pp. 1–18.

40. S. A. Hewlett, *Creating a life: Professional women and the quest for children* (New York: Talk Miramax, 2002).

41. L. R. Brody and J. A. Hall, "Gender and Emotion," in M. Lewis and J. Haviland, eds., *Handbook of emotions* (New York: Guilford, 1993), pp. 442–460.

42. R. C. Barnett and N. L. Marshall, "Men, family-role quality, job-role quality, and mental-physical health," *Health Psychology* 12 (1993). See also Barnett and Rivers, *She works/he works.*

43. E. E. Maccoby, *The two sexes: Growing up apart, coming together* (Cambridge: Harvard University Press, 1998).

44. Maccoby, *The two sexes.*

45. Maccoby, *The two sexes,* p. 58.

46. J. R. Harris, *The nurture assumption: Why children turn out the way they do* (New York: Free Press, 1998).

47. Maccoby, *The two sexes*, p. 50.

48. C. Gilligan, *Psychological theory and women's development* (Cambridge: Harvard University Press, 1982).

49. D. Tannen, *You just don't understand: Women and men in conversation* (New York: Morrow, 1990).

50. M. B. Pipher, *Reviving Ophelia: Saving the selves of adolescent girls* (New York: Putnam, 1994).

51. K. Gerson, *Hard choices: How women decide about work, career, and motherhood* (Berkeley: University of California, 1985); K. Gerson, *No man's land: Men's changing commitments to family and work* (New York: Basic, 1993).

52. B. Thorne, *Gender play: Girls and boys at school* (New Brunswick, N.J.: Rutgers University Press, 1993).

53. Thorne, *Gender play.*

54. Thorne, *Gender play.*

55. Thorne, *Gender play,* p. 108.

56. Thorne, *Gender play.*

57. Z. Luria and E. W. Herzog, "Sorting gender out in a children's museum," *Gender and Society* 5, no. 2 (1991): 224–232.

58. Thorne, *Gender play.*

59. C. Hoff Sommers, *The war against boys: How misguided feminism is harming our young men* (New York: Touchstone, 2000).

60. Gurian, *Wonder of boys.*

61. Thorne, *Gender play,* p. 98.

62. L. Shapiro, "Where little boys can play with nail polish," *Newsweek,* May 28, 1990, p. 62.

63. M. Kimmel, "About a boy," *Vassar,* Winter 2003.

64. M. Lewis, *Altering fate: Why the past does not predict the future* (New York: Guilford, 1997).

Chapter 10

1. C. Gilligan, N. P. Lyons, and T. J. Hanmer, *Making connections: The relational worlds of adolescent girls at Emma Willard School* (Cambridge: Harvard University Press, 1990).

2. M. B. Pipher, Reviving *Ophelia: Saving the selves of adolescent girls* (New York: Putnam, 1994).

3. American Association of University Women, *Shortchanging Girls, Shortchanging America: Full Data Report* (Washington, D.C., 1990).

4. E. Hooper, "Guidance for Ophelias' moms," *St. Petersburg Times* (November 8, 2003).

5. E. Gedalius, "Ophelia project builds self-esteem," *Tampa Tribune,* March 15, 2003.

6. D. Eiucher, "Bonding with books," *Denver Post,* May 8, 1997.

7. "Boys and girls clubs teach youth how to take it easy," *Canada Newswire,* June 2, 2000.

8. E. Gleick, "Surviving your teens," *Time,* February 19, 1966.

9. B. Bower, "Teenage turning point: Does adolescence herald the twilight of girls' self-esteem?" *Science News* 139 (1991): 184–186.

10. Bower, "Teenage turning point."

11. D. Baker, "Northeast tall tale," *Hartford Courant Sunday Magazine*, December 27, 1998.

12. Gilligan, Lyons, and Hanmer, *Making connections*.

13. Gilligan, Lyons, and Hanmer, *Making connections*.

14. W. Kaminer, "The trouble with single-sex schools," *Atlantic*, April 1998.

15. Gilligan, Lyons, and Hanmer, *Making connections*, p. 15.

16. Gilligan, Lyons, and Hanmer, *Making connections*, p. 11.

17. Gilligan, Lyons, and Hanmer, *Making connections*, p. 10.

18. K. Torres, "Ophelia girls," *Atlanta Journal Constitution*, December 9, 2003.

19. Pipher, *Reviving Ophelia*, p. 22.

20. Pipher, *Reviving Ophelia*.

21. Pipher, *Reviving Ophelia*, p. 21.

22. Pipher, *Reviving Ophelia*, appendix.

23. AAUW, *Shortchanging girls*.

24. AAUW, *Shortchanging girls*.

25. S. Daley, "Little girls lose their self-esteem on the way to adolescence, study finds," *New York Times,* January 9, 1991.

26. S. Coopersmith, *The antecedents of self-esteem* (San Francisco: Freeman, 1967); D. M. Tice, "The social motivations of people with low self-esteem," in R. Baumeister, ed., *Self-Esteem: The puzzle of low self-regard* (New York: Plenum, 1993).

27. S. Freud, *Psychopathology of everyday life* (New York: Macmillan, 1930).

28. K. Horney, *Our inner conflicts: A constructive theory of neurosis* (New York: Norton, 1945).

29. Horney, *Our inner conflicts*.

30. J. Crocker, B. Major, and C. Steele, "Social stigma," in D. T. Gilbert, S. T. Fiske, G. Lindzey, eds., *The Handbook of social psychology* (Boston: McGraw-Hill; New York: Oxford 1998).

31. Gilligan, Lyons, and Hanmer, *Making connections*, p. 4.

32. Pipher, *Reviving Ophelia*, p. 64.

33. Pipher, *Reviving Ophelia*, p. 64.

34. B. Major et al., *Gender and self-esteem: A meta analysis* (Santa Barbara: University of California Press; Buffalo: State University of New York at Buffalo, 1997).

35. K. C. Kling et al., "Gender differences in self-esteem: A meta-analysis," *Psychological Bulletin* 125, no. 4 (1999): 470–500.

36. Kling et al., "Gender differences."

37. Major et al., *Gender and self-esteem*.

38. AAUW, *Shortchanging girls*.

39. Kling et al., "Gender differences."

40. Kaminer, "The trouble with single-sex schools," p. 9.

41. Kaminer, "The trouble with single-sex schools," p. 10.

42. Kling et al., "Gender differences."

43. Kling et al., "Gender differences."

44. Kling et al., "Gender differences."

45. AAUW, *Shortchanging girls*.

46. A. Kohn, "The Truth About Self-Esteem," *Phi Delta Kappan,* December 1994, pp. 272–301.

47. Kohn, "Truth About Self-Esteem."

48. M. Rosenberg, C. Schooler, and C. Schoenbach, "Self-esteem and adolescent problems: Modeling reciprocal effects," *American Sociological Review,* December 1989, pp. 1004–1018.

49. C. M. Steele and J. Aronson, "Stereotype threat and the intellectual test performance," *Journal of Personality and Social Psychology* 69 (1995): 797–811.

50. Pipher, *Reviving Ophelia,* appendix.

51. D. Pollard, *Separated by sex: A critical look at single-sex education for girls* (Washington, D.C.: Institute for Women's Policy Research, 1998).

52. D. Brady, "Toronto feminists have customized a radical new curriculum for girls," *Maclean's,* April 25, 1994.

53. T. Lewin, "Girls' schools gain, saying coed isn't coequal," *New York Times,* April 11, 1999.

54. M. F. Belenky et al., *Women's ways of knowing: The development of self, voice, and mind* (New York: Basic, 1986).

55. Lewin, "Girls' schools gain."

56. R. Hotakainen, "Single sex schools are separate but not always equal," *Minneapolis Star Tribune,* June 9, 2002.

57. M. R. Davis, "Department aims to promote single sex schools," *Education Week,* May 15, 2002.

58. Belenky et al., *Women's ways of knowing.*

59. C. F. Epstein, *Deceptive distinctions: Sex, gender, and the social order.* (New Haven: Yale University Press; New York: Russell Sage Foundation, 1988).

60. Epstein, *Deceptive distinctions.*

61. L. Shaw, "Powerful lessons: In staying separate, girls learn to be equal," *Seattle Times,* May 11, 2003.

62. M. Talbot, "Girls Just Want to Be Mean," *New York Times Magazine,* February 24, 2002.

63. S. Meadows, "In defense of teen girls," *Newsweek,* June 3, 2002.

64. Talbot, "Girls."

65. B. L. Foster, "The Secret Life of Teenage Girls," *Washingtonian,* November 2000.

66. Quoted in Talbot, "Girls."

67. A. Datnow, L. Hubbard, and E. Woody, "Is single-gender schooling viable in the public sector? Lessons from California's pilot program." Ford Foundation executive summary, May 20, 2001.

68. Datnow, Hubbard, and Woody, "Single-gender schooling."

69. Datnow, Hubbard, and Woody, "Single-gender schooling."

70. V. E. Lee et al., "The culture of sexual harassment in secondary schools," *American Educational Research Journal* 33 (1993): 383—418.

71. Lee, "The culture."

72. Kaminer, "Single-sex schools."

73. Kaminer, "Single-sex schools."

74. Patrick Welsh, "Single-sex schools unbalance education," *USA Today,* May 15, 2002.

75. Welsh, "Single-sex schools."

76. Kling et al., "Gender differences."

77. F. Stewart, "Competitive girls often become successful women," *Cleveland Plain Dealer,* April 27, 1999.

Chapter 11

1. K. Pollitt, "Marooned on Gilligan's Island: Are women morally superior to men?" *Nation,* December 28, 1992, pp. 799–807.

2. C. Hoff Sommers, *The war against boys: How misguided feminism is harming our young men* (New York: Touchstone, 2000).

3. R. D. Putnam, *Bowling alone: The collapse and revival of American community* (New York: Simon & Schuster, 2000).

4. R. Dawkins, *The selfish gene* (New York: Oxford, 1976).

5. S. Blackmore, *The meme machine* (New York: Oxford, 1999).

6. Richard Dawkins first raised the idea of the "meme," a unit of culture spread by imitation. Susan Blackmore, drawing on Dawkins's work, outlined an elaborate theory of memetic evolution in her book, *The Meme Machine.* Blackmore offered some ideas that are relevant to the future of the sexes. Asking the question which ideas, or memes, tend to spread, she notes that those which are more visible travel fastest.

7. M. Sunstrom and A. Duvander, "Gender division of child care and the sharing of parental leave among new parents in Sweden," *European Sociological Review* 18 (2002): 433–447.

Index